THE SUFFERING CANON

How We Learned to Mistake Pain for Profundity—And What It's Costing Us

Table of Contents

Copyright © 2025, C Davert 1

DISCLAIMER 4

A NOTE BEFORE YOU BEGIN 6

PREFACE: Why I Wrote This Book 7

PART ONE: THE CATHEDRAL 11

CHAPTER 1: The Cathedral of Suffering 12

CHAPTER 2: THE DAILY CANON—When News Became Suffering Homework 22

CHAPTER 3: THE ENTERTAINMENT CATHEDRAL—Prestige Means Pain 30

CHAPTER 4: STARTING YOUNG—Children's Media and First Deaths 39

CHAPTER 5: THE CLASSROOM CATHEDRAL—Education as Indoctrination 47

CHAPTER 6: THE SEMINARY OF SUFFERING—The MFA and the Production of Dogma 57

PART TWO: THE FOUNDATIONS 68

CHAPTER 7: FROM GREEKS TO GOD—Ancient Foundations 69

CHAPTER 8: THE ROMANTIC VIRUS—When Artists Became Tortured 76

CHAPTER 9: AFTER THE WARS—Modernism's Despair Mandate 83

PART THREE: THE COST 91

CHAPTER 10: THE MENTAL HEALTH BILL—Quantifying Damage 92

CHAPTER 11: THE IMAGINATION DRAIN—What We Can't Envision 101

CHAPTER 12: THE LOST READERS—Who We Exclude . 111

PART FOUR: THE BLUEPRINT 118

CHAPTER 13: THE FLOURISHING CANON—An Argument for a New Library 119

CHAPTER 14: NEWS THAT NOURISHES—Rebalancing the Daily Canon 135

CHAPTER 15: THE PEDAGOGY OF POSSIBILITY—Teaching Toward Flourishing 147

CHAPTER 16: THE INSTITUTIONAL LEVERS—Awards, Publishing, and Prestige 159

CHAPTER 17: RECLAIMING JOY—A Conclusion 169

CONCLUSION: THE CHOICE 188

APPENDIX A: THE 25 MOST-TAUGHT TEXTS—SUICIDE & SELF-ANNIHILATION CODING 193

APPENDIX B: DATA SOURCES FOR THE "MOST-TAUGHT BOOKS" ANALYSIS 197

APPENDIX C: METHODOLOGICAL NOTE 198

APPENDIX D: METHODOLOGY AND DATA FOR THE ANALYSIS OF BEST PICTURE WINNERS (1975-2024) 200

APPENDIX E: PULITZER PRIZE AND NATIONAL BOOK AWARD ANALYSIS (2004-2024) 208

APPENDIX F: COMBINED PRESTIGE CULTURE ANALYSIS (2004-2024) 217

APPENDIX G: THE FLOURISHING CANON—ANNOTATED LIST OF 100 WORKS 224

APPENDIX H: SUPPLEMENTARY TABLES—SYNTHESIZED STATISTICAL OVERVIEW 245

CONSOLIDATED REFERENCES 249

COMPLETE INDEX - THE SUFFERING CANON 266

Copyright © 2025, C Davert

All rights reserved. No part of this publication may be reproduced, distributed, or transmitted in any form or by any means—whether electronic, mechanical, photocopying, recording, or through an information storage and retrieval system, or any other electronic or mechanical methods—without prior written permission from the publisher. Exceptions apply only in cases of brief quotations included in critical reviews and certain non-commercial uses as permitted by copyright law.

ISBNs:
979-8-9938724-2-1 Soft Cover
979-8-9938724-3-8 Hard Cover
979-8-9938724-4-5 Ebook

Library of Congress Control Number: 2025924316

For permission requests, write to the publisher:

Davert Forest Creek Publishing
1517 Joe Mann Blvd. #1021
Midland, MI 48942
davertforestcreekpublishing@gmail.com

For Rosemary A,
who opened the newsroom door to me and gave me a reporter's job,
edited my pages and my book without mercy,
and stayed my friend through every draft.
You still make me laugh, and your brilliant mind has always made mine work harder.

And to all souls who have moved through this world
across the unfathomable sweep of time:
your joys and griefs still echo through us,
shaping the long arc of human longing.

THE SUFFERING CANON

How We Learned to Mistake Pain for Profundity—And What It's Costing Us

C Davert

Davert Forest Creek Publishing

1517 Joe Mann Blvd. #1021

Midland, MI 48942

davertforestcreekpublishing@gmail.com

DISCLAIMER

The material in this book is provided solely for general informational, cultural, and analytical purposes. It represents interpretations, observations, and arguments about storytelling, media, culture, and documented patterns within them.

The author is not a psychologist, therapist, physician, attorney, or licensed professional in any clinical field. Nothing in this book should be construed as medical, psychological, legal, or professional advice, nor should it replace consultation with qualified professionals.

Except where explicitly noted, all individuals described in this book are composites drawn from multiple real-world experiences, interviews, cultural patterns, and anonymized anecdotes. The Author's Note on Methodology provides detailed explanation of this approach. Any resemblance to identifiable persons, living or dead, is coincidental or the result of deliberate anonymization intended to protect privacy. All examples are illustrative and should not be interpreted as diagnostic assessments of any specific individual or community.

Cultural analysis is inherently interpretive, and reasonable people may disagree about the ideas or conclusions presented. The arguments offered here are invitations to examination and debate rather than definitive claims about any person, institution, discipline, or work of art. No statement in this book should be understood as representing the views of any organization, employer, or institution with which the author is affiliated, past or present.

The author makes no guarantees regarding any outcome that may result from applying, misapplying, or interpreting the concepts discussed, and shall not be held liable for any actions taken, decisions made, or consequences experienced in connection with the material presented. For personal, educational, psychological, or professional guidance, please consult an appropriate licensed or certified expert.

A NOTE BEFORE YOU BEGIN

This book examines stories—specifically, the stories our culture consecrates as "profound," and the potential cost of their near-monopoly on seriousness.

To make this case, the analysis quotes and examines works containing intense themes, including suicide, trauma, abuse, and despair. The intention is not to dismiss these stories, nor to suggest painful experiences are unworthy of artistic treatment, but to question the imbalance of a curriculum and culture that offer so few alternatives to suffering-centered narratives.

Some material discussed may be difficult. Readers should use their own judgment about when and how to engage with it, and prioritize their well-being. This book is not a substitute for professional mental health support.

If you are in emotional distress or thinking about self-harm, please seek support immediately from a qualified professional or crisis service. In the United States, the 988 Suicide & Crisis Lifeline is available 24/7 by calling or texting 988, or via chat at 988lifeline.org. Outside the U.S., please consult local emergency numbers or mental health resources in your area.

The views expressed are based on research, analysis, and documented patterns in cultural production. They are offered in the spirit of opening necessary conversation, not as medical, psychological, or legal advice.

PREFACE: Why I Wrote This Book

I didn't always feel this way about our cultural rituals.

I was eighteen when I walked into a movie theater to see the first Bruce Lee film. It was the early 1970s, and martial arts cinema was exploding into American consciousness. Everyone was going. It was the thing to see.

Fifteen minutes in, I felt sick.

Not metaphorically uncomfortable. Physically ill. The choreographed violence—bodies crashing, bones breaking, blood flowing—triggered something visceral. My stomach turned. My hands went cold. I had to leave the theater.

I was embarrassed. My friends stayed. The culture said this was entertainment, that I was overreacting, that I needed to toughen up. But my body was telling me something my mind hadn't yet articulated: this is not what humans are meant to consume in such concentrated doses.

That was more than fifty years ago.

Today, I can watch the same kind of violence without flinching. I have been, quite literally, culturally conditioned. What once triggered visceral rejection now barely registers. I wish I could say this was growth or maturity—the development of more nuanced understanding of art's purpose. But I've come to recognize it for what it is: desensitization. The inevitable result of decades participating in rituals that have systematically confused intensity with importance and trauma with truth.

The moment I knew I had to write this book came not in a classroom or library, but in my own living room. My husband and I have accumulated somewhere between three and four hundred DVDs over the years—a collection representing decades of "what's worth watching." As I scanned those shelves one afternoon, I realized something unsettling: of those hundreds of films, I genuinely enjoy perhaps forty. Maybe.

The rest—the vast majority, chosen primarily by my husband—center violence, war, moral collapse, or existential despair. Murder mysteries. War epics. Psychological thrillers. Documentaries about atrocities. Films where good intentions lead to ruin and love ends in loss. I don't hate these films. Many are brilliantly made. But they don't nourish me. They don't leave me fuller or more hopeful or better equipped to face the world. They leave me, at best, grimly informed. At worst, depleted.

As I stood there counting—forty out of four hundred, roughly ten percent—I realized I was living inside a statistic I hadn't yet calculated. That ratio wasn't random. It was the predictable output of a system that has spent half a century consecrating exactly those narratives with its highest honors.

The question that haunted me was simple: Is that all there is?

When I began paying attention—really paying attention—to what our culture celebrates, I saw the same pattern everywhere. The films that win Oscars. The books that win major literary prizes. The stories we're told are "important" and "serious." They share a common denominator: they center suffering.

So I began to count.

I analyzed fifty years of Best Picture winners. I coded twenty-two years of Pulitzer Prize and National Book Award winners for fiction. I examined the most-taught books in American high schools. I looked at the structure of television news broadcasts, the language critics use to praise "serious" work, and the pedagogy of MFA programs. What I found was not a preference or a trend. It was a cathedral—a self-reinforcing system of cultural rituals spanning multiple institutions, all defining seriousness in the same narrow way, all teaching the same lesson: that to be important is to hurt.

The data is stark. Over the past twenty-two years, seventy-one percent of the most prestigious awards in American film and literature have gone to narratives centered on suffering, trauma, or existential despair. Only ten percent have gone to narratives centered on flourishing, competence, or joy. In the high school literary canon, sixty-eight percent of the most commonly taught texts feature suicide or deliberate self-annihilation. On the evening news, the vast majority of airtime is devoted to violence, disaster, and political conflict, with only token moments of lightness squeezed into the final seconds.

These are the rituals. This is what we are told matters. This is what we have been trained, systematically and over decades, to accept as sacred.

This book is not an argument against tragedy. Tragic narratives are essential. They help us process grief, understand injustice, grapple with the reality of human suffering. *Hamlet* and *The Road* and *Schindler's List* are profound works that deserve their place in our cultural conversation.

But when tragedy becomes not one voice in a chorus but the only voice we are taught to hear—when seventy-one percent of our most celebrated stories tell us that meaning is found exclusively in collapse—we are not being shown the full range of human experience. We are being indoctrinated into a worldview that mistakes a single emotional register for the entirety of truth.

This book is my attempt to name that worldview, to show how it was built, to demonstrate its costs, and to imagine what it might look like to dismantle it. It is for every reader who has been told their love of hopeful stories is naive. For anyone who has felt exhausted by the insistence that "serious" must mean "bleak." For everyone who, like my eighteen-year-old self, once felt something was fundamentally wrong—and then, over time, learned not to feel it anymore.

That desensitization is not wisdom. It is not sophistication. It is the successful operation of a system that benefits from our belief that the world is primarily a place of suffering and that attempts to build something better are either futile or foolish.

I wrote this book to break that conditioning—in myself, and perhaps in those who read it.

What follows is the evidence. The counting. The patterns. The rituals. The costs.

And, eventually, the possibility of something different.

Because that eighteen-year-old who walked out of the theater? She was right. Her body was telling her the truth.

It is time to stop worshiping at the altar of despair.

PART ONE: THE CATHEDRAL

Diagnosis: Mapping the Suffering Canon

We enter the nave. Here, we trace the architecture of despair—from the required reading list to the nightly news, from the silver screen to the childhood storybook. This is a survey of the sanctuary our culture has built, stone by stone, and the doctrines preached from its pulpits. Before we can imagine a different edifice, we must first understand the contours of this one.
Chapters 1–6

CHAPTER 1: The Cathedral of Suffering

Seventeen.

In the twenty-five most-taught books in American high schools, seventeen center on a protagonist whose story ends in suicide or deliberate self-annihilation. Not seventeen deaths—seventeen deliberate choices by characters to end their own lives, or engage in acts of self-annihilation, rather than continue existing in the worlds their authors created.

Romeo and Juliet drink poison and stab themselves. Anna Karenina throws herself under a train. Ophelia drowns in a Danish stream. Willy Loman deliberately crashes his car. Emma Bovary swallows arsenic. Edna Pontellier walks into the sea.

And you are still reading.

The hook was set with seventeen deaths, and now you are being reeled in. You didn't close this book when it opened with a body count. You leaned in. Because I knew—the same way every publisher, editor, and news producer knows—that death commands attention in a way joy almost never does.

I opened with corpses because decades of cultural conditioning taught me that suffering equals seriousness, that depth requires damage. You would likely dismiss a book beginning with "Only eight of the twenty-five most-taught books end hopefully" as sentimental fluff. Even while writing against our cultural death obsession, I instinctively lead with the very thing I decry.

That's how deep the conditioning runs. So deep that even those of us who see the trap are compelled to use its bait.

We didn't accidentally create a culture drawn to dark content. We manufactured it. From the last straight comedy to win Best Picture in 1977 to prestige television built around antiheroic despair, we have spent decades rewarding stories that equate pain with profundity and sidelining those that take happiness, repair, or simple endurance seriously.

I am not arguing for the elimination of tragic literature. I am arguing for balance—for the radical idea that stories which make us glad to be alive might be as worthy of serious attention as those that make us question whether life is worth living at all.

If this analysis cannot escape using death to secure its own credibility, what chance do the fourteen-year-olds required to read these stories have? We ask them to analyze why these characters chose death, to write essays exploring their despair, to be tested on their understanding of self-destruction. We are grading them on how well they can articulate why someone would choose to die.

This is the cathedral we have built: a monument to suffering so imposing that even those attempting to dismantle it must first worship at its altar just to be heard.

But this book was not born from a statistic. It was born from a question, one that echoed in the space after a bell had rung.

The Tremor

It began not as a thesis but as a tremor of unease in a sun-drenched classroom. Jennifer Westbridge, a teacher with two decades of service, had just concluded a carefully crafted lesson on the "profundity" of Hamlet's despair. Her students, a group of high-achieving eleventh-graders, could parse the symbolism of Yorick's skull with the clinical precision of medical examiners. They knew which lines signaled existential crisis, which metaphors foreshadowed tragedy. Their essays would be tight, textually supported, and ready for the rubric.

After the bell rang, one student lingered. Emma Brightwater, whose insights were usually sharp and swift, hovered by the corner of Jennifer's desk, backpack slung over one shoulder, eyes clouded by a different kind of understanding.

"Ms. Westbridge," she asked, her voice quiet but clear, "this is the fifth book this year where the main character dies. And in three of them, it's suicide. Is… is that all there is?"

The question—a window into a student's soul—would not close. It haunted Jennifer as she graded elegant essays on Gatsby's futile yearning and lesson-planned the predetermined mutilation of Oedipus. By every metric her district provided—test scores, evaluations, college recommendations—she was a successful teacher. But Emma's disillusionment had exposed a fissure in the very foundation of her life's work.

Is that all there is?

Not "Is Hamlet profound?" but "Is profound suffering the only kind of profound there is?"

A few nights later, after posting another round of grades, Jennifer opened a new document. Instead of writing the next lesson plan, she began a list. Not of standards. Not of themes. A list of bodies.

Counting the Curriculum

What started as a teacher's private audit evolved into this book's first striking dataset. In the twenty-five most-taught books in American high schools, self-destruction is not an anomaly. It is the curriculum.

To assemble that list, Jennifer drew from three primary sources: the College Board's AP English Literature free-response question data, which reveals the novels and plays students most frequently write about; the Common Core State Standards' text exemplars; and state-level curriculum guides. From these, she constructed a representative set of the texts that, in various combinations, shape the majority of American students' literary education.

The construction of that list and the coding of each text are described in Appendices A–C. Each text was coded using a three-part system that captures everything from explicit suicide to what I call thematic self-annihilation: endings in which the protagonist deliberately erases their own agency, identity, or existence, even if the method is not labeled "suicide" in the text.

The data were stark. The analysis found that sixty-eight percent of these cornerstone texts feature either a suicide or a central, deliberate self-annihilation.

Let's be clear about what this means. This analysis focuses on the most commonly required texts—the books that shape the core of high school literary education. Individual teachers may supplement with more varied works, and some schools have begun experimenting with alternative curricula. But the dominant pattern in the canon is unmistakable: we have systematically elevated tragedy and marginalized hope.

This is not a mere subjective impression; it is what emerges when systematic counting reveals the pattern. We are not teaching tragedy as one color on the palette of human experience. We are teaching a monochrome of despair.

Even the way I have presented these numbers is shaped by the cathedral we inhabit. I led this chapter with the deaths, just as Jennifer led her list with the bodies. I might have told you first that only eight of the twenty-five most-taught books end with anything resembling constructive hope, or that barely a third of the most-assigned works offer models of endurance, repair, or communal flourishing. But I knew "seventeen suicides or self-annihilations" would carry more cultural weight than "eight hopeful endings."

The cathedral trains us all.

This book will mirror the pattern it critiques—not because I couldn't imagine another way, but because to reach you, I must first speak the language you've been trained to hear. The first half of this book will feel heavy, because that's what seriousness sounds like in our current cathedral. But if I've done my job, by the time you reach the solutions section, you'll be ready to hear a different kind of depth—one that doesn't require darkness to prove its worth. The tonal shift you'll feel isn't an accident. It's the argument.

The Annual Journey Through Catastrophe

Consider the year of a student like Ashley Pennbrook. She is fifteen, navigating the natural turbulence of adolescence, a period now marked by a documented national crisis in teen mental health. Her brain is still under construction, particularly the systems that regulate emotion and weigh future consequences. She is exquisitely sensitive to threat, to rejection, to any suggestion that she does not belong.

Her literary education, however, is a sustained immersion in catastrophe.

In the fall, she analyzes *Frankenstein*'s obsessive pursuit of knowledge and the eventual collapse of his life, family, and moral world—a self-inflicted ruin presented as inevitable, as if once the monster is alive the rest of the dominos can only fall one way.

By winter, she traces the psychological self-flagellation in *The Scarlet Letter*, learning that moral victory is found in public shame and private anguish. The most virtuous characters suffer the most. The story ends not with a healed community, but with graves.

In spring, she witnesses Jay Gatsby shot, face down, in his pool, a testament to the American Dream as a lethal illusion. Loyalty is betrayed, idealism is punished, and the people who go on living are the ones "who smash things up and then retreat back into their money."

Sprinkled in between may be *Romeo and Juliet*, where love is a prelude to a double death; *Lord of the Flies*, where the veneer of civilization burns away into murder; *Hamlet*, returning once more to a prince who cannot find a way to live but can, at last, find a way to die.

I am not arguing that any of these works are valueless. They are potent, often brilliant explorations of obsession, guilt, hypocrisy, and grief. The problem is not any single text. The problem is the pattern.

What Ashley never encounters in her required reading is a protagonist who builds something lasting. A community that solves a problem together. A character who chooses hope after understanding despair. Not because these stories don't exist, but because the curriculum has consecrated a different kind of narrative as the only one worthy of serious attention.

Over four years, Ashley will become fluent in the language of suffering. She will be functionally illiterate in narratives of hard-won joy.

The Catharsis Defense: A Fossil Argument

The most common counterargument, and the most ancient, is catharsis. We invoke Aristotle, claiming that tragedy purges pity and fear. We point to our own experiences as readers: the way encountering *King Lear* or *Death of a Salesman* or *Beloved* felt like being shattered and remade into deeper, more compassionate people. We reassure ourselves that confronting suffering on the page arms students against suffering in the world.

But this defense is a fossil, unearthed to justify a system it no longer describes.

Greek tragedy was never intended as a solitary reading assignment for developmentally vulnerable individuals consumed alone in a bedroom at midnight. It was a civic ritual. Performances took place in daylight, in public, with music, masks, and a chorus. The audience was not a single teenager in a hoodie; it was an entire city watching itself.

The Greek chorus provided context and communal response. Their tragedies reinforced social bonds and shared ethical questions. As Martha Nussbaum observes, Greek tragedy was never meant to be absorbed in isolation, stripped of its religious and communal framework.[1] And as middle-school teacher Claire Needell Hollander argues in *The New York Times*, assigning such concentrated misery to teenagers can be pedagogically reckless.[2]

For an adult with a fully formed prefrontal cortex and a lifetime of experiences, *King Lear* is a profound exploration of folly and love. For a sixteen-year-old whose brain is hypersensitive to threat and social rejection, whose cognitive schemas are still forming, it can read as a simple, brutal truth: that the world is a place where love turns to betrayal and the only sane response is to go mad.

We have extracted the ritual framework that made Greek tragedy functional and kept only the suffering. We offer the poison without the antidote.

The Parallel Trends

The correlation is not causation, but the parallel trends demand attention. As the CDC reports a forty percent increase in persistent feelings of sadness and hopelessness among high school students between 2009 and 2019,[3] the literary canon we require of them has remained a static gallery of the doomed.

When our most celebrated novels teach students, over and over, that love ends in ruin, ambition in betrayal, and idealism in gunfire—when they model suicide as a reasonable, sometimes even noble, response to human suffering—we are not simply teaching literature. We are training cognitive patterns. We are rehearsing despair.

This is not about "trigger warnings" or protecting fragile sensibilities. This is about recognizing that stories are not neutral. They are cognitive training exercises. When sixty-eight percent of required texts center on self-destruction, we are systematically teaching students what kinds of endings matter, what kinds of responses are "deep," and what kinds of lives are worth literary attention.

The cathedral's liturgy begins here, in ninth-grade English classrooms, where students learn their first formal lesson in what "serious" literature looks like.

Emma's Meta-Analysis

Emma Brightwater was not failing to understand the literature. She was understanding it all too well. She was performing a meta-analysis her teacher had missed, because her teacher was standing inside the cathedral, leading the service without questioning the creed.

Jennifer knew the themes and structures of each work. She could map tragic arcs, identify motifs, guide students through close readings of metaphors and symbols. She had years of professional development on how to differentiate instruction and align assessments with standards. What she had not been trained to do was step back and see the cumulative psychological world her curriculum constructed.

Emma did that instinctively. She looked not at *Hamlet* in isolation, but at *Hamlet* and *The Great Gatsby* and *Of Mice and Men* and *Romeo and Juliet* and whatever other texts her district had chosen. She looked at them all together and asked a devastatingly simple question about the world they reflected back to her: *Is that all there is?*

Not "Is Hamlet profound?" but "Is profound suffering the only kind of profound we are allowed to study here?"

The full list of texts, and the methodology behind their classification, appear in the appendices. What matters here is not the elegance of the spreadsheet. What matters is the pattern—and what that pattern quietly teaches young people to expect from life, from literature, and from themselves.

The Liturgy Begins

The counting of the bodies in the library was only the beginning. It was the tolling bell of a curriculum that confuses despair for depth and tragedy for truth.

This is where the cathedral's liturgy begins: in ninth-grade English classrooms, where students attend their first formal services. The rituals are familiar. Take out your notebook. Underline the foreshadowing. Identify the tragic flaw. Write a thesis about why the protagonist's demise was inevitable. Reflect on how the character's death "gives meaning" to the story. Now share with the class.

By the time they graduate, students like Ashley and Emma will have participated in hundreds of hours of such rituals, all consecrating the same creed: that meaning is found at the edge of self-destruction, that depth requires damage, and that hope is for children who haven't yet learned to read seriously.

The ritual is complete when students like Emma stop asking "Why is everything so sad?" and start asking "What's wrong with me for wanting something else?"

That transformation—from question to shame—is not education. It is indoctrination.

And it begins here, in Chapter One of their required reading, with seventeen out of twenty-five cornerstone texts centering on suicide or self-annihilation waiting in the pages ahead.

CHAPTER 1 ENDNOTES
1. Martha C. Nussbaum, *The Fragility of Goodness: Luck and Ethics in Greek Tragedy and Philosophy*, rev. ed. (Cambridge: Cambridge University Press, 2001), 15–17.

2. Claire Needell Hollander, "Why Are We Teaching Sad Books to Teens?" *The New York Times*, July 6, 2013.
3. U.S. Centers for Disease Control and Prevention, *Youth Risk Behavior Survey Data Summary & Trends Report: 2009–2019* (Atlanta: U.S. Department of Health and Human Services, 2020).
4. College Board, "AP English Literature and Composition Free-Response Questions 1971–2022," accessed November 2025.
5. Common Core State Standards Initiative, *Appendix B: Text Exemplars and Sample Performance Tasks* (Washington, DC: National Governors Association Center for Best Practices and the Council of Chief State School Officers, 2010).
6. Arthur N. Applebee, *Curriculum as Conversation: Transforming Traditions of Teaching and Learning* (Chicago: University of Chicago Press, 1996).

CHAPTER 2: THE DAILY CANON— When News Became Suffering Homework

If the literary canon is the foundation of our cathedral, laid brick by brick in the classrooms of our youth, then the evening news is its daily liturgy. Here, the equation of suffering with significance is not absorbed over semesters but administered in a potent, concentrated ritual—a ceremony we have mistaken for civic duty.

The scene is familiar. Mike Ironwood, a composite representing millions of Americans, settles into his recliner at 6:30 PM for the same devotion he has performed for forty years: the network evening news. The screen flickers. For the next half hour, he is a conscientious citizen, "informing himself." But what is the actual content of this information?

Media scholars have quantified what Mike is really consuming. Content analyses of television news over months of broadcasts routinely find that a majority of stories focus on violence, conflict, crime, and disasters. As political scientist Stuart Soroka notes in his research on media negativity, the gatekeeping function of news consistently prioritizes threatening information, a pattern documented for decades.[1] Studies by Lichter and Amundson of local and national newscasts have reported that roughly half to two-thirds of items are "negative" in this sense, with violence, crime, accidents, and political conflict dominating the limited airtime.[2] The details differ by outlet and era, but the overall pattern is remarkably consistent: when time is scarce, bad news crowds everything else off the stage.

The modern newscast is a masterpiece of condensed tragedy. Its structure has evolved into a kind of secular three-part mass, as predictable and ritualized as any cathedral service:

The Three-Part Mass of Catastrophe

The Opening Catastrophe. The broadcast almost invariably opens with what producers call a "tentpole" story—a major disaster, a mass shooting, a geopolitical crisis—often accompanied by dramatic, often chaotic, footage. This is the lead, signaling to the viewer what matters most: imminent threat. The music is urgent, the cadence grave. We are taught, from the first second, that significance is synonymous with emergency.

The Political Theater. The second act shifts to Washington or a state capital, framing civic life not as a complex process of governance but as bloodsport. The language is of "battles," "gridlock," "scandals," and "bitter debate." The segment relies on split-screen arguments and short, decontextualized soundbites designed to highlight conflict rather than illuminate policy. The lesson: our government is a theater of futility.

The Chronicle of Chaos. The final act is a rapid-fire sequence of lesser tragedies—a local fire, a fatal car crash, a random act of violence. These stories are rarely situated in a broader statistical context (for instance, whether crime is actually rising or falling), making the anomalous seem normative. The effect is a sensory bombardment of isolated misfortunes, creating the impression of a world spinning into entropy.

This tripartite liturgy is as reliable as the anchor's suit and tie. And then, the reprieve. The "And finally..." token—a single, brief, whimsical story about a rescued cat or a talented dog, usually squeezed into under a minute. This is not balance; it is a psychological pressure valve, a tiny, sanctioned glimpse of light that only emphasizes the overwhelming darkness of the preceding segments. It is the journalistic equivalent of offering a single flower at a funeral and calling it a celebration of life.

The Historical Shift: From News to Threat

This relentless concentration on catastrophe is a historical anomaly. As media historian David T. Z. Mindich notes in *Tuned Out*, the half-hour broadcast of the 1960s and '70s, under the FCC's Fairness Doctrine and with a stronger mandate for objectivity, allowed for longer segments and a broader conception of news that could include scientific discovery or cultural achievement.[3] The tectonic shift began with the rise of 24-hour cable news in the 1980s, which weaponized anxiety for ratings—a tactic the legacy networks eventually adopted to compete in a fractured media landscape.

The physics are simple and brutal: less time, more death.

We have moved from a broadsheet of the day's events to a distilled shot glass of catastrophe, served neat, every evening at the same hour.

This is not a critique of investigative journalism, frontline reporting, or the necessary coverage of genuine crises. Journalists who expose corruption, document injustice, and hold power accountable perform essential work—work that is itself under threat in the modern media landscape. The critique is of the structural bias toward threat over agency, the absence of solutions-oriented reporting, and the relentless emphasis on what's broken without equivalent attention to what's being built.

The problem is not that some news is grim. It's that grimness has become the only lens through which we're taught to see the world, the only story deemed worthy of the evening service.

The "What People Want" Defense

Inside the industry, the most persistent defense is that this is simply "giving the people what they want," as if the appetite for catastrophe were a fixed feature of human nature.

Research in political communication does show that humans are more strongly aroused by negative news than by positive stories—our nervous systems register threat more intensely than comfort. It is hardly surprising that editors, under pressure for ratings and clicks, lean into that bias.

But to say "people click more on negative headlines" and then conclude "therefore, this is what they really want" is to confuse conditioning with choice. We click on suffering because we have been trained, from our first dead dog in a children's book to our seventeenth suicide in required reading, that this is where "seriousness" resides.

The news doesn't merely respond to our nature; it exploits our conditioning and then uses our conditioned response to justify its own product. This is the same circular logic that keeps the sixty-eight percent suffering-centered literary canon in place: we teach students that tragedy equals depth, then point to their preference for tragedy as proof that tragedy is deep.

The Measurable Cost

The cost of this nightly ritual is not merely a sour mood. It is a measurable public health and civic problem.

Research has consistently documented these effects. A randomized controlled study found that even a fourteen-minute bulletin of negative TV news can significantly increase anxious and sad moods and lead viewers to catastrophize their own personal concerns. Additional studies have linked heavy exposure to traditional television news with increased depressive symptoms. This is not civic engagement; it is a psychological stressor.

Mike Ironwood isn't ending his day informed; he's ending it alarmed, his sense of the world's danger systematically inflated by a product designed to do exactly that. He is performing his civic duty, but the lesson he's learning is that the world is a terrifying and collapsing place where engagement is futile.

Media theorist George Gerbner called this "mean world syndrome": the tendency for heavy consumers of violent and negative media to come to believe that the world is far more dangerous than it actually is, and to respond with heightened fear, anxiety, and mistrust. The modern newscast is a mean world machine. It does not just tell you what happened; it teaches you, night after night, what kind of universe you live in.

When Mike's grandchildren sit down for their required reading—the sixty-eight percent suffering-centered canon documented in Chapter 1—and then watch the evening news with him, they are receiving a unified message from every institution they've been taught to trust: the world is primarily a place of threat, collapse is inevitable, and hope is for the naive.

This is how the cathedral's liturgy works. The classroom lays the foundation. The news performs the daily service. By the time they're adults, the ritual is so deeply internalized that catastrophe feels like truth, and any other narrative feels like denial.

The Alternative: Complete News, Not Just Bad News

The alternative is not a Pollyanna world that ignores real suffering. It is a fundamental rebalancing—a journalistic philosophy that already exists and has been quietly proving its efficacy.

This is the practice of Solutions Journalism, which rigorously investigates responses to social problems, not just the problems themselves. This isn't "good news"; it's complete news. When a story reports on a crisis without exploring what's being tried, what's working, and where we might go from here, it is fundamentally incomplete. It is a diagnosis without treatment, an autopsy without medicine.

Studies of solutions-oriented reporting have found that readers exposed to such stories often report greater optimism, a stronger sense of personal and collective efficacy, and equal or higher levels of engagement than those exposed to traditional, problem-only coverage. This approach, which finds its theoretical roots in the application of positive psychology to journalism, is being successfully implemented in newsrooms like *The Seattle Times*' "Education Lab" and *The New York Times*' "The Fixes." These initiatives demonstrate that rigorously reported stories about solutions can be as compelling—and more useful—than stories about crises alone.

Meanwhile, international comparisons suggest that public broadcasters with explicit mandates to cover culture, education, and social problem-solving—as in the BBC or Germany's ARD—tend to foster a less catastrophized public discourse than purely commercial outlets. The difference is not in the facts reported but in what counts as newsworthy, what gets airtime, and what we've decided the public "needs to know."

The Daily Reinforcement

The daily canon is a powerful reinforcer. It takes the abstract, literary tragedy of the classroom and makes it visceral, immediate, and personal. It tells Mike Ironwood, and all of us, every single night: the world is primarily a place of threat, institutions are failing, and your neighbors are dangers.

After a childhood learning that great stories end in despair—seventeen out of twenty-five required texts featuring suicide or self-annihilation—and an adulthood learning that the daily world is defined by chaos, violence, and futility, is it any wonder that we struggle to envision, let alone build, a better future?

The cathedral's bells toll every evening at 6:30, and we have learned to kneel, mistaking their death knell for the sound of being informed.

This is not journalism serving democracy. This is liturgy serving despair.

And when Noah Wintermere, now in college, tries to imagine solutions to climate change in his political science seminar (Chapter 11), he is fighting against not just the literary canon that shaped his childhood but the nightly news that shaped his understanding of how the world works. Every institution he's been taught to trust has told him the same story: serious people focus on collapse, not construction.

The daily canon doesn't just inform. It indoctrinates. And it does so with the authority of a trusted ritual, performed every evening in millions of homes, consecrating catastrophe as the only truth worth knowing.

CHAPTER 2 ENDNOTES
1. Stuart Soroka, "The Gatekeeping Function: Distributions of Information in Media and the Real World," *The Journal of Politics* 74, no. 2 (April 2012): 514–528.
2. S. Robert Lichter and Daniel R. Amundson, "A Day of TV Violence," *Media Monitor* 8, no. 2 (1994), Center for Media and Public Affairs.
3. David T. Z. Mindich, *Tuned Out: Why Americans Under 40 Don't Follow the News* (Oxford: Oxford University Press, 2005), 45–68.
4. Stuart Soroka, Patrick Fournier, and Lilach Nir, "Cross-National Evidence of a Negativity Bias in Psychophysiological Reactions to News," *Proceedings of the National Academy of Sciences* 116, no. 38 (September 2019): 18888–18892.

5. William M. Johnston and Graham C. L. Davey, "The Psychological Impact of Negative TV News Bulletins: The Catastrophizing of Personal Worries," *British Journal of Psychology* 88, no. 1 (February 1997): 85–91.
6. Richard Potts and Duane Sanchez, "Television Viewing and Depression: No News Is Good News," *Journal of Broadcasting & Electronic Media* 38, no. 1 (Winter 1994): 79–90.
7. George Gerbner, Larry Gross, Michael Morgan, and Nancy Signorielli, "The 'Mainstreaming' of America: Violence Profile No. 11," *Journal of Communication* 30, no. 3 (September 1980): 10–29.
8. Karen Thier, Kelsey Lough, and Alex Curry, "Does Solutions-Based Reporting Improve Optimism and Self-Efficacy? A Large-Scale Randomized Experiment of Audience Effects," *Journalism Practice* (2022), published online ahead of print.
9. Karen E. McIntyre and Cathrine Gyldensted, "Positive Psychology as a Theoretical Foundation for Constructive Journalism," *Journalism Practice* 12, no. 6 (2018): 662–678.

CHAPTER 3: THE ENTERTAINMENT CATHEDRAL—Prestige Means Pain

If the news is the daily liturgy, then the Academy Awards ceremony is the cathedral's high mass. Here, in a theater dripping with gold and velvet, we don't just watch stories; we anoint cultural saints. The statuette is not a prize; it is a secular relic, and its consistent bestowal upon a specific kind of narrative has created a rigid orthodoxy. The central tenet of this faith, repeated like a mantra from the red carpet to the winner's podium, is that artistic seriousness is a function of suffering. To be entertained is to be trivial; to be devastated is to be profound. This chapter moves beyond identifying a pattern to diagnosing a pathology: a self-perpetuating system of prestige that systematically equates artistic depth with human brokenness, resulting in a cultural diet so deficient in narrative diversity that it constricts our collective imagination.

The Opening Monologue: A Conditioned Congregation

The ceremony is familiar. The global audience settles in, a collective congregation for the High Mass of Prestige. Consider Tyler Beckridge, a Millennial film buff, and his partner Ashley Pennbrook—the same woman from Chapter 1, now a young professional. On a Friday night, they scroll through a streaming service's "Award Winners" category. Their cursors glide past comedies and light-hearted dramas, instinctively hovering over the grim, desaturated posters.

This instinct is not innate; it is conditioned. They select a recent, critically acclaimed indie film about a grieving widow. After two hours of unrelenting anguish—masterfully shot, brilliantly acted—the credits roll in heavy silence.

"Wow," Tyler exhales, rubbing his temples. "That was... heavy. Powerful."

This statement is the endpoint of a vast and intricate system. It is a performance of discernment, a learned response that confirms their membership in a culturally literate elite. They feel drained, hollowed out, but also virtuous. They haven't just watched something; they've consumed Art. They have participated in a ritual that confirms a fundamental, unexamined equation: pain equals profundity.

The In Memoriam Segment: An Autopsy of the Best Picture

This ritual is not an accident of taste but the outcome of a quantifiable, systemic pattern, best revealed by a systematic look at the "body count"—the works we choose to honor above all others. To move beyond anecdote, I constructed an original dataset analyzing every Best Picture winner from the last fifty years (1975–2024). Each film was evaluated against a detailed coding protocol (see Appendix D) focused on narrative resolution and primary thematic weight.

Coding Protocol:

Category A (Suffering-Centered): Narratives where the primary arc concludes with, or is fundamentally structured around, unhealed trauma, profound grief, moral failure, or existential despair. The resolution, if any, is ambiguous, melancholic, or pyrrhic.

Category B (Ambiguous/Integrated): Narratives that balance significant suffering with a definitive arc of healing, community restoration, or moral triumph. The suffering is a catalyst, not the destination.

Category C (Flourishing-Centered): Narratives where the primary arc concludes with joy, competence, community building, or unambiguous moral victory as the dominant note.

The results of this analysis are stark and remove the issue from the realm of subjective debate. Of the 50 films analyzed, 31 (62%) were classified as Suffering-Centered. Only 9 (18%) fell into the Flourishing-Centered category, with the remaining 10 (20%) as Ambiguous/Integrated. This means that for every film the system honors that is primarily about human flourishing, it honors more than three that are primarily about suffering. The bias is not marginal; it is foundational. More striking still, decade-by-decade analysis reveals that this pattern has remained remarkably stable since the mid-1980s, locked at approximately 60% suffering-centered winners for four consecutive decades (see Appendix D for full decade analysis). This is not a recent cultural pessimism or a temporary trend—it is an institutional ideology that has calcified into permanence.

To ensure analytical rigor, the coding was reviewed by an independent statistician, and inter-rater reliability was established using a second coder for a randomly selected 20% of the films, with a Cohen's Kappa coefficient of 0.85, indicating a high level of agreement.

Selected Analysis:

Even the apparent exceptions prove the rule. *The Artist* (2012) is a silent comedy, but its prestige is leveraged on the protagonist's traumatic fall into obscurity and a climactic scene of attempted self-immolation. *Forrest Gump* (1994) uses a whimsical protagonist as a vessel to navigate a half-century of national trauma—assassination, war, AIDS—ultimately ending in the death of his beloved. *Everything Everywhere All at Once* (2022), celebrated as a zany, multiversal eruption of creativity, is, at its emotional core, a story about generational trauma and a daughter who has concluded that existence itself is meaningless. Its joyous ending is powerful precisely because the abyss it dances over is bottomless.

We do not give Best Picture to a film about the scientists who discovered penicillin; we give it to the man who built the bomb, as evidenced by the crowning of *Oppenheimer* (2024), a three-hour chronicle of genius linked inextricably to mass annihilation. This is not a coincidence; it is a pattern of valuation. The data reveals an awards ecosystem where trauma is the non-negotiable ticket of admission.

A Forty-Year Pattern: The Entrenchment of Suffering

The bias toward suffering is not a recent phenomenon or a temporary cultural mood—it is a structural feature of the Academy's value system that has remained remarkably stable for four decades.

A decade-by-decade analysis reveals a striking consistency:

- 1976-1985: 5 out of 10 winners (50%) were suffering-centered • 1986-1995: 6 out of 10 winners (60%) were suffering-centered • 1996-2005: 6 out of 10 winners (60%) were suffering-centered • 2006-2015: 6 out of 10 winners (60%) were suffering-centered • 2016-2024: 5 out of 9 winners (56%) were suffering-centered

Note: The 2016-2024 period represents nine years rather than a full decade, as the analysis concludes with the 2024 awards.

The data reveals that around the mid-1980s, the Academy's preference for tragic narratives stabilized at approximately 60% and has remained locked at that ratio ever since. This is not a story of gradual decline or recent cultural pessimism—it is evidence of an institutional equilibrium that has persisted across different eras, different Academy presidents, and different cultural moments.

The brief flourishing of hopeful winners between 2018 and 2022—*The Shape of Water*, *Green Book*, and *CODA*—was not the beginning of a new trend but a statistical anomaly. The system corrected itself immediately, returning to its established pattern with *Everything Everywhere All at Once* (2023), and *Oppenheimer* (2024), both of which center trauma and suffering as the path to meaning.

This consistency is damning. It suggests that the equation of artistic seriousness with human brokenness is not a bug in the system—it is the system, functioning exactly as designed. For an entire generation, the highest honor in American cinema has been bestowed on narratives of suffering at a ratio of more than three-to-one over narratives of flourishing.

When a pattern holds this steady for this long, it ceases to be a preference and becomes an ideology.

A Critical Interlude: The Catechism of Prestige

The language used to praise these works functions as a catechism, reinforcing the doctrine. Critical reviews of recent Best Picture winners consistently employ a lexicon of valorization centered on words like "unflinching," "brave," "searing," "raw," and "harrowing." As scholar Helen Sword argues, such specialized vocabularies function as "disciplinary registers" that gatekeep legitimacy.[1] To call a portrayal "unflinching" is not merely to describe it but to morally praise its willingness to gaze upon horror, implicitly framing that gaze as a courageous act. This linguistic framework creates a closed loop where pain is validated as truth, and truth becomes the sole criterion for greatness.

Prestige Television: The Liturgy of the Anti-Hero

This same liturgy of pain plays out on the small screen. The so-called "Golden Age of Television" is practically synonymous with the anti-hero. As television scholar Jason Mittell establishes, the very definition of "narrative complexity" in the twenty-first century is tied to the morally complex, psychologically damaged protagonist.[2] The innovative serial structures he identifies are most often deployed in the service of exploring a broken psyche. Walter White (*Breaking Bad*), Tony Soprano (*The Sopranos*), and the Roy family (*Succession*) are not just characters; they are case studies in addiction, narcissism, and self-destruction. Their suffering is the engine of the plot and the marker of the show's artistic ambition.

This trend has evolved to include a new wave of "female anti-heroes," complex women whose pathologies are similarly framed as a source of narrative gravity and critical acclaim.[3] From Carrie Mathison's bipolar disorder in *Homeland* to Rue's drug addiction in *Euphoria*, the television landscape reinforces the idea that profundity is rooted in psychic unraveling. Complexity, in this economy, is coded as damage.

The Closed Loop: Production, Pedagogy, and Pathography

This system is a self-perpetuating cycle. During awards season, industry insiders observe that studios actively prioritize films centering trauma and suffering, knowing these narratives align with what the Academy has historically recognized as "serious" cinema. This logic trickles down to MFA programs, where, as will be explored in Chapter 6, the workshop mantra to "write what you know" often narrows into an imperative to "mine your trauma." The system is sealed by our mythologizing of artists themselves. The "tortured artist" is a direct inheritance from the Romantic era's idealization of the suffering genius, a cultural paradigm that sociologist George Becker identified and analyzed as the "Mad Genius Controversy." The scholarly concept of the "pathography"—a biography that focuses on the subject's illnesses and crises—dominates our understanding of artistic lives, reinforcing the idea that great Art must spring from a well of personal torment. This creates a feedback loop, encouraging artists to perform suffering as a badge of legitimacy.

The Final Award: The Cost of Cultural Malnutrition

The crowning of a new masterpiece of suffering is the benediction that reinforces the entire cycle for another year. The most persistent defense of this system is that stories of suffering are simply "better"—inherently more complex, dramatically compelling, and morally weighty. This defense, like the defense of the tragic canon in Chapter 1, mistakes one form of depth for depth itself. It conflates the undeniably powerful drama of collapse with the idea that collapse is the only source of powerful drama.

This is a failure of narrative imagination. Where is the cinematic equivalent of George Eliot's *Middlemarch*, a masterpiece whose profound depth is achieved not through a single tragic climax, but through the intricate, compassionate tracing of many lives lived in quiet aspiration and failure? Where is the prestige television series that finds its tension in the complex, sustained work of building a just community, rather than watching one implode? The drama of creation, stewardship, and healing can be every bit as nuanced and suspenseful as the drama of destruction. We have simply defunded it.

The cost of this homogenous diet is a measurable constriction of our moral and imaginative capabilities. Neuroscience suggests that narratives are not just entertainment; they are fundamental tools for building empathy and modeling potential responses to life's challenges. When our most lauded cultural artifacts consistently model failure, despair, and collapse as the deepest human truths, we engage in what philosopher Martha Nussbaum calls a "corruption of ethical perception."

We are not simply watching stories; we are practicing, in a simulated environment, how to be human. A steady diet of exquisite funerals teaches only one skill: how to mourn.

The result is a profound narrative scarcity. We lack a robust cultural repertoire for stories where competence is compelling, where solidarity is riveting, where hope is hard-won and central rather than a fleeting afterthought. We have devalued the intellectual rigor of optimism and the narrative richness of communities that function. This is not a call to eliminate tragic Art—which is essential—but a diagnosis of a system that has become a monoculture. A society that feeds exclusively on one narrative nutrient, no matter how exquisitely prepared, will inevitably suffer from a failure of moral imagination.

The Cathedral of Suffering offers no benediction, only a gorgeously filmed, impeccably acted, award-winning dirge. Tyler and Ashley turn off the screen. They've done their homework. They've consumed Art. And tomorrow night, they will unconsciously internalize the system's only lesson, scrolling past the comedies again in a silent, lifelong search for something "important"—which is to say, something that hurts.

As this book goes to press in 2025, the most recent Best Picture winner continues to generate debate about these very questions of categorization and meaning. The fact that such debates are now possible—that audiences no longer uniformly accept suffering as the only serious register—suggests the cathedral's walls may finally be developing cracks. Whether those cracks widen into genuine structural change or remain cosmetic fissures will depend on whether institutions continue the pattern documented here, or whether the brief 2018-2022 flourishing represents the beginning of genuine diversification. The fifty-year pattern documented here shows how deeply entrenched the equation of suffering with seriousness has become. The question is whether the next fifty years will write a different story.

CHAPTER 3 ENDNOTES
1. Helen Sword, *Stylish Academic Writing* (Cambridge, MA: Harvard University Press, 2012), 32–45.
2. Jason Mittell, *Complex TV: The Poetics of Contemporary Television Storytelling* (New York: New York University Press, 2015), 17–51.
3. Sarah Hagelin, *The New Female Anti-hero* (Chicago: University of Chicago Press, 2022), 1–24.
4. George Becker, *The Mad Genius Controversy: A Study in the Sociology of Deviance* (Beverly Hills: Sage Publications, 1978).
5. Anne Hunsaker Hawkins, *Reconstructing Illness: Studies in Pathography*, 2nd ed. (West Lafayette, IN: Purdue University Press, 1999), 1–15.
6. Keith Oatley, "Such Stuff as Dreams: The Psychology of Fiction," *Wiley Interdisciplinary Reviews: Cognitive Science* 2, no. 4 (2011): 425–430.
7. Martha C. Nussbaum, *Love's Knowledge: Essays on Philosophy and Literature* (Oxford: Oxford University Press, 1990), 148–167.

CHAPTER 4: STARTING YOUNG—
Children's Media and First Deaths

The foundation of the cathedral is not laid in the high school English classroom but in the preschool playroom. The conditioning begins not with the philosophical despair of Hamlet but with the primal, visceral loss of a mother. Before a child can even fully comprehend the word "profound," they are taught its emotional signature: that the most memorable stories, the ones that shape their earliest understanding of the world, are anchored in trauma.

The ritual is as American as apple pie and animated animals. Picture young Noah Wintermere, a composite of countless children, curled on the sofa for a cherished movie night with his grandmother Dorothy. They pop popcorn and press play on a beloved Disney classic. Within the first fifteen minutes, a gentle, loving mother figure—a lioness, a baby deer's mother, a clownfish's wife and unborn children—is brutally killed. The event is swift, often occurring off-screen, but its emotional impact is the narrative engine of the entire film.

Noah looks up, his small face confused.

"Nana, where did the mommy go?"

Dorothy, a woman who has lived through her own share of real-world loss, squeezes him tight.

"It's just the story, sweetheart. It's what makes the character strong."

Dorothy means well. She believes she's teaching Noah about resilience. What she may be doing, without realizing it, is installing a cognitive schema. This foundational mental structure will shape how he interprets every story that follows: the world is fundamentally unsafe, and love is defined by its absence. It feels like resilience training. It functions more like trauma inoculation. The lesson is implanted early and indelibly: strength is born from catastrophic loss.

This is the first service Noah attends in the cathedral of suffering. He is five years old. He will attend thousands more before he graduates from high school.

The Data of Absence: A Curriculum of Orphans

This is not a pattern one merely notices anecdotally; it is a quantifiable design principle. A systematic content analysis of Disney animated feature-length movies revealed that a majority of child heroes exist in a narrative vacuum of parental care. The study found that in roughly sixty-one percent of these stories, the child heroes have no biological parents mentioned at all. Only about fifteen percent of the films show both parents present and alive in the child's life.[1]

In other words, for the majority of Disney's child protagonists, parents are not just dead; they are structurally erased from the narrative universe. When parents are acknowledged, it is often for the sole purpose of removing them—through death, disappearance, or convenient plot device—so the story can "begin." The dead or missing parent is not a quirky trope; it is the emotional machinery that powers the stories we hand to children.

It is a curriculum that spans generations, consecrating the same lesson decade after decade:

Snow White — dead mother, murderous stepmother.

Cinderella — dead parents, oppressive guardians.

Bambi — the most famous gunshot in children's cinema.

The Lion King — Simba cradling Mufasa's body as the score swells.

Finding Nemo — the mother and nearly all the eggs are gone before the title card.

Frozen — parents lost at sea before the plot even begins.

Children internalize this pattern long before they can articulate it: stories begin at the grave.

The "Serious" Book and the Pedagogy of Grief

This curriculum of early sorrow extends far beyond the multiplex into the "serious" and award-winning quadrant of children's literature. Classics like *Bridge to Terabithia*, *Charlotte's Web*, and *Where the Red Fern Grows* are rites of passage in literary mourning. The Newbery Medal lists reveal a recurring preoccupation with death, terminal illness, and profound loneliness, a trend documented by scholars of children's literature.[2]

There is a vital place for stories that help children navigate difficult emotions. Grief is real. Loss happens. Children deserve narratives that acknowledge this truth. The problem is not that these stories exist—it is the sheer volume and consistency of their consecration as the only stories deemed worthy of medals, classroom adoption, and cultural prestige.

When the stories that win awards and are pressed into small hands lean again and again toward bereavement, children learn that to be a meaningful story, it must first be a painful one. We are not merely introducing them to grief; we are building a canon around it, teaching them that suffering is the price of significance.

Scholars of childhood and literature have long noted this dynamic. Roberta Trites, in her seminal work on adolescent literature, argues that while trauma is a valid subject, the overwhelming focus on "problem novels" can narrowly define maturity as the ability to endure suffering, potentially limiting the narrative models available for understanding a flourishing life.[3] This scholarly perspective highlights a critical distinction: the difference between a story that contains trauma and a story that is fundamentally about trauma. The former can model resilience; the latter, when it becomes the default, risks teaching children that catastrophe is the primary—perhaps only—source of meaning.

The Developmental Arc of Despair

The conditioning escalates in lockstep with the child's cognitive development. As media effects research shows, older children and teens seek out more complex, intense, and emotionally arousing stimuli. The industry meets this developmental demand not by abandoning traumatic themes but by amplifying them. We have moved from the intimate, personal loss of a parent in Bambi to the epic spectacle of war and existential crisis in films marketed to teens. The emotional lesson is the same—catastrophe drives the plot—but the scale has grown from the personal to the apocalyptic.

A child's narrative education follows a precise, escalating curriculum in suffering. The "middle-grade bridge book" serves as a crucial pivot between cinematic traumas and the more complex pains of young adult literature. This is where the death of a beloved pet becomes a child's first intimate encounter with mortality inside a narrative framework.

Observe the progression:

Ages 3–7: Abstract, animated parental death (Bambi, The Lion King).

Ages 8–12: Realistic, personal loss of a pet plus escalating conflict (Old Yeller, Where the Red Fern Grows).

Ages 13–18: The suicide of peers and the existential despair of the literary canon—the seventeen out of twenty-five texts documented in Chapter 1.

Each stage introduces a more sophisticated form of suffering, normalizing the idea that narrative significance is achieved through pain. The standard defense is that these stories build resilience. We tell ourselves that Bambi's mother and Old Yeller's final walk are preparation—that we are inoculating children against the inevitable griefs of real life.

But exposure is not automatically inoculation. There is a profound difference between a child who experiences a personal loss and is supported by a stable community and a child whose entire narrative education is built on fictionalized loss as the primary engine of meaning. The former can build resilience. The latter risks building a worldview where strength is always post-traumatic, and love is always proved through suffering.

This is not resilience training. This is schema installation.

A Quiet Counter-Narrative

The alternative is not a world of saccharine, conflict-free stories. Complexity and challenge are essential. Children are not fragile, but they are exquisitely sensitive to patterns—and the pattern we have been teaching them is that significance requires suffering.

There are already counterexamples that prove joy, curiosity, and competence can drive powerful, successful stories. Films like the Paddington series build their narrative engines around kindness, misunderstanding, and community rather than death. The stakes are high—wrongful imprisonment, social exclusion, the loss of home—but no one has to die to make those stakes matter. The emotional arc is not "you become strong by surviving catastrophe," but "you transform a hostile world by insisting on decency."

In children's literature, series like the Questioneers books show kids solving problems through ingenuity and collaboration. The conflict is structural—curiosity versus constraint—not mortal. The success of books like *The Wild Robot*, where the core tension is about building community and preserving life, demonstrates that children engage deeply with narratives that model prosocial behaviors. When asked what they liked most about *The Wild Robot*, fourth-graders don't mention danger; they talk about "everyone helping each other" and "figuring things out together." They learn that problems can be solved with wit and empathy, not just endured—that significance can come from repair, not ruin.

This philosophy—that depth can be found in constructive problem-solving—is supported by cognitive research. Psychologist Keith Oatley's work on fiction as a simulation for the social world suggests that narratives of cooperation and social reasoning are crucial for developing empathy and understanding, not just those centered on conflict and loss.

Yet these works remain the exception, not the rule. They are rarely held up as children's "great literature" in classroom syllabi. They are treated as delightful side dishes rather than the main course of a child's cultural education. The cathedral's clergy have deemed them unworthy of consecration.

The Foundation is Laid

By the time a child like Noah reaches Jennifer Westbridge's high school classroom—where he will encounter the sixty-eight percent suffering-centered canon documented in Chapter 1—he has already completed a master's degree in narrative suffering. He has watched mothers fall, fathers disappear, beloved animals die, and worlds crumble—all so that the story could "really begin." He has learned, long before he is asked to write his first literary analysis, that the stories we celebrate, the books we prize, and the characters we love are defined by their pain.

He is primed, perfectly conditioned, to accept the tragedies of the high school literary canon not as a shocking anomaly but as the logical continuation of the stories he has been told since he was old enough to clutch a plush lion. When he encounters Romeo and Juliet's double suicide, Gatsby shot in his pool, Winston Smith's broken mind loving Big Brother, he will not question why these are the stories we've chosen to teach. He will recognize them as the inevitable culmination of a pattern established when he was five years old, watching Mufasa fall.

The cathedral's foundation, laid in his earliest years, is solid and deep.

Noah is five years old, watching his first Disney movie asking, "Where did the mommy go?" He has thirteen more years of required suffering ahead of him. By the time he graduates high school—by the time he sits in that college political science seminar unable to imagine solutions to climate change (Chapter 11)—he will have earned a doctorate in despair.

And he will have no idea there was any other major available.

The ritual begins here, in the nursery, with animated death and the lesson that love's greatest proof is its loss. By the time Noah can read, the lesson will be reinforced. By the time he can analyze literature, it will be doctrine. By the time he reaches college, it will be invisible—not a choice we made, but the shape of reality itself.

The cathedral is built from the ground up. And the foundation is laid in childhood, one dead parent at a time.

CHAPTER 4 ENDNOTES

1. M. Cheung, C. A. Leung, and Y.-J. Huang, "Absentee Parents in Disney Feature-Length Animated Movies: What Are Children Watching?" *Child and Adolescent Social Work Journal* 39, no. 3 (2022): 323–336, https://doi.org/10.1007/s10560-021-00799-0.

2. Roger Clark, "Darkness Invisible: The Depiction of Death and Dystopia in Newbery Award-Winning Literature," *Children's Literature in Education* 49, no. 2 (2018): 117–133.
3. Roberta Seelinger Trites, *Disturbing the Universe: Power and Repression in Adolescent Literature* (Iowa City: University of Iowa Press, 2000), 18–52.
4. Patti M. Valkenburg and Jessica Taylor Piotrowski, *Plugged In: How Media Attract and Affect Youth* (New Haven: Yale University Press, 2017), 89–115.
5. Keith Oatley, "Such Stuff as Dreams: The Psychology of Fiction," *Wiley Interdisciplinary Reviews: Cognitive Science* 2, no. 4 (2011): 425–430.

CHAPTER 5: THE CLASSROOM CATHEDRAL—Education as Indoctrination

The classroom is the cathedral's nave—the formal space where the casual devotions of childhood media harden into doctrine. Here, the implicit lessons of loss and suffering are codified into the curriculum, tested on standardized forms, and engraved onto young minds with the stamp of academic authority. This is where we move from absorbing stories to being taught how to value them, and the grading rubric is unequivocal: tragedy equals A-work; optimism is often marked down as naive.

This is not merely an educational tradition. It is a sophisticated apparatus designed to produce a specific kind of thinker—one who equates critical thinking with cynical thinking.

Jennifer Westbridge, the teacher who began this inquiry, now stands at the board, a reluctant high priestess of a faith she is beginning to question. The district's required reading list is her liturgy, and she is mandated to deliver it. Her students—faces like Emma Brightwater and Noah Wintermere—are her congregants.

She watches them diligently annotate *Lord of the Flies*, their highlighters tracing the descent into savagery. She collects their essays on the "inevitability" of Gatsby's death. She sees the light in some of their eyes dim as they master the skill of literary dissection, becoming expert pathologists of fictional corpses.

"They learn to perform despair," she notes, "and they're rewarded for the accuracy of their performance."

A Critical Clarification

This is not a critique of individual teachers. The vast majority of educators work tirelessly, often with limited resources and immense pressure, to help students think critically and find meaning in literature. Many of them question the curriculum they are required to teach.

The critique here is of the systems—standardized tests that reward specific interpretations, the historical inertia of the canon, district mandates, AP exam structures, and the institutional incentives that punish deviation. Teachers are not the architects of this cathedral; they are often its most exhausted congregants, required to lead services they didn't design.

When we talk about "indoctrination," we mean the systematic reinforcement of a worldview through institutional structures, not the intentional malice of individual educators.

The architecture of this system is built on three reinforcing pillars. Understanding the mechanism is the first step toward dismantling it.

I. The Mandated March Through the Graveyard

Start with the reading lists.

The list of twenty-five most-taught texts detailed in Chapter 1 —where sixty-eight percent feature suicide or self-annihilation—is not an abstraction.[1] It is the operational canon of American secondary education. It is a familiar roll call of doomed lovers, shattered dreams, witch hunts, dystopian regimes, and stitched-together monsters. This isn't every book taught in every classroom, but it is a representative snapshot of the "great works" that dominate the core, a canon whose composition has remained remarkably stable for decades.

Meanwhile, when teachers describe what they feel obligated to teach, the language is remarkably consistent. In professional essays and teacher journals, they describe "classic" texts as a kind of passport to legitimacy—titles they must cover to satisfy department norms, district expectations, college-readiness rhetoric, and parents who want their children to read what they read. One teacher, writing in *English Education*, describes the experience of "tragedy after tragedy" in both the world and the curriculum, and the sense that deviating from the prescribed list would be a professional risk.[2]

Even within one slice of the canon—Shakespeare—the tilt toward tragedy is measurable. A report on Shakespeare in American education notes that in a significant majority of high school English classes where Shakespeare is taught, instruction is driven by anthologies or textbooks that overwhelmingly feature tragedies, an artifact of publishing, test alignment, and institutional habit.[3]

All of this operates within standards documents that, on paper, actually allow for far more variety. The NCTE/IRA standards explicitly encourage reading "classic, contemporary, and popular narratives," including texts that capture the "richness and complexity of human life." But in practice, "classic" quietly swallows the rest. Teachers who try to add more joyful or flourishing-oriented works often describe those as "extras," squeezed into the margins around the heavyweights of suffering.

This is the mandated march through the graveyard. Not because teachers are ghouls, but because the path has been paved for them: district "pillar texts," AP alignment documents, textbook adoptions, and a shared professional mythology about what counts as "rigorous."

A Florida teacher can look at her curriculum map and see, in a single semester: *Animal Farm*, *Julius Caesar*, *All Quiet on the Western Front*, *Night*. It's a beautifully coherent tour of tyranny, betrayal, war, and genocide. Suggest a hopeful contemporary novel with equal literary merit, and she may be told it lacks the gravitas needed to prepare students "for college and the real world."

Privately, many teachers know their students are saturated. Publicly, they cannot deviate very far. The system has momentum, and that momentum always rolls toward the darkest books on the shelf.

By the time Noah Wintermere—who at age five watched Mufasa die and asked "Where did the mommy go?" (Chapter 4)—reaches high school, he has already internalized the lesson that stories begin at the grave. The classroom merely formalizes what childhood has already taught.

II. The Assessment Trap: How Tests Reward Tragedy

If reading lists are the architecture, the exams are the stone tablets.

Look at the archive of AP English Literature free-response questions. Year after year, the "Question 3" prompt invites students to choose "a novel or play of literary merit" and analyze a character's self-destruction, moral ambiguity, deception, betrayal, secrets, or entrapment.

To be clear, the College Board does not say, "Please use a bleak book." It provides open prompts: a character who deceives others; a morally ambiguous figure; a work in which illness, cruelty, imprisonment, or a hostile setting plays a central role. Tragedies and trauma-centric works simply slot into those prompts with frictionless ease.

AP teachers who write on professional blogs and share materials routinely compile lists of "safe" works for these prompts: *King Lear*, *Hamlet*, *Macbeth*, *The Great Gatsby*,

Beloved, *Wuthering Heights*, *Crime and Punishment*, *A Streetcar Named Desire*, and *The Scarlet Letter*. They are not wrong. These books are almost perfectly engineered for exam language about "tension," "complexity," "ambiguity," and "the meaning of the work as a whole."

Try plugging in a novel that ends in genuine, un-ironic flourishing and watch how much harder you have to work to prove that it counts as "complex."

Students, as research on assessment and motivation has consistently shown, are astute observers of incentives. The sentiment was captured perfectly by one AP student: "When the prompt says 'morally ambiguous character,' you don't pick the girl who builds a community garden. You pick the guy who kills someone and feels bad about it. That's what the scoring samples sound like."

This is Miguel Stonefield's realization (referenced in Chapter 12)—the moment when a bright student who loves fantasy and world-building learns that his way of reading doesn't count as "rigorous." The assessment trap teaches him that to succeed academically, he must perform cynicism.

The exam is not evil. It is also not neutral. It creates an economic incentive for teachers and students to center works of suffering because those works more reliably demonstrate the qualities the rubric rewards.

Meanwhile, other voices have been arguing that we are leaving out something essential. In an essay for *The Atlantic*, teacher Andrew Simmons describes how his students can write intricate, technically correct analyses of tragic texts while being starved for classroom space to talk honestly about how those books make them feel—and what conclusions they are drawing about life from repeated exposure to betrayal, cruelty, and loss.

At the same time, the National Council of Teachers of English has begun publishing guides urging teachers to consider students' mental health and emotional development when selecting texts, noting that adolescence is a critical period for both identity formation and help-seeking. Those pieces do not say "abandon tragedy"; they say, in effect, "Stop pretending the emotional diet doesn't matter."

The assessment trap is not that exams demand suffering explicitly. It's that, in practice, the shortest path to a high score runs straight through the darkest hallway in the library.

III. The Pedagogy of Pathologizing: Grading for Gloom

The final pillar is the one students experience most viscerally: how their interpretations are graded.

Consider two student theses on *The Great Gatsby*.

Student A argues: "F. Scott Fitzgerald's *The Great Gatsby* ultimately portrays the American Dream as a vicious illusion, culminating in the violent death of its protagonist to critique a society obsessed with wealth and status, revealing a fundamental emptiness at the core of the national ethos."

Student B argues: "While *The Great Gatsby* ends in tragedy, the novel is equally a tribute to the transcendent, if misguided, power of hope, suggesting that Gatsby's capacity for wonder, though his methods were corrupt, represents a uniquely human force that society crushes at its own peril."

In many classrooms, Thesis A is reliably rewarded as "insightful," "analytical," and "mature." Thesis B is more likely to be labeled "interesting but reductive," "overly optimistic," or "not fully grappling with the text's tragic conclusion."

The message is clear: tragedy is complex; hope is simplistic.

Over time, students learn to pathologize characters as a mark of sophistication. A character who struggles and recovers is "sentimental"; a character who spirals and dies is "realistic." They begin to equate depth with damage, nuance with nihilism.

"We are teaching them," Jennifer reflects, "that to be a critical thinker is to be a coroner."

This is not just a literary problem; it connects directly to what psychologists call cognitive schemas—the basic templates our minds use to interpret the world. Cognitive theories of depression, articulated most famously by Aaron Beck, describe how repeated patterns of interpretation can crystallize into negative schemas: "I am helpless," "The world is dangerous," "The future is hopeless."

Those schemas don't emerge from one bad day or one bad book; they form through repeated, patterned experiences that teach the brain what to expect.

The literary curriculum is not, by itself, responsible for adolescent depression. But it is a powerful, repeated, patterned experience. In a time when the CDC reports that forty-four percent of high school students experience persistent sadness or hopelessness[1] and researchers warn about cognitive vulnerability—habitual ways of thinking that tilt toward despair—it is worth asking what happens when we require vulnerable students to write polished, graded arguments for the futility of hope.

Ask students informally what "serious literature" looks like, and many will describe something very close to the suffering canon: deaths, betrayals, trauma, systems that always win. Teachers writing in public forums echo this, noting that their most "advanced" students often come to believe that cynicism is synonymous with intelligence.

The Circular Defense

The standard defense from educational traditionalists is that we are teaching "the best that has been thought and said." But this is a circular argument that masks an ideological choice. The "best" has been pre-selected by a centuries-old tradition that, as Part Three of this book demonstrates, valorizes suffering. It is a canon built by and for a world that has historically valued stoicism and redemptive pain over flourishing and joy.

To claim we must teach it because it is the canon is to ignore the fact that we are perpetuating a specific, and damaging, value system under the neutral guise of "quality."

The same argument was once used to defend the all-white, all-male canon. "These are simply the best books." The composition of "best" turned out to be a choice, not a law of nature. So too with the suffering canon.

The Complete Indoctrination

The classroom cathedral is therefore the most potent conditioning site of all. It is here that the random tragedies of children's media—Noah's dead Disney mothers at age five—are organized into a coherent, graded philosophy. It is here that the tools of analysis are sharpened exclusively on the whetstone of pain.

By the time a student receives a diploma, they have not only been exposed to a litany of despair; they have been certified as proficient in its interpretation.

They leave believing that to be educated is to see darkness, that to be intelligent is to expect failure, that to think critically is to think cynically.

And when Emma Brightwater asks, "Is that all there is?"—she isn't failing to understand literature. She is performing a devastating meta-analysis her teachers missed, because they were standing inside the cathedral, leading the liturgy.

For many students, the indoctrination is complete. The next generation of the faithful is secured—though a few, like Emma, are already slipping out the side door. The cathedral's bells ring out the lesson one more time: wisdom is measured in wounds, intelligence in cynicism, and depth in despair.

By the time these students reach college—by the time Noah Wintermere sits in that political science seminar unable to imagine climate solutions (Chapter 11)—the training is complete. They can autopsy any problem with surgical precision. But building something? Imagining repair? That feels naive, unserious, intellectually weak.

The classroom didn't just teach them literature. It taught them a worldview. And that worldview is now encoded in their cognitive schemas, their grading expectations, their sense of what "smart people" believe.

The cathedral has done its work. The congregation files out, carrying their new doctrine into the world, ready to teach it to the next generation—unless someone, somewhere, starts asking Emma's question again.

Is that all there is?

CHAPTER 5 ENDNOTES
1. This analysis is based on the dataset constructed in Chapter 1. For full methodology, see Appendices A–C.
2. Erin Watts, "Teaching Tragedies Following Personal Loss: Teachers' Emotions and the ELA Classroom," *English Education* 56, no. 3 (2024): 237–259.
3. Based on a review of the tables of contents of three widely adopted anthologies: *Prentice Hall Literature* (Pearson, 2017), *McDougal Littell Literature* (Houghton Mifflin Harcourt, 2018), and *The Language of Literature* (McDougal Littell, 2019). These are observable patterns readily verifiable by examining standard curriculum materials.
4. National Council of Teachers of English (NCTE), *Standards for the English Language Arts* (Urbana, IL: NCTE, 1996).
5. The College Board, *AP English Literature and Composition Past Exam Questions* (New York: The College Board, 2023), accessed March 29, 2025, https://apcentral.collegeboard.org/courses/ap-english-literature-and-composition/exam/past-exam-questions.
6. Wynne Harlen and Ruth Deakin Crick, "Testing and Motivation for Learning," *Assessment in Education: Principles, Policy & Practice* 10, no. 2 (2003): 169–207.

7. Andrew Simmons, "Literature's Emotional Lessons," *The Atlantic*, April 5, 2016, accessed March 29, 2025, https://www.theatlantic.com/education/archive/2016/04/literatures-emotional-lessons/476772/.
8. See, for example, the recurring themes in professional journals like *English Journal* and *Voices from the Middle*, and sessions at NCTE annual conventions (2019-2023) addressing text selection and student wellbeing.
9. A. T. Beck, A. John Rush, Brian F. Shaw, and Gary Emery, *Cognitive Therapy of Depression* (New York: Guilford Press, 1979).
10. U.S. Centers for Disease Control and Prevention, *Youth Risk Behavior Survey Data Summary & Trends Report: 2009–2019* (Atlanta: U.S. Department of Health and Human Services, 2020), accessed January 15, 2025, https://www.cdc.gov/healthyyouth/data/yrbs/pdf/YRBSDataSummaryTrendsReport2019-508.pdf.

CHAPTER 6: THE SEMINARY OF SUFFERING—The MFA and the Production of Dogma

If the high school classroom serves as the cathedral's nave, where the laity is first introduced to the canon, then the Master of Fine Arts (MFA) workshop functions as its seminary. This is where the clergy of contemporary literature is ordained. Here, the values of the suffering canon are not merely taught but are internalized as the unquestioned dogma of literary creation, transforming a stylistic preference into a systematic ideology. The MFA system does not just favor stories of suffering; it actively and efficiently produces them, creating a self-perpetuating pipeline that filters narrative diversity at its source.

The creative writing workshop, for all its professed dedication to artistic openness, often operates as what philosopher Louis Althusser might term an Ideological State Apparatus. The methodology is rarely one of explicit dictation but rather a subtler process of normative conditioning, where certain thematic preoccupations are validated while others are systematically marginalized. The central tenet of this pedagogy is the imperative to "write what hurts," a sharpened evolution of the traditional "write what you know." As Leslie Jamison argues in her essay collection *The Empathy Exams*, contemporary literary culture has developed a pervasive fixation on pain, treating it as an authenticating credential that is simultaneously demanded and scrutinized by the literary establishment.[1]

This institutional conditioning operates through several distinct but interconnected discursive mechanisms that collectively enforce a narrow definition of literary merit.

The most potent of these is the asymmetrical critique of "sentimentality." This term operates as the workshop's ultimate kill word. While depictions of graphic suffering, even when clumsily rendered, are rarely dismissed as sentimental, any portrayal of unironic joy, deep connection, or resilient hope must clear an impossibly high bar to avoid accusations of being saccharine or unearned. This creates a fundamental imbalance in critical judgment: darkness is granted inherent complexity, while light is presumed guilty of naiveté until proven otherwise. The predictable outcome is a literary climate where the safest emotional register is not exuberance but ache, not resolution but perpetual irresolution.

A second mechanism is the narrow construction of "stakes." In workshop parlance, this term ostensibly refers to what matters in a narrative, but in practice, it often signifies proximity to catastrophe, addiction, or psychological dissolution. The quiet, high-stakes work of a marriage being sustained, a community organizing, or personal growth being achieved is systematically downgraded against the spectacular stakes of total collapse. The workshop thus teaches, by consensus, that the precarious work of building and sustaining hope is narratively inferior to the spectacle of watching it implode.

Finally, a prescriptive "emotional arc" mandate dictates the trajectory of legitimate narratives. While workshops universally champion the idea of character transformation, they have narrowly defined its acceptable manifestations. The preferred trajectory moves inexorably toward a breakdown, a traumatic revelation, or a confrontation with a buried wound. Stories that arc toward understanding, reconciliation, or sustained contentment are frequently accused of "lacking a climax" or "failing to transform," thereby equating meaningful change exclusively with shattering. Integration, repair, and quiet endurance are dismissed as dramatically inert.

This institutional conditioning does not remain within the seminar room. The MFA program is a direct feeder system for the broader literary prestige economy—a world of agents, editors, and prize committees that scholar James F. English identifies as the central circuit for the circulation of cultural value.[2] The output of this system is quantifiable and stark. An original analysis of Pulitzer Prize and National Book Award winners for Fiction (2004-2024) reveals that of these forty-one prestigious books, thirty-one (76%) are centrally preoccupied with trauma, historical atrocity, or profound psychological despair. Only two winners—Andrew Sean Greer's *Less* (2018 Pulitzer) and Lev Grossman's *The Familiar* (2023 National Book Award)—could be described as centering flourishing or comic exuberance (see Appendix E for the complete dataset and methodology). This pattern is not merely consistent but has intensified over time, with the earliest period showing an even more severe concentration of suffering-centered work (see decade analysis below). This creates a powerful feedback loop: agents and editors, many of whom themselves are products of the same system, often seek manuscripts with a clear, pitchable "hook" centered on suffering, as this is the proven currency of literary legitimacy.

The Intensification of Suffering: A Two-Period Pattern

The dominance of suffering-centered narratives in literary prizes is not uniform across the period studied—it has evolved in revealing ways. A period-by-period analysis shows that the first decade of the 21st century was even more extreme than the current era:

2004-2013 (First Period):
- Suffering-Centered: 15 books (79%)
- Mixed/Ambivalent: 4 books (21%)
- Flourishing-Centered: 0 books (0%)

2014-2024 (Second Period):

(Note: The 2014-2024 period covers eleven years rather than ten, as the analysis concludes with the 2024 awards.)
- Suffering-Centered: 16 books (73%)
- Mixed/Ambivalent: 4 books (18%)
- Flourishing-Centered: 2 books (9%)

The data reveals a striking reality: for the entire first period of this analysis (2004-2013), the American literary establishment awarded its two most prestigious prizes to exactly zero narratives centered on flourishing or comic exuberance. Every single winner was either primarily about suffering or, in four cases, balanced suffering with ambivalent resolution. This represents not merely a bias but a near-total exclusion of hopeful narratives from the definition of literary seriousness.

The second period shows marginal improvement—the appearance of *Less* (2018) and *The Familiar* (2023) as flourishing-centered winners represents a small but notable shift. However, even in this "improved" period, nearly three out of four winners remain suffering-centered. The system has loosened slightly but not fundamentally changed. Two flourishing winners in twenty-one years—less than 5% of the total—does not constitute diversity; it constitutes tokenism.

This pattern is particularly significant because it coincides with the period of maximum MFA influence on American literary culture. The number of MFA programs quadrupled between 1975 and 2020, with the most dramatic expansion occurring in the 1990s and 2000s.[3] By 2004, the MFA had become the de facto credentialing system for serious literary fiction in America. The prizes awarded during this era thus reflect not a natural or inevitable literary preference but the output of a specific institutional pipeline that systematically trains writers to equate depth with damage and seriousness with suffering.

The human cost of this system is paid by the writers themselves. MFA graduates and emerging authors have become increasingly candid about the psychic toll of being expected to perform their wounds for institutional validation. The boom in "trauma memoir" and anthologies such as *What My Mother and I Don't Talk About*, edited by Michele Filgate, has sparked necessary conversations about the ethics and exhaustion of commodifying personal crisis. As novelist Brandon Taylor has articulated, there is a palpable pressure, particularly for writers from marginalized backgrounds, to become a "trauma spokesperson," a role that can feel fundamentally at odds with the full spectrum of their creative and personal identities.

Underpinning this entire system is not merely a stylistic preference but a profound philosophical error. By enshrining "write what hurts" as the highest form of authenticity, the literary establishment has adopted a worldview in which the real is synonymous with the broken. Beauty, stability, and joy are treated as illusions or, at best, as narrative destinations that lack the complexity of the journey. This is a curated and distorted reality. Human life encompasses marriages that endure, communities that collaborate, and the complex, nuanced drama of building a life that works. When our most prestigious institutions refuse to treat these experiences as worthy of serious art, they are not being more truthful; they are propagating a partial and deeply pessimistic vision of human existence.

The Ritual Convergence: The Combined Prestige Ecosystem

The MFA industrial complex is not an isolated problem—it is one pillar of a cathedral whose architecture spans multiple institutions. To understand the full scope of the suffering canon's dominance, we must view the prestige ecosystem as a whole, examining not just literary prizes in isolation, but how they operate in concert with the film industry analyzed in Chapter 3.

When we combine the datasets—the twenty-one Best Picture winners from 2004 to 2024 with the forty-one Pulitzer Prize and National Book Award winners for fiction over the same period—a stark pattern emerges. These sixty-two works represent the pinnacle of American prestige culture: the films and books that received the most institutional validation, the most media coverage, the most curriculum adoption, and the most cultural authority during the era of maximum MFA influence.

The combined analysis reveals that **seventy-one percent of all prestige winners across film and literature centered narratives of suffering, trauma, or existential despair**. Only **ten percent** centered on narratives of flourishing, competence, or joy. For every prestige work that told us life can be built, seven told us it will be broken.

This is not a preference. This is an orthodoxy.

Two Periods, One Liturgy

Breaking the data into periods reveals how this orthodoxy has evolved—and how it began even more restrictively than its current state:

First Period (2004-2013):
- Total prestige winners: 29 (10 Best Picture + 19 literary prizes)
- Suffering-centered: 22 works (76%)
- Mixed/ambivalent: 6 works (21%)
- Flourishing-centered: 1 work (3%)

In the first period of the 21st century, American prestige culture crowned one flourishing-centered work in ten years. That single work was *Slumdog Millionaire* (2009), a film whose "feel-good" label was often deployed with a tinge of condescension, as if its joyful resolution required explanation or apology.

Meanwhile, seventy-six percent of prestige winners centered on suffering. If you participated only in award-sanctioned culture during this period, you encountered tragedy, trauma, or despair three out of every four times. This was not merely a trend—it was a near-total gatekeeping of hope from the definition of excellence.

Second Period (2014-2024):
- Total prestige winners: 33 (11 Best Picture + 22 literary prizes)
- Suffering-centered: 23 works (70%)
- Mixed/ambivalent: 5 works (15%)
- Flourishing-centered: 5 works (15%)

The second period shows marginal improvement. Five flourishing-centered works won major prizes: *Less* (2018 Pulitzer), *The Shape of Water* (2018 Best Picture), *Green Book* (2019 Best Picture), *CODA* (2022 Best Picture), and *The Familiar* (2023 National Book Award). This represents a shift from three percent to fifteen percent—a notable change that suggests the possibility of evolution in institutional values.

However, even in this "improved" period, nearly seven out of ten winners still centered on suffering. At the current rate of change—a twelve-percentage-point improvement over eleven years—it would take more than half a century to reach anything resembling balance between narratives of suffering and narratives of flourishing.

The Reinforcing Echo

The combined analysis reveals something more troubling than the individual patterns: the two systems perform the same ritual. While film awards have held steady at approximately sixty percent suffering-centered winners for four decades, literary prizes have been even more restrictive, awarding seventy-six percent of prizes to suffering-centered works and going an entire period (2004-2013) without a single flourishing-centered winner.

This creates a cultural echo chamber with no escape route. A film like *Oppenheimer* wins Best Picture, validating the equation of genius with mass destruction. That same year, novels like *Demon Copperhead* (Pulitzer) and *The Rabbit Hutch* (National Book Award) won top literary honors, both centering on poverty, addiction, and systemic neglect. The year before, *Everything Everywhere All at Once* takes Best Picture—celebrated for its zany creativity but emotionally anchored in generational trauma and suicidal nihilism—while *Demon Copperhead* claims the Pulitzer for its unflinching portrait of Appalachian despair.

The message from every prestige institution is identical: seriousness requires suffering. For the culturally engaged consumer—the person who watches the Oscars, follows book prize announcements, and uses these institutions as guides—there is no alternative voice. Whether they turn to film or literature, the liturgy is the same: if it matters, it hurts.

What These Rituals Do

A seventy-one percent suffering-centered prestige culture is not simply unbalanced—it is systematically restrictive. It creates what psychologists call an "availability heuristic," where repeated exposure to a specific pattern causes us to perceive that pattern as representative of reality. When the vast majority of "important" stories center on suffering, we begin to believe that suffering is the primary—perhaps only—path to meaning.

This is not merely an aesthetic problem. As explored in earlier chapters, heavy exposure to negative media content is associated with increased anxiety, catastrophic thinking, and pessimistic worldviews. While a single tragic film or novel is not harmful—and can indeed be profound and necessary—the cumulative effect of a seventy-one percent tragic prestige culture, consumed year after year across an entire generation, shapes not just individual mood but collective imagination.

We are not merely watching or reading these stories. We are learning, through repetition and institutional validation, what kinds of lives are worthy of serious attention. We are building cognitive schemas—mental templates for interpreting the world—that treat flourishing as trivial and suffering as profound. We are practicing, in the simulator of narrative, how to respond to life's challenges. And the lesson, delivered consistently across film and literature, across fiction and nonfiction, across entertainment and education, is that the appropriate response to difficulty is despair, that love ends in ruin, and that attempts to build something lasting are narratively inert.

The Cathedral Complete

The individual chapters of this section have shown the patterns in isolation—the literary canon taught in schools, the structure of news broadcasts, the Academy Awards, the children's films, the high school curriculum, and now the MFA-to-prize pipeline. But here, in the aggregate, we see the full architecture of the cathedral.

It is a self-reinforcing system spanning multiple institutions and media, all performing the same ritual, all defining seriousness in the same narrow way, all systematically marginalizing narratives of flourishing. The high school student who learns that *Hamlet* and *The Great Gatsby* are the pinnacle of literary achievement grows into the college student who is taught in MFA workshops to "write what hurts." That student becomes the author whose trauma memoir wins the National Book Award, which is then taught in high school alongside *Hamlet* and *The Great Gatsby*, and the cycle continues. Meanwhile, that same student watches the Oscars and sees *Oppenheimer* and *Everything Everywhere All at Once* crowned, reinforcing the lesson: suffering is where seriousness lives.

The seventy-one percent statistic is not just data. It is a portrait of a culture that has mistaken a single emotional register for the full spectrum of human experience. It is evidence of a system that has taught an entire generation that to be serious is to suffer, that to hope is to be naive, and that the only stories worth consecrating are stories of collapse.

The MFA industrial complex is the capstone of this cathedral, but it is not the cause. It is one ritual among many, all performed in service of the same creed. The feedback loop—from workshop to agent, to prestigious publication, to prize committee, and back to the classroom as required reading—is so tightly sealed that resistance requires extraordinary luck or stubbornness. We are left, once again, staring at a shelf of beautifully crafted elegies, having been taught to forget that other kinds of stories were ever possible, or that they could ever be considered profound.

The question that haunts us now is not merely "How did this happen?" but "Why?"

To answer that, we must leave the contemporary landscape and return to the ancient world, to the moment when suffering first became synonymous with profundity, when the equation was first inscribed into Western consciousness. We must trace the lineage of this belief—from the Greeks who gave us tragedy as civic ritual, to the Christians who made suffering redemptive, to the Romantics who made the artist a martyr, to the Modernists who made despair mandatory.

The cathedral bells ring in perfect harmony across film and literature, across education and entertainment, across past and present. Their toll is always the same: this is what matters, this is what is real, this is all there is.

But to understand why we built this cathedral—and how we might dismantle it—we must first understand where its foundations were laid.

CHAPTER 6 ENDNOTES
1. Leslie Jamison, *The Empathy Exams: Essays* (Minneapolis: Graywolf Press, 2014), 5–7.
2. James F. English, *The Economy of Prestige: Prizes, Awards, and the Circulation of Cultural Value*

(Cambridge, MA: Harvard University Press, 2005), 33–58.
3. Association of Writers & Writing Programs (AWP), "The MFA in Creative Writing: A History and Statistical Overview," report, 2021, accessed May 8, 2025, https://www.awpwriter.org/mfa_programs/history_overview.
4. Michele Filgate, ed., *What My Mother and I Don't Talk About: Fifteen Writers Break the Silence* (New York: Simon & Schuster, 2019).
5. Brandon Taylor, "I Don't Want to Be a Spokesperson for Trauma," *The Guardian*, February 16, 2021, accessed May 8, 2025, https://www.theguardian.com/books/2021/feb/16/brandon-taylor-trauma-spokesperson-racial-expectations.

PART TWO: THE FOUNDATIONS

History: How We Built This Cathedral

Every cathedral rests upon a foundation. To understand why the walls are built as they are, we must excavate the bedrock. This section delves into the philosophical, cultural, and historical footings—from ancient tragedy to Romantic agony to modern fragmentation—that established suffering as the cornerstone of artistic seriousness.
Chapters 7–9

CHAPTER 7: FROM GREEKS TO GOD
—Ancient Foundations

To dismantle the cathedral, we must first understand its bedrock. The valorization of suffering is not a modern invention, nor is it a mere cultural accident. Its foundations were laid with immense care and profound purpose in the ancient world, where two powerful streams of thought—the Greek theory of tragic catharsis and the Judeo-Christian narrative of redemptive suffering—converged to establish pain as a primary conduit to meaning, wisdom, and even holiness. We have inherited these structures but live in them long after the original philosophical and theological roofs have caved in, leaving us with the crumbling walls of suffering but not the shelter they were meant to provide.

I. The Athenian Stage: Catharsis and Its Modern Misreading

In fifth-century Athens, the theater of Dionysus was not a place of entertainment but a civic and religious ritual. The tragedies of Aeschylus, Sophocles, and Euripides were performed during state festivals, attended by the entire citizenry as a function of their democratic and spiritual life. At the heart of this practice was Aristotle's concept of *catharsis*—a term from his *Poetics* that has been perhaps the most misappropriated and diluted concept in Western aesthetics.

Aristotle postulated that tragedy, through pity (*eleos*) and fear (*phobos*), accomplishes a catharsis of such emotions.

The precise meaning of *katharsis* is debated, but it is best understood not as a mere "purgation" in the medical sense but as a clarification or purification. As philosopher Martha Nussbaum argues, tragedy does not simply evacuate emotions but refines them through a complex intellectual and emotional process, leading to a deeper understanding of the human condition and its vulnerabilities.[1] The audience witnessing Oedipus's self-blinding or Agamemnon's murder did not leave the theater clinically purged of feeling; they left with a sobered, communal understanding of the fragility of happiness, the limits of human knowledge, and the consequences of hubris.

Greek tragedy, in its original context, was profound and necessary. Performed during religious festivals, attended by the entire polis, framed by ritual and communal meaning-making, these plays served a civic and spiritual function. The chorus provided a communal response. The festival context provided catharsis. The theological and mythic framework provided an explanation. Aristotle's analysis assumes this rich cultural ecosystem.

The problem is not Sophocles but what we've done with Sophocles—stripping away the ritual, the communal catharsis, the civic function, and the theological framework, leaving only the suffering. We teach the tragedy but not the culture that made sense of it. We've extracted the wound and discarded the medicine. The plays remain brilliant, but we've turned them into something their creators never intended: isolated encounters with despair, consumed alone, without communal processing or spiritual context.

The modern error lies in extracting this ritual from its context. We have taken the tool—the depiction of suffering—and discarded the purpose—the communal, philosophical clarification. We assign *Oedipus Rex* to fifteen-year-olds in a vacuum, treating the catharsis as an automatic, individual psychological event rather than the civic function it was designed to serve. We present the suffering without the surrounding framework of myth, civic religion, and shared public discourse that gave it meaning. We offer the poison without the antidote.

II. The Jerusalem Codex: The Sanctification of Pain

Simultaneously, but in a radically different key, the Judeo-Christian tradition was performing its own alchemy on suffering. In the Hebrew Bible, pain is often interpreted as a form of chastisement or a test of faith, as in the Book of Job, where profound, inexplicable suffering becomes the grounds for a cosmic confrontation over righteousness and divine justice. But it is in the New Testament that suffering is transformed from a puzzle to be endured into a path to be embraced.

The central figure of Christianity is a tortured and executed man. The crucifixion is not merely a tragic event in the story; it is the pivotal moment of cosmic salvation. Through Christ's passion—his physical and spiritual agony—humanity is offered redemption. This establishes a powerful new template: redemptive suffering. Pain is no longer just a punishment or a random affliction; it is imbued with transcendent meaning. As the Apostle Paul writes, "Now I rejoice in my sufferings for your sake, and in my flesh I am filling up what is lacking in Christ's afflictions for the sake of his body, that is, the church" (Colossians 1:24).[2]

This theology gave birth to the cult of the martyr, where the ultimate act of faith was to suffer and die *imitatio Christi* (in imitation of Christ). The blood of the martyrs was seen as the seed of the church; their agony was a testament so powerful that it confirmed the truth of their belief. As theologian and critic Elaine Scarry observes in *The Body in Pain*, intense physical pain can destroy language, but in Christian martyrdom it is re-fashioned into a world-making script, a testament to an otherworldly kingdom.[3]

This sanctification of pain seeped deep into the Western psyche. It created a cultural schema where enduring suffering could be seen as noble, virtuous, and spiritually significant. To suffer was to participate in a grand, divine narrative. Even as Western society has secularized, this underlying code remains. We have largely discarded the theology of redemption, but we have retained the valorization of the suffering itself.

The tortured artist, the misunderstood genius, the writer who "mines their trauma"—these are our secular saints, their pain still tacitly understood as a sign of depth and authenticity, a secular echo of a sacred script.

III. The First Required Reading: The Secular Martyrdom of Romeo and Juliet

The fusion of these classical and theological traditions did not remain abstract. It found its perfect, enduring vessel in a story that remains a cornerstone of our educational rituals: *Romeo and Juliet*. This is where the ancient foundations become a mandatory lesson for fourteen-year-olds.

The play operates as a crucial bridge. From the Greek tradition, it borrows the structure of inescapable fate—the "star-crossed" destiny that functions as a secularized version of the Moirai. The tragic ending is not a random accident, but the inevitable conclusion foretold in the prologue, promising the audience a cathartic journey.

But its profound influence on our suffering canon comes from how it transforms Christian martyrdom for a secular age. Romeo and Juliet do not die for God; they become martyrs for love. Shakespeare elevates their suicides from tragic mistakes into a sacred, symbolic ritual. Romeo descends into a tomb, which he reframes as a "lantern," a place of light —a direct inversion of the martyr's narrative where the place of death becomes a site of spiritual triumph. He dies by poison, a secular echo of Eucharistic wine, consuming his death willingly. Juliet completes the ritual with his dagger, uniting them in a death that is also a consummation.

Their double suicide is presented not as the futile act of impulsive teenagers but as the logical, necessary, and even beautiful proof of their devotion. Critics like Robert Watson have argued that early modern drama is haunted by anxieties around annihilation and the possibility of death as absolute extinction; in that context, *Romeo and Juliet* systematically sanctifies the lovers' deaths, making their double suicide the ultimate proof of the authenticity of their love.

This is the misread lesson we drill into adolescents. We are not teaching a simple cautionary tale. We are teaching that true love is worth dying for; that the ultimate expression of authenticity is self-annihilation in the face of an imperfect world. The "profundity" we ask them to analyze is this very martyrdom structure, stripped of its divine context but retaining all its emotional and moral weight. *Romeo and Juliet* thus bequeath to us a modern, devastating formula: Significance = Suffering = Love.

The Cathedral's Foundation Stones

The seventy-one percent suffering-centered prestige culture documented in Chapter 6 did not emerge from nowhere. Its roots reach back twenty-five hundred years to the moment when two powerful civilizations—Athens and Jerusalem—independently discovered that suffering could be made sacred.

The Greeks gave us the ritual framework: communal gathering, dramatic presentation, emotional catharsis through witnessing pain. The Christians gave us the theological framework: redemption through suffering, meaning through martyrdom, authenticity proven by sacrifice. When these traditions merged in the European cultural consciousness, they created an irresistible formula.

But here is what we have forgotten: both traditions provided more than just the suffering.

The Greeks provided:
- Communal context (the entire polis gathered)
- Ritual framing (religious festivals)
- Choral commentary (communal processing)
- Civic discourse (public discussion and debate)
- Mythic distance (gods and heroes, not ordinary lives)

The Christians provided:
- Theological explanation (why suffering matters)
- Promise of redemption (suffering leads to salvation)
- Community of believers (shared meaning-making)
- Afterlife consolation (death is not the end)
- Liturgical context (suffering within a broader spiritual narrative)

We have kept the suffering. We have discarded everything else.

We teach *Oedipus Rex* without the festival. We assign *Romeo and Juliet* without the theological framework that makes martyrdom meaningful. We present the crucifixion narrative stripped of resurrection. We have built a cathedral of suffering on ancient foundations, but we removed the roof that once sheltered those who entered.

The result is not wisdom. It is not catharsis. It is not redemption. It is simply exposure to trauma, presented as education, consumed in isolation, without the communal or spiritual apparatus that once gave it purpose.

The Liturgy We Inherited

The ancient foundations are therefore not relics. They are alive in the very texts we mandate for our children, in the rituals we perform in every high school English classroom across America. The Greek sense of tragic fate and the Christian template of redemptive suffering were synthesized into a secular scripture that primes the psyche for the entire suffering canon to come.

We have been taught, from our first encounter with "great literature," that the deepest truths are written in blood, and that the purest emotions are proven in the grave. This is the liturgy we inherited: that suffering sanctifies, that pain authenticates, that death gives meaning to love.

The ancient world gave us powerful tools to make meaning from pain. Our modern failure is not in using these tools but in treating them as blunt instruments, forgetting the intricate philosophical and theological frameworks meant to guide them. We have kept the scalpel but lost the art of surgery, and we wonder why the patient is bleeding out.

The cathedral was built on solid foundations. But we have mistaken the crypt for the sanctuary, the altar of sacrifice for the altar of transformation. We worship at the foundation stones, having forgotten that they were meant to support something higher—not to become the destination themselves.

To understand how this cathedral grew from ancient foundations into the massive institutional structure we documented in Part One, we must trace the next phase of construction: the Romantic movement's transformation of the suffering artist from a tragic figure into a sacred calling.

CHAPTER 7 ENDNOTES
1. Martha C. Nussbaum, *The Fragility of Goodness: Luck and Ethics in Greek Tragedy and Philosophy* (Cambridge: Cambridge University Press, 1986), 378–394.
2. *The Holy Bible, English Standard Version* (Crossway Bibles, 2001), Colossians 1:24.
3. Elaine Scarry, *The Body in Pain: The Making and Unmaking of the World* (Oxford: Oxford University Press, 1985), 27–59.
4. Robert N. Watson, *The Rest Is Silence: Death as Annihilation in the English Renaissance* (Berkeley: University of California Press, 1994), 89–118.

CHAPTER 8: THE ROMANTIC VIRUS
—When Artists Became Tortured

The ancient world made suffering meaningful. The Christian world made it holy. But it was the Romantics who made it fashionable—and in doing so, transformed it from a tragic necessity into a creative credential. In the ferment of the late eighteenth and early nineteenth centuries, a new orthodoxy emerged, one that would permanently rewire our understanding of artistic genius. This was the birth of the cult of the tortured artist: a figure who no longer suffered for fate or God but for the sake of art itself. In this new theology, agony became the hallmark of authenticity, and the artist's inner turmoil was enshrined as the only valid subject worth exploring.

The scene shifts from the public stage of Athens and the martyr's stake to the solitary, storm-lashed crag. Here stands the archetypal Romantic hero, a figure like Lord Byron's Childe Harold, whose world-weariness and brooding sensitivity establish a new emotional aristocracy. "I stood / Among them, but not of them," Byron wrote, defining the artist not as a craftsman serving a community but as a solitary, superior being, alienated by the very depth of his feelings.[1] This was a radical departure. The artist was no longer the interpreter of shared myths but a genius whose own suffering was the myth.

The Romantics did not invent the association between creativity and pain—the Greeks and Christians had established that foundation. But the Romantics performed a crucial alchemical transformation: they made suffering not just meaningful or holy, but necessary. They established the template we still follow: that genius is not simply compatible with anguish but requires it, that the artist who does not bleed has nothing worth saying.

This revolution was powered by three interconnected ideological shifts that, together, created a self-reinforcing system—one that would eventually calcify into the institutional orthodoxy we documented in Part One.

I. The Cult of Sensibility: Feeling as Credential

The Romantic movement elevated raw, unfiltered emotion—"sensibility"—to the highest form of truth. Reason, the Enlightenment's idol, was dethroned. Passion took the throne. This shift alone was not fatal; emotion is a legitimate source of knowledge and art. But the Romantics did not simply add feeling to the palette—they created a hierarchy within emotion itself, and placed suffering at its apex.

Sorrow, heartbreak, and melancholy were considered the deepest and most complex of emotions, the ones that revealed the most about human nature. Joy was shallow, easily achieved, and available to anyone. But profound sadness? That required a refined sensibility, a soul attuned to frequencies ordinary people could not perceive. Pain became the emotional gold standard, the feeling that proved you were feeling correctly.

A feedback loop emerged, elegant and devastating:
- Suffering proved sincerity
- Sincerity proved depth
- Depth proved genius
- Genius justified suffering

The artist's internal landscape—especially its storms—became the new frontier of exploration. Emotional turbulence was not a hazard to be managed; it was a credential to be cultivated. To be happy was to be shallow. To be content was to be unaware. To suffer was to see.

II. The Beautiful Death: Keats and the Consumptive Ideal

Few figures embody the Romantic conflation of suffering, beauty, and artistic genius as perfectly as John Keats. His tuberculosis was not simply a medical tragedy; it was alchemized into cultural mythology, transforming a young man's slow death into proof of his transcendent sensitivity. The "consumptive aesthetic"—the fevered flush, the trembling fragility, the brilliant mind housed in a dying body—was romanticized as a superior artistic state. The disease became inseparable from the art. Keats's own letters fed this myth; he wrote that a "World of Pains and troubles" was necessary to "school an Intelligence and make it a Soul."[2] Suffering was not an obstacle to artistic development but its precondition. Without anguish, there could be no soul; without a soul, there could be no art worth making.

His death at twenty-five was framed not as a devastating loss of potential but as the fitting, inevitable finale of a soul too luminous for the dullness of ordinary life. The tragedy was not that he died young; the tragedy would have been if he had lived to grow old, settled, and happy. Better to burn out than fade away—a romanticization that would echo through centuries, from James Dean to Kurt Cobain, establishing an unspoken rule: the artist's suffering is not incidental but essential.

The work became the symptom. The suffering became the masterpiece.

III. The Byronic Hero: Performance as Identity

If Keats gave us the passive, consumptive ideal—the artist as beautiful victim—Byron gave us its opposite: suffering as spectacle, pain as performance, anguish as brand.

The "Byronic hero"—moody, charismatic, cynical, darkly irresistible—was not simply a literary archetype. It was a persona Byron performed with unmatched theatrical flair, collapsing the boundary between fiction and autobiography until they became indistinguishable. His scandals were as carefully crafted as his verse. His exile was as dramatic as any plot. His brooding melancholy was consumed voraciously by a public eager to believe that the man was the poem.

As biographer Benita Eisler argues, Byron understood intuitively what would become a foundational principle of modern celebrity: the artist's life had become inseparable from the art itself.[3] The biographical details were not mere context—they were authentication. A happy, stable Byron would have been a fraud. A tortured, self-destructive Byron was real.

The Romantic age thus birthed the modern concept of the artist as brand—and the brand was pain. A contented life became a biographical liability. A tortured one became a seal of legitimacy. The equation was complete: to be an artist was to suffer; to suffer publicly was to be an authentic artist; to be authentic was to be great.

The Gendered Cathedral: Who Gets to Be a Martyr?

This aesthetic was profoundly, systematically gendered—a pattern that persists in the seventy-one percent suffering-centered prestige culture we documented in Chapter 6.

Mary Wollstonecraft's emotional suffering—her unrequited attachments, her two suicide attempts—was used to undermine her philosophical work both in her lifetime and posthumously. Where Byron's turmoil enhanced his mystique, Wollstonecraft's became a weapon against her credibility. As scholars of Romanticism like Anne K. Mellor have documented, women writers were framed not as philosophical agents but as emotional phenomena—their pain was not profound but pathological, not artistic but hysterical.

The template hardened into an institutional pattern:
- A tortured man is a genius
- A tortured woman is unstable
- Male suffering is universal
- Female suffering is personal

This gendered double standard did not die with the Romantics. It structures the contemporary literary marketplace, where male authors writing about depression are celebrated as unflinching truth-tellers while women writing about the same experiences are dismissed as "navel-gazing" or writing "women's fiction"—a genre label that functions as an aesthetic demotion.

The cathedral of suffering has always had separate entrances.

The Operating System We Inherited

Romanticism did not merely add "sadness" to the palette of artistic themes. It installed a new operating system, a set of background assumptions so deep we rarely notice them running:

Genius is a function of personal anguish.

We now inherit this belief without question, and it structures every institution we examined in Part One:
- **Award committees** gravitate toward the autobiographically tragic (seventy-six percent of literary prizes, eighty percent of Pulitzers)
- **Publishers** assume memoirs about devastation are more "serious" than memoirs about recovery
- **MFA programs** orbit around pain as if it were a craft element, teaching "write what hurts" as a fundamental technique
- **Critics** treat happiness with suspicion, requiring it to "earn" its place in ways suffering never must

Literary scholars have traced this inheritance with precision. Lionel Trilling wrote about the modern obsession with "authenticity" as suffering-driven sincerity, where alienation from society became the only honest stance. Virginia Jackson has explored how the lyric "I" became fused with the idea of the wounded subject, so that to speak in the first person became synonymous with speaking from pain.

These scholarly threads confirm that we didn't imagine this cultural drift—we have been swimming in it for two centuries, so immersed we mistake it for water itself.

The Virus Escapes

The Romantics aestheticized the wound and made it the signature of artistic worth. What began as a philosophical movement—a rebellion against Enlightenment rationalism, a celebration of individual feeling—metastasized into an orthodoxy as rigid as any it replaced. The virus escaped the laboratory of nineteenth-century literary salons and lodged itself in Western creative culture at every level.

By the time the cataclysms of the twentieth century arrived—the trenches of World War I, the death camps, the mushroom clouds—the groundwork was already laid. The Romantics had taught us that suffering was the price of genius, that pain authenticated art, that happiness was for people who weren't paying attention. Modernism would take these premises and institutionalize them completely, building the cathedral whose dimensions we measured in Part One.

The Romantics handed us a new liturgy: that art requires blood, that authenticity demands anguish, that to create without suffering is to create without substance. We have been performing that ritual ever since, in every MFA workshop that teaches students to mine their trauma, in every literary prize that crowns another elegy, in every review that treats hope as naive and despair as wise.

The wound became holy. The artist became a priest. And the altar of suffering—already ancient, already sanctified—found its perfect modern clergy.

CHAPTER 8 ENDNOTES
1. George Gordon Byron, *Childe Harold's Pilgrimage* (London: John Murray, 1812), Canto III, stanza 113.
2. John Keats, Letter to George and Georgiana Keats, April 21, 1819, in *The Letters of John Keats, 1814–1821*, ed. H. E. Rollins, vol. 2 (Cambridge, MA: Harvard University Press, 1958), 102.
3. Benita Eisler, *Byron: Child of Passion, Fool of Fame* (New York: Alfred A. Knopf, 1999), 234–267.
4. Anne K. Mellor, *Romanticism and Gender* (New York: Routledge, 1993), 24–51.
5. Lionel Trilling, *Sincerity and Authenticity* (Cambridge, MA: Harvard University Press, 1972), 1–25; 93–134.
6. Virginia Jackson, *Dickinson's Misery: A Theory of Lyric Reading* (Princeton, NJ: Princeton University Press, 2005), 1–34.

CHAPTER 9: AFTER THE WARS—
Modernism's Despair Mandate

The Romantic virus, for all its power, remained a voluntary affliction, a pose available to the sensitive few. Then came the twentieth century and the industrial-scale slaughter of the World Wars. The machine gun, the gas attack, the concentration camp, and the atomic bomb did not just kill millions; they murdered the very premises of Western civilization—reason, progress, order, and the inherent value of the individual.

In the smoldering crater left by this violence, Romantic suffering was no longer a fashionable pose; it became the only honest response. The problem is not that Modernism existed or that it responded to genuine horror, but that its aesthetic of fragmentation and despair became the only acceptable stance for "serious" art, creating a monopoly that persists to this day. Modernism, the art that emerged from the rubble, did not just depict despair; it institutionalized it as the only intellectually respectable position for the serious mind.

The shift was not merely thematic but formal. The world had been broken; so too would be its art. The elegant, linear narratives of the nineteenth-century novel, which implied a coherent world and a knowable self, came to seem like a lie. In their place, Modernism offered fragmentation, alienation, and a pervasive, ontological uncertainty. This was no longer the beautiful, consumptive death of Keats; it was the anonymous, mechanized death of millions, and its aesthetic was not the sublime but the absurd.

I. The Great War as Cultural Breaking Point

World War I was the primordial rupture. The staggering loss of life—a generation of young men fed into the insatiable maw of trench warfare—shattered the illusion of progressive civilization. The war poets, like Wilfred Owen, did not write of glory but of visceral horror:

If you could hear, at every jolt, the blood *Come gargling from the froth-corrupted lungs...*[*1]

This was a new voice: stripped of romanticism, choked with the mud of the real.

The trauma demanded new forms. T. S. Eliot's *The Waste Land* (1922) became the definitive monument of the era, a poem that is itself a literary battlefield, littered with the fragments of a shattered culture. Its famous opening, "April is the cruellest month," is a direct inversion of Chaucer's life-affirming spring, establishing a world where regeneration is more terrifying than sterility.[2]

Eliot does not tell a story; he diagnoses a collapse. The poem's difficulty—its dense allusions, jagged shifts in voice, and sudden changes in language—is not mere elitism but a formal representation of a world that no longer makes coherent sense. To be "easy" or "accessible" in such a climate was to be complicit in the old lies.

II. The Institutionalization of Alienation

In the aftermath of such a cataclysm, optimism became impossible. It was not just unfashionable; it was intellectually suspect. A new orthodoxy hardened, one that equated artistic and philosophical sophistication with a relentless critique of all systems, all meanings.

This found its purest philosophical expression in existentialism, with Jean-Paul Sartre declaring that man is "a useless passion" and Albert Camus framing life as the absurd struggle of Sisyphus pushing his rock up the hill forever.[3] The serious thinker was now the one who stared into the void without flinching.

In literature, this despair mandate crystallized around two dominant modes:

The Stoic Nihilism of Hemingway.

Hemingway's sparse prose is often praised as "reflecting a world stripped of illusion," but this reading itself becomes a form of canonization—treating his despair as inevitable wisdom rather than as one possible response among many. What we call his "honesty" is actually a highly selective filter: he wrote obsessively about wounded soldiers and broken men, but rarely about the nurses who patched them up, the communities that rebuilt, or the marriages that endured. His style didn't strip away illusion; it stripped away alternatives, leaving only the wound as "real."

In *A Farewell to Arms*, his protagonist, Frederic Henry, concludes:

That was what you did. You died. You did not know what it was about. You never had time to learn. They threw you in and told you the rules, and the first time they caught you off base, they killed you.

The so-called "Hemingway code"—grace under pressure—was a way to endure a universe devoid of inherent meaning. The heroism was not in triumph but in the way one carried oneself under the weight of meaninglessness. But this, too, was a choice—to write only about those who break, never about those who build.

The Fragmented Psyche of Faulkner and Woolf.

If Hemingway responded with stoic compression, others mirrored the internal collapse through stream-of-consciousness and radical subjectivity. Faulkner's South is a haunted, decaying psyche; his narrative structures are as convoluted and trapped by the past as his characters.

Woolf's characters, by contrast, grasp for ephemeral "moments of being" against a terrifying backdrop of flux and death. In *To the Lighthouse*, the central section, "Time Passes," coolly reports the death of a major character in a bracketed aside. Mrs. Ramsay's death is narrated almost as an afterthought—grammatically minimized, emotionally devastating. The brutality of the world is conveyed through its stylistic indifference.

This was no longer just one artistic movement among many; it was the establishment of a new default.

Critic Lionel Trilling, in *Sincerity and Authenticity*, traced this cultural shift, arguing that the modern self came to be defined by its "authenticity," which was increasingly measured by its alienation from a sick society. To be well-adjusted to a pathological world was itself a form of sickness. The only "healthy" response was a profound and unyielding disaffection. Sadness became not just an emotion but a credential—a way of proving that one saw the world clearly enough to be devastated by it.

The publishing and academic industries, emerging in their modern form during this period, canonized this stance. The New Critics, who came to dominate literary studies in mid-century, championed the very texts that embodied complexity, irony, and ambiguity—qualities overwhelmingly found in tragic and pessimistic works. As we saw in Chapter 5, this pedagogical preference was eventually codified, ensuring that the Modernist vision of a broken world would become the foundational lens through which subsequent generations were taught to read.

The Romantic virus had found its ultimate host in the institutions of culture. What began as a personal, emotional stance was now the official doctrine of high art. The wars had made despair a necessary response, and Modernism's institutions made it the only acceptable response for serious art.

III. Depressive Realism and the "Smart" Sad Person

Meanwhile, psychology was telling its own, unsettling story. In the late twentieth century, a controversial line of research proposed something that sounded like the ultimate Modernist punchline: depressed people, under certain conditions, might see aspects of reality more accurately than their non-depressed peers. This idea—often summarized under the label "depressive realism"—came from studies suggesting that mildly depressed individuals sometimes made more accurate judgments about their level of control over events than non-depressed individuals, who showed a slight "illusory optimism."

The data is contested, and no responsible clinician would prescribe depression as a path to wisdom. But culturally, the idea landed with a thud of recognition. Of course, the saddest people see most clearly. Of course, the cheerful ones are deluded. It was the scientific-sounding confirmation of a story Modernism had already told: if you are not at least a little bit hopeless, you must not be paying attention.

At the same time, clinical psychology was mapping how certain patterns of thinking deepen and sustain depression. Susan Nolen-Hoeksema's work on rumination, for example, showed how repetitive, passive focus on one's distress—turning the same bleak thoughts over and over—predicts both the onset and the persistence of depressive episodes. Yet in our cultural aesthetics, that same rumination is often rebranded as depth, as seriousness, as the mark of the thoughtful soul.

Put simply: some of the very cognitive habits that make people clinically miserable—global negative conclusions, selective attention to what's broken, relentless replay of what hurts—overlap almost perfectly with the interpretive habits we reward in "serious" readers and "serious" artists.

In this sense, the depression aesthetic is not only a description of art; it is a training regimen for a particular way of thinking:
- assume the worst,
- expect betrayal,
- find the fatal flaw,
- distrust anything that looks like hope.

When those habits show up in a therapist's office, we call them distortions. When they show up on the page, we call them genius.

The Liturgy of Despair

The cost of this profound and necessary artistic response to genuine horror has been a long afterlife of cynicism. The twentieth century needed art that could look directly at trench warfare, genocide, and nuclear annihilation without flinching. That art was indispensable.

But its aesthetic—alienation as authenticity, despair as intelligence—outlived the moment that made it necessary. It bled from the page into the psyche, creating a cultural climate where imagining a better future came to seem not just difficult but delusional, where sadness itself became a kind of status symbol, proof that you were not naive enough to hope.

This is how Modernism's necessary response to genuine trauma became a permanent ritual. The seventy-one percent suffering-centered prestige culture documented in Chapter 6 is not an accident—it is the direct descendant of Modernism's institutional triumph. When the Academy Awards choose *Oppenheimer* over lighter fare, when the

Pulitzer Prize crowns *Demon Copperhead*'s portrait of Appalachian despair, when MFA workshops teach writers to "write what hurts," they are all performing the same liturgy established a century ago: that seriousness requires suffering, that authenticity demands alienation, that hope is for those who haven't been paying attention.

The wars shattered the world. Modernism built a cathedral in the ruins. And we have been worshiping there ever since, long after the original necessity has passed, treating the aesthetic of despair not as one valid response among many but as the only intellectually honest position available to the serious mind.

The cathedral had found its modern stained glass: shattered, dark, and treated as the only serious way to see the light.

CHAPTER 9 ENDNOTES
1. Wilfred Owen, "Dulce et Decorum Est," in *Poems* (London: Chatto & Windus, 1920). Original poem written in 1917.
2. T. S. Eliot, *The Waste Land* (New York: Boni & Liveright, 1922), line 1.
3. Jean-Paul Sartre, *Being and Nothingness* (Paris: Gallimard, 1943); Albert Camus, *The Myth of Sisyphus* (Paris: Gallimard, 1942).
4. Ernest Hemingway, *A Farewell to Arms* (New York: Charles Scribner's Sons, 1929), 327.
5. Virginia Woolf, *To the Lighthouse* (London: Hogarth Press, 1927), Part II.
6. Lionel Trilling, *Sincerity and Authenticity* (Cambridge, MA: Harvard University Press, 1972), 93–134.
7. Lauren B. Alloy and Lyn Y. Abramson, "Judgment of Contingency in Depressed and Non-depressed Students: Sadder but Wiser?" *Journal of Experimental Psychology: General* 108, no. 4 (1979): 441–485.
8. Susan Nolen-Hoeksema, "The Role of Rumination in Depressive Disorders and Mixed Anxiety/Depressive

Symptoms," *Journal of Abnormal Psychology* 109, no. 3 (2000): 504–511.

PART THREE: THE COST

Consequences: What It's Costing Us

A cathedral casts a long shadow. The shadow of this one falls across our imagination, our mental well-being, and our very capacity for hope. Here, we step into that shadow to measure the toll—the constricted imagination, the psychological burden, and the readers who turn away—of a culture that has lit its candles before a single, sorrowful altar.
Chapters 10–12

CHAPTER 10: THE MENTAL HEALTH BILL—Quantifying Damage

For decades, the defense of the suffering canon has rested on a noble abstraction: it builds resilience, it fosters empathy, it prepares the young for a difficult world. That's the story we tell ourselves as we assign seventeen out of twenty-five texts featuring suicide or self-annihilation, as we beam daily catastrophe into living rooms, as we consecrate prestige stories that end with ash and wreckage.

But at some point, the bill for all this "preparation" comes due.

It doesn't arrive as a philosophical treatise. It arrives as a guidance counselor's office with a waitlist. As a parent sitting in an ER after a self-harm scare. As a teenager, head down on a desk, mumbling, "If even the heroes are doomed, what chance do I have?"

We live in a moment when we no longer have to guess about the state of adolescent mental health. We can count it. The question this chapter asks is not whether books and media single-handedly cause this crisis—they don't—but whether our rituals of despair constitute a meaningful part of the ecosystem that's making it worse.

I. The Crisis We Can Measure

Let's start with the part that is not in dispute.

According to the U.S. Centers for Disease Control and Prevention's Youth Risk Behavior Survey (YRBS), the share of high school students reporting persistent feelings of sadness or hopelessness rose from approximately 26% in 2009 to 37% by 2019.[1]

By the 2021 survey cycle, those numbers had climbed even higher: almost 44% of high school students—more than two in five—said they had felt so sad or hopeless almost every day for at least two weeks in a row that they stopped doing their usual activities. Among girls, that figure reached nearly 60%.[2]

This is not a blip. It's a trend line pointing in one direction: up. And up in a way that is historically unusual.

Psychologist Jean Twenge, in *iGen* and later work, has argued that rates of depression and anxiety among teens began to rise sharply around 2012–2013, alongside the spread of smartphones and social media.[3] Researchers debate the size and mechanics of that effect. But almost no one disputes the direction of the curve.

Every serious analysis of this crisis points to multiple culprits:
- Social media and the comparison economy
- Sleep deprivation and academic pressure
- Economic precarity and climate anxiety
- The erosion of in-person community

What I'm adding here is not a new smoking gun but an uncomfortable co-conspirator: the stories we require, reward, and revere.

While we track these rising graphs, we are simultaneously schooling teens in an intellectual liturgy that treats hopelessness as insight and despair as sophistication. We teach them to perform the same cognitive rituals that clinical psychology identifies as risk factors for depression. The data doesn't prove that the suffering canon causes the crisis. But it does make it increasingly difficult to claim that a culture built on institutionalized despair is a neutral backdrop.

II. Stories as Cognitive Training

To understand why this matters, we have to talk briefly about how minds—especially adolescent minds—learn to interpret the world.

In cognitive psychology, a "schema" is a mental template: the brain's shorthand for "how things usually go." Aaron Beck's foundational work on depression showed that people who develop depressive disorders often operate on negative schemas: the world is dangerous, I am inadequate, the future is hopeless. These aren't conscious slogans; they're background assumptions that shape how every new event is interpreted.

Beck identified this pattern—pervasive negative conclusions about self, world, and future—as the "cognitive triad" that both predicts and sustains depressive disorders.

Another relevant piece is rumination: the tendency to dwell repetitively on distressing thoughts and events. Susan Nolen-Hoeksema's research demonstrated that rumination both predicts and prolongs depressive episodes. It's not just that something bad happened—it's that the mind learns to loop endlessly on the worst possible meanings of that event, rehearsing catastrophe until it becomes the dominant narrative.

Now overlay those concepts on Emma Brightwater, the student whose question haunted her teacher back in Chapter 1. Emma is not a research subject; she's a composite of the countless teens who have looked at a reading list and quietly asked, "Is that all there is?"

By the time Emma reaches her junior year, she has:
- Watched a parade of dead or disappearing parents in children's media
- Spent middle school with dead dogs and dying grandparents in "serious" novels

- Hit high school and met Gatsby in his pool, Macbeth on his battlefield, Romeo and Juliet in their tomb

She is now asked—not just to read these stories—but to write polished essays arguing that these endings are inevitable and profound. She is graded on how convincingly she can make the case that futility is the deepest truth available to the serious mind.

That is not neutral content. That is cognitive training.

The suffering canon functions as a semester-long seminar in depressive schemas:
- People are fundamentally corrupt
- Institutions are inherently futile
- Love ends in betrayal or death
- Hope is, at best, delusion; at worst, complicity

This is precisely the pattern Beck identified as the cognitive triad of depression: negative views of self (I am powerless), world (people and institutions are corrupt), and future (hope is delusion). If you presented this list to a clinician familiar with cognitive models of depression, they would recognize these not as intellectual rigor but as the very schema patterns that both predict and sustain depressive episodes—the patterns cognitive therapy works to interrupt.

We are, in effect, training students to think as depressed people think, and then praising them for doing it well.

III. The Daily Canon as Chronic Stressor

What happens in the classroom doesn't stay in the classroom. It syncs up with the daily liturgy of the news—the "Daily Canon" we examined in Chapter 2—which functions as a mood disorder in broadcast form.

A 2020 study in the *Journal of Broadcasting & Electronic Media* found that even brief exposure to negative television news significantly increased anxious and sad mood, and that those emotional effects lingered. Other work on "negativity bias" in news has shown that stories framed around threat, conflict, and outrage are more likely to be clicked and shared, reinforcing an editorial focus on catastrophe as the only story worth telling.

The teenager who spends the day in a curriculum of catastrophe and the evening in a feed of crisis is not just "being informed." They are experiencing a repeated pairing, reinforced hundreds of times: the important thing is the terrible. The brain learns that if something is calm, cooperative, and hopeful, it is by definition trivial. Suffering becomes synonymous with seriousness. Despair becomes indistinguishable from depth.

We don't need a bespoke lab study titled "Required Reading vs. Depression" to see why this matters. We already know—from decades of research—that:
- Repeated exposure to negative, uncontrollable events increases stress responses
- Rumination on those events amplifies risk for depression and anxiety
- Cognitive schemas about the world's danger and futility shape how new experiences are interpreted

Our cultural institutions—schools, newsrooms, awards committees, publishing houses—are extraordinarily efficient at supplying the raw material for all three.

IV. Correlation, Not Culpability—But Still Responsibility

Let's be very clear about what I am not saying.

I am not saying that reading Macbeth gives you major depressive disorder, or that watching one prestige drama about a doomed family will send you to therapy. Human beings are more complex than that, and serious stories about suffering can be meaningful, even life-saving, especially for readers who see their own pain finally named and validated.

What I am saying is that when:
- More than two in five high school students report persistent sadness and hopelessness
- Emergency rooms are seeing unprecedented spikes in teen self-harm
- Schools are scrambling to provide enough counselors to triage the fallout

...then it is no longer intellectually honest to treat the suffering canon as a harmless aesthetic preference, a matter of taste disconnected from consequences.

Stories are part of the environment. They are inputs, not wallpaper. When the environment is already saturated with stressors—phones, feeds, pressure, precarity—we cannot continue pretending that a school-sanctioned, award-validated, institutionally enforced monopoly on despair is just "rigorous education."

At a minimum, we should be able to acknowledge this:

Correlation is not causation. The mental health crisis has many drivers, most of them systemic and outside any individual teacher's or parent's control.

But correlation does imply responsibility. If we are choosing, year after year, to feed young minds almost exclusively on narratives of futility and self-annihilation—if we are requiring them to perform rituals of despair in order to earn the credential of "serious student"—then we are not innocent bystanders. We are active participants in shaping the cognitive terrain on which this crisis plays out.

The seventy-one percent suffering-centered prestige culture we documented in Chapter 6 is not a random aesthetic development. It is a choice, repeated daily in thousands of classrooms, newsrooms, and award ceremonies. And choices have consequences.

V. Cleaning the Water

Right now, our primary response to rising adolescent distress is individual: therapy, medication, mindfulness apps, "resilience training." These are good things. I am in favor of kids getting every tool available.

But imagine discovering that a town's water supply was contaminated and deciding the most sensible response was to put every resident on a low-dose medication while leaving the pipes exactly as they are. That would be absurd. We would fix the water.

That is roughly what we are doing with culture.

The pipes, in this metaphor, are the stories we institutionalize:
- The required reading lists mandate seventeen out of twenty-five texts featuring suicide or self-annihilation
- The exam passages that test comprehension of despair
- The shows we shower with Oscars and Emmys
- The books we crown with Pulitzers and National Book Awards
- The workshop pedagogy teaches aspiring writers that "serious" means "suffering."

This chapter is not an argument for disinfected, conflict-free art. Tragedy has its place. Difficult stories matter. But there is a difference between having access to tragic narratives and being force-fed them as the exclusive diet, as the only stories deemed worthy of institutional consecration.

We cannot fix social media, climate anxiety, or economic precarity by swapping out a few books. But we can stop acting as if seventeen out of twenty-five texts featuring suicide or self-annihilation in the high school canon, an awards ecosystem that crowns suffering at a seventy-one percent rate, and a news culture optimized for panic are somehow disconnected from the graphs that keep climbing.

The mental health bill of the suffering canon is not a single line item. It is a surcharge added quietly and repetitively every time we teach a young mind that despair is depth and hope is childish, every time we require them to perform cognitive rituals identical to the ones that sustain clinical depression, every time we tell them that to be taken seriously, they must worship at the altar of despair.

VI. The Hopeful Paradox

The good news—the genuinely hopeful news, which I am contractually obligated by my own thesis to believe—is that if stories can help train brains toward hopelessness, they can also help train them toward something else.

Schemas can be built. They can also be rebuilt.

Rumination can be practiced. So can reflection that moves toward integration rather than dissolution.

The cognitive habits that make us vulnerable to depression are not hardwired. They are learned. And what is learned can be unlearned.

But only if we change what we canonize. Only if we stop treating the ritual performance of despair as the sole credential for intellectual seriousness. Only if we recognize that the water is part of the problem—and that we have more control over the water than we admit.

The cathedral's stained glass may be dark, but glass can be replaced.

The question is whether we have the courage to let in the light.

CHAPTER 10 ENDNOTES

1. U.S. Centers for Disease Control and Prevention, *Youth Risk Behavior Survey Data Summary & Trends Report: 2009–2019* (Atlanta: U.S. Department of Health and Human Services, 2020), https://www.cdc.gov/healthyyouth/data/yrbs/index.htm.

2. U.S. Centers for Disease Control and Prevention, *Youth Risk Behavior Survey: Data Summary & Trends Report, 2011–2021* (Atlanta: U.S. Department of Health and Human Services, 2023).
3. Jean M. Twenge, *iGen: Why Today's Super-Connected Kids Are Growing Up Less Rebellious, More Tolerant, Less Happy—and Completely Unprepared for Adulthood* (New York: Atria Books, 2017), 79–108.
4. Aaron T. Beck, *Cognitive Therapy and the Emotional Disorders* (New York: International Universities Press, 1976), 47–89.
5. Susan Nolen-Hoeksema, "The Role of Rumination in Depressive Disorders and Mixed Anxiety/Depressive Symptoms," *Journal of Abnormal Psychology* 109, no. 3 (2000): 504–511.
6. Donald L. Diefenbach, "The Impact of Television News on Mood and Mood Regulation," *Journal of Broadcasting & Electronic Media* 64, no. 3 (2020): 393–411.
7. Christopher E. Robertson, Stuart Soroka, and Tanya Collins, "Negativity Drives Online News Consumption," *Proceedings of the National Academy of Sciences* 120, no. 15 (2023): e2217563120.

CHAPTER 11: THE IMAGINATION DRAIN—What We Can't Envision

The most insidious cost of the suffering canon is not what it makes us feel but what it prevents us from seeing. A culture that consecrates narratives of inevitable decline, inherent human corruption, and futile struggle is a culture that systematically dismantles its own capacity to imagine alternative futures. This is not an abstract literary concern; it is a critical failure of collective cognition. When we cannot envision a viable pathway to a better world, we cannot build one.

The suffering canon has become a cage for our imagination. Its bars are made of "realism," its lock is prestige, and its wardens are all the voices—teachers, critics, algorithms, award committees—that reward breakdown while treating repair as unserious. The consequences show up everywhere from policy seminars to private therapy sessions, from climate activism to personal life planning.

Noah Wintermere, now a college freshman in a political science seminar, is one of those consequences. (Like other named students in this book, he's a composite—a real pattern in a single, readable body.) The class is discussing climate policy. Noah's peers eloquently deconstruct the failures of the Paris Agreement, the intransigence of the fossil fuel industry, and the psychological barriers to collective action. The analysis is sharp, sophisticated, and profoundly bleak.

When the professor asks for solutions-oriented proposals, the room falls silent.

Noah finally offers, "Maybe we need a story about how we fix this, not just how we fail."

Another student snorts. "That's just science fiction. We have to be realistic."

The word *realistic* hangs in the air, automatically synonymous with cynical. The imagination has been shamed into silence.

This is what it looks like when a culture has trained an entire generation to autopsy problems but never to architect solutions. Noah has spent eighteen years—from Mufasa's death at age five to Oppenheimer's atomic horror at eighteen—learning that serious narratives end in collapse. He can describe, with academic precision, every way a system might fail. But asking him to imagine how one might succeed feels, even to him, like intellectual weakness.

He has been taught to mistake diagnosis for wisdom.

I. The Policy Implication: Cynicism as Default Setting

The dominance of tragic, corrosively ironic narratives has reshaped our political and policy discourse. We have become fluent in the language of breakdown, but nearly illiterate in the language of repair.

You can hear it in how we talk about almost everything that matters: climate, democracy, inequality, technology, and health care. Our public conversation is saturated with threat, scandal, and unmasking—*What's broken? Who lied? How bad is it, really?*—and comparatively barren when it comes to concrete, believable "What if we..." futures.

This isn't because human beings are incapable of imaginative, hopeful thinking. History demonstrates otherwise. No major social advance has ever been powered by despair alone. Abolitionists imagined a world without legal slavery long before it was politically plausible. Civil rights organizers imagined integrated schools and voting booths while "realists" told them to be patient. Even something as apparently technocratic as the moon landing required a wildly optimistic act of collective imagination: we pictured ourselves standing on another celestial body and then reverse-engineered reality until the image came true.

Sociologist Ruth Levitas has argued that utopian thinking—the imaginative reconstitution of society—is not childish escapism but a method, a way of testing possible futures against our deepest values.[1] The suffering canon has quietly made this method suspect. Today, the same kind of forward-leaning imagination is often treated as an embarrassment, something you grow out of once you've read enough bleak novels and watched enough prestige television.

The suffering canon has rewritten the rules of intellectual status: pessimism reads as sophistication; hope reads as naiveté. Political theorists and psychologists have a term for what happens next: learned helplessness at scale.

When every "serious" narrative ends in corruption, collapse, or martyrdom, imagining a functional institution starts to feel childish. Our mental picture of "how things go" has been trained by a thousand tragic arcs—the seventy-one percent suffering-centered prestige culture we documented in Chapter 6. So even when we sit in rooms explicitly tasked with generating policy—commissions, think tanks, legislative committees—we default to critique and risk assessment, not to narrative design.

We know how to autopsy a failing system. We are far less practiced at drafting a living one.

II. Climate Despair vs. Climate Solutions

Nowhere is this imagination drain more catastrophic than in our response to climate change.

The dominant cultural stories are apocalyptic: drowned cities, dust-bowl famines, roaming bands of survivors fighting over dwindling resources. These books and films are usually written with moral urgency—*wake up before it's too late*—but the emotional takeaway for many readers is closer to *we're doomed, and there's nothing we can do.*

Psychologists who study climate emotions have documented this cluster of feelings: climate anxiety or climate distress—a mix of fear, grief, anger, and hopelessness that can paralyze rather than mobilize. In a ten-country survey of 10,000 young people aged 16–25, nearly 60% reported being "very" or "extremely" worried about climate change, and almost half said that these feelings negatively affected daily life—sleep, concentration, even the willingness to plan for the future.[2]

Hope, in this context, is not a Hallmark sentiment; it's a psychological variable with measurable effects. Research on young people and environmental engagement has found that certain kinds of hope—vague, "I'm sure it will all work out" optimism—do very little to foster action. But constructive hope—hope tied to a sense of personal and collective agency, concrete pathways, and belief that one's efforts matter—predicts greater willingness to act, especially among youth.[3]

Our cultural output, however, heavily favors the doom side of the equation. We mass-produce end-of-the-world scenarios and treat stories that linger on solutions as suspiciously "soft." A novel that focuses on how communities successfully transition to renewable energy, redesign cities, or restructure economies sounds, in many editorial meetings, like a pamphlet, not a story—not "literary" enough for the seventy-seven percent of Pulitzers that go to suffering-centered narratives.

So we get two dominant modes:

Collapse Porn: Exquisitely detailed visions of how everything falls apart, rendered with all the aesthetic prestige the cathedral can bestow.

Techno-Magic: A single miracle invention or billionaire savior that fixes it all offstage, requiring no messy democratic process or collective action.

What we almost never get are rigorous, emotionally compelling narratives about the messy, incremental, democratic work of actually changing systems: policies fought for and passed, coalitions formed, habits shifted, infrastructures reimagined. In other words, the very things we most desperately need to see modeled.

The result is a perverse emotional economy. A teenager who binge-reads climate dystopias is praised for being "awake" and "engaged," even if those stories leave them more immobilized than before. A teenager who dares to sketch a believable, hopeful climate future—how governance could work, what technology and culture might look like—is likely to have their work dismissed as unrealistic.

We have confused grim with mature so thoroughly that any other tone feels like a violation of the liturgy.

III. The Lost Stories: The Creativity Cost

This imagination drain is not only political; it is creative.

Whole categories of stories have been pushed to the margins by the prestige machinery that enforces the suffering canon.

Writers feel it as a kind of invisible fence. They may start with an idea full of wonder, competence, or communal triumph—and then hear the internalized workshop voice: *Where's the trauma? Where's the wound? Raise the stakes. Make it hurt more.* That voice is not just aesthetic; it's economic. It whispers, *If you want an agent, a review, a prize, this needs to bleed.*

So the joyful heist turns into a heist born of childhood abuse. The curious scientist gets a tragic backstory. The community garden has to be bulldozed by a corrupt corporation in Act III so the ending can taste "serious" enough—serious enough to join the seventy-seven percent of literary prize winners that center on suffering.

Meanwhile, the genres that unapologetically center flourishing—romance, cozy mystery, certain strains of science fiction and fantasy—are often walled off in the critical ghetto. They are wildly popular with readers, but they are coded as "guilty pleasures," not as part of the conversation about what literature and cinema can do for a culture's imagination.

This matters. Stories are not just entertainment; they are tools. They teach us what kinds of problems exist, what kinds of people matter, and what kinds of endings are possible. They function like mental simulations, letting us rehearse possible futures and emotional responses in low-risk environments. If almost all our "serious" simulations end badly, we start to treat "things end badly" as a law of nature rather than a storytelling choice.

The cost is subtle but profound:
- Young activists who can describe every way a movement might fail but struggle to picture how it might succeed
- Young artists who can brilliantly parody institutional rot but feel cheesy trying to depict institutional repair
- Young readers who can map the anatomy of a nervous breakdown but have never seen a convincing portrayal of long-term, hard-won mental health

We have taught a generation to perform postmortems on worlds that don't yet exist, instead of architecting the ones we need.

IV. The Shrinking of Personal Possibility

The imagination drain doesn't only operate at the level of policy and art; it infiltrates the most intimate questions of personal life.

Ask a teenager what kind of world they expect to live in at forty, and you will often hear some variation of: "If we're not underwater or in a fascist state by then." Ask what kind of life they picture for themselves, and many will shrug. They can enumerate possible careers, but it's hard for them to conjure a *felt image* of a life that is not either precarious or performatively extraordinary. The middle registers—stable, meaningful, quietly joyful—rarely show up in the stories they've consumed.

When every memorable protagonist is either a tragic genius, a traumatized survivor, or an antihero circling the drain, wanting an ordinary, decent, flourishing life can feel like wanting nothing at all.

The suffering canon has so successfully colonized our sense of depth that "I want to build something good and live in it" sounds, to many young adults, like a confession of cowardice.

Reports on climate-related mental health echo this narrowing of possibility. Young people describe not just fear, but a sense that the future is "frightening," that adults have "failed to take care of the planet," and that the burden of a damaged world has been shifted onto their shoulders. When the future feels both terrifying and already decided, why bother imagining anything different, let alone working toward it?

This is not just sad; it's dangerous. A citizenry that cannot imagine itself into a livable future is a citizenry that will either disengage entirely or cling desperately to whoever offers the most vivid dystopia to rail against. Outrage, after all, is easier to sustain than constructive vision. Anger can feed on bad stories. Hope needs better ones.

V. Opening the Windows

The point of this diagnosis is not to argue that we should ban tragedy, outlaw dystopia, or mandate happy endings. A culture without the ability to face darkness honestly would be as distorted as the one we have now.

The argument is about balance, and about repertoire.

We need stories that do what tragedy has always done at its best: tell the truth about suffering, injustice, and loss. But we also need stories that do something our current canon has almost entirely ceded to children's programming and "guilty pleasure" genres: give us credible visions of repair, solidarity, and flourishing that are not saccharine, not simplistic, and not restricted to individual salvation.

We need:
- Climate stories that linger on the mechanics of transition, not just the aesthetics of collapse
- Political stories that dramatize coalition-building and institutional reform, not only corruption and coups
- Personal stories in which therapy works, communities hold, and love persists—not perfectly, but believably

Most of all, we need to recover the sense that imagining better is not childish, but one of the most adult acts available to us.

The suffering canon has had centuries to establish its prestige. It will not vanish, and it shouldn't. But we can refuse to let it be the only liturgy. We can stop treating cynicism as the cover charge for seriousness. We can build a flourishing canon alongside the suffering one—a counter-tradition that trains the imagination toward possibility, not just postmortem.

The Cathedral's Windows

A cathedral, after all, is not only stone and shadow. It is also windows.

Right now, our cultural cathedral feels like a building where someone boarded most of those windows up from the inside. Light does sneak in—through the odd romantic comedy, the hopeful science-fiction novel, the community theater production about neighbors who actually solve a problem together—but it arrives in narrow, guilty beams. We stand in the half-dark, squinting at the stained glass of martyrdom and ruin, and tell ourselves this dimness is depth.

It doesn't have to stay this way. We can choose, window by window, to pry the boards loose.

A teacher who pairs a tragic novel with a reparative one is opening a window. A filmmaker who lets their characters build something that lasts, instead of burning it all down for gravitas, is opening a window. A teenager who writes fanfiction where their favorite doomed heroine lives, heals, and starts a mutual-aid garden? That's a window.

Imagine walking a young person—Noah, or someone like him—into this rebuilt cathedral. Not the old one, echoing with prestigious dirges, but a living structure where tragedy sits alongside comedies of competence, where dystopias share shelf space with carefully imagined better worlds.

Instead of the familiar hush of resignation, there's a low, humming energy: the sound of people asking, *What if...?* and *Why not...?*

He looks up, and instead of a single, enormous panel of a saint in agony, he sees a riot of scenes: people at city council meetings hammering out policy; friends repairing a broken friendship instead of ghosting; communities retreating from the brink and redesigning how they live. There are storms in the glass, yes. But there are also bridges, gardens, and ships that actually make it to shore.

This is what it means to open the windows: not to deny the storm, but to let in enough light that we can see our own hands, our own tools, our own capacity to build.

Until we do, we will keep mistaking the dim interior of our narrative architecture for the shape of reality itself. When we start, we give ourselves—and the Noahs of the world—something better than diagnosis. We give them blueprints. We give them glass. We give them a view.

The suffering canon has taught us how to mourn. It's time we learned how to build.

CHAPTER 11 ENDNOTES

1. Ruth Levitas, *Utopia as Method: The Imaginary Reconstitution of Society* (London: Palgrave Macmillan, 2013), 1–35.
2. Caroline Hickman, Elizabeth Marks, Panu Pihkala, Susan Clayton, R. Eric Lewandowski, Elouise E. Mayall, Britt Wray, Catriona Mellor, and Lise van Susteren, "Climate Anxiety in Children and Young People and Their Beliefs About Government Responses: A Global Survey," *The Lancet Planetary Health* 5, no. 12 (2021): e863–e873.
3. Maria Ojala, "Hope and Climate Change: The Importance of Hope for Environmental Engagement Among Young People," *Environmental Education Research* 18, no. 5 (2012): 625–642.
4. Data derived from the author's analysis of Pulitzer Prize for Fiction and National Book Award for Fiction winners, 2004–2024. See Appendix E for the complete dataset and methodology.
5. American Psychological Association and ecoAmerica, *Mental Health and Our Changing Climate: Impacts, Implications, and Guidance* (Washington, DC: American Psychological Association, 2017), accessed February 15, 2025, https://www.apa.org/news/press/releases/2017/03/mental-health-climate.pdf.

CHAPTER 12: THE LOST READERS—
Who We Exclude

The suffering canon is not merely a collection of texts; it is a filtering mechanism. Its relentless focus on trauma and tragedy does not elevate all readers—it actively selects for a specific kind of reader while gently, and sometimes not so gently, nudging countless others toward the exits. The cost is measured not only in mental health statistics, cultural imagination, or policy paralysis, but in a vast, silent diaspora of people who decide somewhere along the way: *This world is not for me.*

The cathedral of suffering, for all its grandeur, has a tiny door. We seem shocked to discover how few people fit through it.

Consider Miguel Stonefield—the composite student introduced in Chapter 5, who learned to game the AP exam by pathologizing characters. Miguel is bright and empathetic, a teenager who devours fantasy novels with genuine intellectual passion. He lights up while explaining the political systems of fictional kingdoms, or how a ragtag fellowship triumphs not because of destiny but because they learn to cooperate. His engagement with these stories is sophisticated: he tracks narrative structures, analyzes power dynamics, and questions authorial choices.

But in English class, he struggles. The internal agonies of Hamlet feel alien; the suburban despair of *The Catcher in the Rye* feels myopic. His essays—brimming with patterns of connection, resilience, and world-building logic—come back with comments urging him to "engage more deeply with the tragic core" and "avoid reducing the text's complexity."

The message is clear: his way of reading doesn't count.

By senior year, Miguel concludes that literature simply "isn't for him." He stops reading for pleasure altogether.

That loss is not anecdotal. It echoes through classrooms everywhere. And it represents a catastrophic failure of cultural stewardship—not because Miguel lacks intellectual capacity, but because the cathedral has declared his cognitive orientation heretical.

I. The Voluntary Exiles: Students Who Stop Reading

This pattern has been documented for decades. The National Endowment for the Arts has tracked steady declines in voluntary reading among teens and young adults, with their landmark report *Reading at Risk* noting that the drop begins sharply in late adolescence—precisely when students encounter the sixty-eight percent suffering-centered canon documented in Chapter 1.[1] Pew Research Center has likewise found that large segments of U.S. adults rarely read books at all, and many cite school reading experiences as their turning point away from the habit.[2]

Teachers report the same pattern: students who love reading outside school lose that love inside school. And it's not because the stories are "too hard"—it's because the stories are relentlessly grim, and the classroom consecrates only one kind of engagement with them.

When the curriculum implies that "good literature" is synonymous with "depressing literature," a predictable sorting happens. Students who can metabolize tragedy, who find intellectual satisfaction in dissecting despair, remain in the congregation. Those fueled by curiosity, wonder, or communal problem-solving drift away.

They are not failing to grasp complexity. They are rejecting the premise that complexity requires despair.

Miguel didn't need simpler books. He needed permission to value what he was already doing—reading stories as models for how communities function, how systems change, how cooperation overcomes obstacles. But the cathedral doesn't consecrate those readings. It calls them naive, insufficiently critical, a failure to engage with "the text's darkness."

So Miguel leaves. And with him goes a particular kind of intelligence—one that looks for patterns of repair, not just patterns of ruin.

II. The Ashamed Audience: The Guilty Pleasure Hierarchy

The exclusion doesn't end with graduation—it calcifies into a cultural hierarchy that follows readers for life.

Consider Siobhan Moorley, a composite representing countless readers. Siobhan is a successful professional, a problem-solver by training and temperament, who relaxes with cozy mysteries and space operas about functional starship crews navigating complex situations with competence and wit.

But she hides this part of herself.

"After a day of solving real problems," she explains, "I want a story where problems get solved, where competence is rewarded, and community matters. But at dinner parties, you don't mention that. That's when you talk about the latest bleak limited series on war or addiction. If I bring up the mystery where an elderly baker solves a crime with her cat, people assume I'm unserious."

This shame around joy—this quiet self-censorship—is the guilty pleasure's origin story. The suffering canon didn't just crown tragedy as our highest art form; it made other modes feel frivolous, lesser, embarrassing. Even when they are what actually nourish us, what help us navigate the world, what model the cognitive skills we desperately need.

Romance readers hide their books. Science fiction fans apologize for their genre. Anyone who admits to preferring stories where things get better is immediately coded as intellectually soft, insufficiently willing to face "reality."

We have built a system in which people hide the books that heal them and express enthusiasm for the books that drain them. This is not a healthy literary culture. This is a collective delusion sustained by institutional prestige—the seventy-one percent combined suffering dominance in film and literary prizes documented in Chapter 6.

III. The Silenced Stories: Whose Trauma Counts?

The suffering canon doesn't just dictate what readers should value; it dictates what writers—especially marginalized writers—are allowed to create.

The pressure is subtle but omnipresent: *Your story matters most when you bleed.*

Writers of color discuss this repeatedly in essays and interviews. Many describe an unspoken expectation that their work must highlight trauma—racism, violence, generational pain—as if those are the only stories from marginalized communities that "count" as serious literature.

Amara Goldmere, a composite representing this pattern, puts it this way:

"There's an unspoken rule. If I write Black joy, Black triumph, Black communities solving problems together, it's seen as less authentic. Less literary. Like, I'm not being honest about the Black experience. But if I write about suffering, suddenly everyone thinks it's profound and important."

The suffering canon turns marginalized authors into archivists of their people's wounds while sidelining narratives of joy, ingenuity, community, everyday life, and hard-won triumph. Pain becomes marketable. Flourishing becomes niche. Trauma becomes the entry fee for literary prestige.

This is not representation; it is a curated museum of trauma, endlessly restaged for a presumed audience that needs to be educated in darkness. It tells marginalized writers: *We will listen to you, but only when you perform your pain. Show us your wounds, and we will call you authentic. Show us your joy, and we will call you escapist.*

The result is a canon that claims to be more diverse than ever while still consecrating the same old creed: suffering equals significance. We have changed who gets to suffer on the page, but not the fundamental equation that makes suffering the only path to literary legitimacy.

IV. The Democracy Problem

A healthy democracy depends on a plurality of voices, experiences, and imaginative pathways. It needs cultural ecosystems in which all kinds of readers feel at home, and all kinds of stories are considered legitimate tools for thinking about the world.

But when our literary culture privileges only one emotional register—bleakness, breakdown, cynicism—it narrows who participates. And a narrowed public square is a weakened one.

The lost readers are not just lost customers for the publishing industry. They are lost citizens.

They are the Miguel Stonefields, trained to believe their orientation toward hope and collaboration disqualifies them from being serious thinkers. By the time Miguel reaches the college political science seminar where Noah Wintermere sits, unable to imagine climate solutions (Chapter 11), Miguel won't even be in the room. He stopped believing his thinking mattered years ago.

They are the Siobhan Moorleys, who internalize the idea that pleasure is embarrassing, competence is unpoetic, and problem-solving narratives are intellectually lightweight. When she's called to serve on a civic committee, she unconsciously mimics the cathedral's liturgy: critique everything, build nothing, because building feels naive.

They are readers who might have approached public life with pragmatism, creativity, and communal imagination—but were taught those qualities don't belong in "serious" discourse.

A public square dominated by cynicism is not neutral; it is impoverished. It becomes a place where outrage is easier than problem-solving, where despair masquerades as realism, where imaginative solutions struggle to gain traction because they sound like fiction—like the naive fantasies the suffering canon taught us to dismiss.

When Emma Brightwater asked, "Is that all there is?" in Chapter 1, she wasn't just asking about literature. She was asking about life, about possibility, about whether intelligence requires despair. The cathedral answered: Yes. And students like Miguel heard that answer and walked away, taking their particular forms of intelligence with them.

The Cost of Exclusion

The exclusion of readers who hunger for wonder, humor, competence, connection, or constructive problem-solving is not a minor footnote in literary culture. It is a catastrophic failure of stewardship.

It impoverishes our artistic landscape. It narrows our cognitive diversity. It undermines our collective ability to imagine futures worth inheriting. It weakens our democracy by driving away the very people whose ways of thinking we most desperately need—people who believe problems can be solved, who see patterns of repair, who imagine communities that work.

In a culture where only pain is permitted to be profound, we lose not just readers. We lose direction home. We lose blueprints for repair. We lose the cognitive models that show us how things get better, not just how they fall apart.

The cathedral stands, magnificent and oppressive, consecrating the same service it has performed for centuries. And outside, in the growing darkness, stand all the readers we've exiled—people like Miguel, like Siobhan, like Amara, like everyone who ever looked at the tiny door and decided they didn't fit.

They are still there, reading in secret, hiding their joy, apologizing for their hope. Waiting for someone to open a window. Waiting for permission to come home.

The question is not whether we can afford to welcome them back. The question is whether we can afford to keep them out.

CHAPTER 12 ENDNOTES

1. National Endowment for the Arts, *Reading at Risk: A Survey of Literary Reading in America* (Washington, DC: National Endowment for the Arts, 2004), accessed March 10, 2025, https://www.arts.gov/sites/default/files/ReadingAtRisk.pdf; National Endowment for the Arts, *To Read or Not to Read: A Question of National Consequence* (Washington, DC: National Endowment for the Arts, 2007), accessed March 10, 2025, https://www.arts.gov/sites/default/files/ToRead.pdf.
2. Pew Research Center, "Who Doesn't Read Books in America?," September 21, 2021, accessed March 10, 2025, https://www.pewresearch.org/short-reads/2021/09/21/who-doesnt-read-books-in-america/;
"Reading Habits in the Digital Age," January 26, 2023, accessed March 10, 2025, https://www.pewresearch.org/internet/2023/01/26/reading-habits-in-the-digital-age/.

PART FOUR: THE BLUEPRINT

Solutions: Building What Comes Next

Diagnosis is not destiny. History is not a prison. Having mapped the cathedral and traced its foundations, we now turn to the drafting table. This final section offers tools, texts, and tactics—a flourishing canon, a pedagogy of possibility, a rewired culture—for the necessary work of construction. The question is no longer what we have built, but what we will build next.
Chapters 13–17

CHAPTER 13: THE FLOURISHING CANON—An Argument for a New Library

The diagnosis is complete. The evidence of damage wrought by the suffering canon is overwhelming. But to simply dismantle the old cathedral is to leave a void—a fenced-off ruin where something living ought to be. The revolution requires not just critique but construction. It demands a new library, stocked with texts that prove complexity need not be born of catastrophe, that technical excellence can marry profound joy, and that the full, magnificent spectrum of human experience is worthy of our deepest artistic and intellectual attention.

This is the Flourishing Canon: a testament to lives lived in connection, curiosity, courage, and ongoing repair.

Building this canon requires a radical redefinition of "profundity." We are not seeking mere happiness—a state just as simplistic as unrelenting despair. We are seeking works that explore the intricate textures of human fulfillment: the struggle for understanding, the grace of community, the resilience of hope, the quiet triumph of competence, the hard work of forgiveness, the discipline of joy.

The criteria for inclusion are as rigorous as any applied to the suffering canon:

Technical Excellence: Masterful craft in language, structure, or form.

Central Exploration of Flourishing: The narrative is organized around connection, growth, discovery, or repair.

Intellectual and Emotional Complexity: The work embraces real challenges and ambiguities, avoiding sentimentality.

A NOTE ON BORDERLINE CASES

Some works resist easy categorization. They contain significant suffering but ultimately organize their meaning around repair, connection, or sustained life rather than collapse. Others end ambiguously, requiring interpretive judgment about where the narrative locates its deepest truth.

Works that straddle categories:

The Overstory (Richard Powers): Contains ecological devastation and personal tragedy, yet its deepest argument is for interconnection and the patient, revolutionary work of cultivation. We include it in the Flourishing Canon while acknowledging its tragic elements. What matters is where the book's emotional and intellectual weight finally rests—not in collapse, but in the stubborn, interwoven persistence of life.

Olive Kitteridge (Elizabeth Strout): Centers a difficult, depressed woman navigating loss and alienation, yet finds connection in jagged, surprising forms that refuse both sentimentality and despair. The complexity here is in the refusal of easy resolution while still insisting on the possibility of human contact.

Gilead (Marilynne Robinson): Written by a dying man, shadowed by mortality and loss, yet organized as a catalog of blessing. The novel's profound depth comes not from denying death but from the discipline of noticing grace within the limits of a finite life.

These borderline cases demonstrate that the distinction between suffering-centered and flourishing-centered narratives is not always binary. What matters is the dominant emotional and thematic arc—where the narrative locates meaning, what it presents as the most important human work, and what cognitive patterns it trains readers to practice.[1] A story can contain immense pain and still ultimately argue that the most serious response is not breakdown but the ongoing labor of repair, attention, and connection.

This acknowledgment is not a weakness in the framework but a feature of it. The suffering canon's error was not in depicting pain—it was in treating pain as the only path to profundity.[2] The Flourishing Canon does not commit the opposite error by denying suffering's reality. It simply insists that other responses are equally worthy of rigorous artistic and intellectual attention.

What follows is a map, not a mandate. It is a curated argument that profundity and joy are not opposites. These are not "guilty pleasures." They are masterworks that have been systematically marginalized not because they lack merit, but because they threaten the suffering canon's monopoly on depth.[3] This is the library we might build if we stopped worshipping at the altar of despair.

I. THE INTELLIGENCE OF REPAIR

Works where the central drama is mending what is broken—in relationships, communities, ecologies, or the self.

Spotlight: Their Eyes Were Watching God by Zora Neale Hurston

Their Eyes Were Watching God follows Janie Crawford's journey toward a hard-won autonomy that does not deny loss but refuses to be defined by it. Hurston does not spare Janie suffering: a loveless arranged marriage, years of being silenced, the death of her beloved Tea Cake. Yet the novel's deepest energy is not organized around trauma as revelation, but around Janie's gradual reclamation of her own voice. The ending refuses both sentimental closure and canonical despair. Janie returns alone, carrying Tea Cake in memory without dissolving into self-annihilation. Crucially, Hurston frames Janie's telling of her story as an act of generative transmission. Depth here resides in the ability to integrate grief into a continuing, relational existence—a script where suffering is real, but the most serious work is learning how to live meaningfully after it.

Other Key Works:
- *Gilead* (Robinson): A dying minister's letter cataloging the blessings of an ordinary life.
- *A Gentleman in Moscow* (Towles): A man builds a meaningful life of work and chosen family under house arrest.
- *The Guernsey Literary and Potato Peel Pie Society* (Shaffer & Barrows): Literature and community as binding agents for healing after war.
- *The Stone Diaries* (Shields): An "ordinary" life rendered as an epic of friendship and quiet self-making.

II. THE DRAMA OF COMPETENCE

Stories that find narrative tension and intellectual satisfaction in skill, craftsmanship, and problem-solving.

Spotlight: All Creatures Great and Small by James Herriot

In a cultural landscape that often equates high stakes with life-or-death betrayal, Herriot builds breathtaking suspense around a breech calf delivery in the middle of the night. The drama is not in psychological collapse, but in the precise application of knowledge, the tension of a difficult procedure, and the profound satisfaction of a problem solved. The narrative is warm and often hilarious, but its core is a celebration of expertise, kindness, and work done well. It is proof that competence itself—the ability to understand a complex system and intervene to set it right—can be a profoundly engaging and deeply human subject, offering a model of agency that is both practical and uplifting.

Other Key Works:
- *Lab Girl* (Jahren): A scientist's memoir where persistence and curiosity are the driving forces.
- *The Martian* (Weir): A masterclass in problem-solving and resilient ingenuity.
- *The No. 1 Ladies' Detective Agency* (McCall Smith): Solving problems through patience, intuition, and cultural wisdom.
- *Shop Class as Soulcraft* (Crawford): A philosophical argument for manual competence as a source of meaning.

III. THE COMPLEXITY OF SUSTAINED CONNECTION

Works that explore the difficult, ongoing work of building and maintaining relationships and communities.

Spotlight: Middlemarch by George Eliot

Middlemarch is a monumental refutation of the idea that breadth requires breakdown. Eliot traces dozens of lives in a provincial town, her omniscient eye following the intricate web of their aspirations, compromises, and interconnectedness. The novel's profound depth is achieved not through a single tragic climax, but through the cumulative weight of "unhistoric acts." Its famous finale argues that the "growing good of the world" is dependent on the number of lives lived in quiet "well-doing." Here, complexity is found in the ethical nuances of a long marriage, the moral courage of a doctor fighting disease, and the quiet heroism of perseverance. It is a masterwork that finds the universe in a grain of provincial life, modeling a worldview where meaning is built incrementally through connection and responsibility.

Other Key Works:
- *Crossing to Safety* (Stegner): The fifty-year friendship of two couples as a narrative of loyalty and forgiveness.

- *The Joy Luck Club* (Tan): Mothers and daughters navigating misunderstanding and migration.
- *Jayber Crow* (Berry): A barber's lifelong meditation on vocation and love of community.
- *Pride and Prejudice* (Austen): A romance driven by humility, conversation, and self-correction.

IV. BLUEPRINTS FOR BETTER WORLDS

Works that imagine not only what might go wrong, but what might go right—and how we might build systems and societies worth inhabiting.

Spotlight: A Psalm for the Wild-Built by Becky Chambers

This novella is a quiet revolution. Set in a post-capitalist society that has solved its basic material needs, it follows a "tea monk" and a robot on a journey to ask, "What do people need?" The answer is not more productivity, but a sense of "enoughness." Chambers builds tension not from conflict or violence, but from the profound, unsettling nature of this question. The book is a blueprint for a different kind of story: one where the stakes are philosophical and emotional, where the goal is not to defeat an enemy but to understand a friend, and where the resolution is found in mutual recognition and care. It demonstrates that the most radical act of imagination is not depicting a dystopia, but sketching a believable, desirable utopia.

Other Key Works:
- *The Dispossessed* (Le Guin): A thought experiment comparing capitalist and anarchist societies.
- *The Lord of the Rings* (Tolkien): A fellowship defeating evil through persistence, friendship, and mercy.
- *The Ministry for the Future* (Kim Stanley Robinson): A dense, realistic novel crammed with actionable climate solutions.
- *The Long Way to a Small, Angry Planet* (Chambers): Diplomacy and conversation as daily practice on a spaceship.

Deep Dive: A Psalm for the Wild-Built and the Theology of Enough

Cultural Position:

A landmark of the contemporary "solarpunk" or "hopepunk" movement, Becky Chambers's novella has achieved critical acclaim, including a Hugo Award, but exists largely outside the traditional literary classroom canon. It is often shelved as genre fiction, a categorization that has historically marginalized works from being considered for "serious" academic study, despite its profound philosophical engagement with post-capitalist, ecological, and existential themes.

Core Arc:

The narrative follows Sibling Dex, a non-binary tea monk experiencing a crisis of purpose in a post-industrial, ecologically balanced society called Panga. They feel a deep, inarticulate need for something more, which drives them to leave their urban sanctuary and journey into the wilderness. There, they encounter Mosscap, a robot who has emerged from the wild to check on humanity centuries after the robots gained consciousness and peacefully departed human society.

The arc is not one of conflict and resolution, but of shared journey and dialogue. Dex and Mosscap travel together, their conversations exploring the nature of need, purpose, satisfaction, and what it means to be a living being in a world that has stepped back from the brink of ecological collapse. The story culminates not in a dramatic climax, but in a moment of quiet mutual understanding: Dex's undefined need is acknowledged as valid, and Mosscap's mission to ask "What do you need?" is accepted as a beginning, not an end.

Meaning Framework:

Chambers constructs a world where meaning is derived from presence, curiosity, and care, rather than conquest, accumulation, or dramatic transformation.

Cognitive Training:

For a reader, *A Psalm for the Wild-Built* is a masterclass in a different kind of cognitive schema:
- **Purpose is Process, Not Product:** Dex's journey refutes the notion that one must have a single, grand, world-changing purpose. Their value is found in their capacity to listen and provide comfort through the ritual of tea, and their restlessness is treated not as a failure but as a valid part of their human experience.
- **Enoughness is Abundance:** The society of Panga operates on a principle of sustainable sufficiency. The drama of scarcity that fuels most narratives is replaced by the more complex, nuanced drama of figuring out what to do once survival is guaranteed. The book frames a life of "enough" not as a compromise, but as a liberation.
- **Curiosity is the Highest Stakes:** The primary engine of the plot is not danger, but intellectual and emotional curiosity. The central question—"What do people need?"—is treated with the same narrative weight as a thriller's central mystery. The "action" is the act of paying deep attention.
- **Interdependence is Strength:** The relationship between Dex and Mosscap is a model of cross-species (or cross-entity) alliance based on mutual respect, not utility. They help each other not because they have to, but because they choose to. Their connection is the narrative's central achievement.
- **Your Needs Are Legitimate:** The book validates the feeling of being safe, fed, and housed yet still feeling a nameless yearning. It models that this isn't a personal failing, but a question worth exploring with compassion.
- **Complexity Resides in Peace:** The novella trains readers to find depth and nuance in quiet moments, in careful conversation, and in the internal landscape of a

character who is not in mortal peril but is on a quest for meaning. It redefines "narrative tension" as the tension of understanding, not of survival.
- **Repair Is the Default:** The world of Panga is one that has already done the hard work of ecological and social repair. The narrative isn't about achieving utopia, but about learning to live within it. This models a forward-looking imagination where the goal is not just to avert catastrophe, but to envision what comes after.
- **Dialogue Is Action:** The long, meandering conversations between Dex and Mosscap *are* the plot. This teaches readers to value the exchange of ideas and the building of understanding as a primary form of narrative movement.

For a young person like Noah Wintermere, mired in collapse narratives, the lesson is revolutionary: the future doesn't have to be a dystopia or a failed utopia; it can be a complex, messy, but fundamentally kind place where the central work is learning how to live with ourselves and each other. For Emma Brightwater, it offers a script where feeling lost is the beginning of a conversation, not a symptom of brokenness.

Pedagogical Pairing:

Pair *A Psalm for the Wild-Built* with *Death of a Salesman* to create a profound dialogue about the meaning of work, success, and personal value. Where Willy Loman is destroyed by his failure to achieve a hollow, materialistic version of the American Dream, Sibling Dex finds their identity challenged but not shattered by a society that has moved beyond such dreams. *Salesman* frames a life without conventional success as a tragic waste; *Psalm* frames it as a potential site of deep, meaningful inquiry.

This pairing forces the question: What are the real "stakes" of a human life? Is it the dramatic failure to achieve an impossible standard, or the quiet, ongoing work of figuring out how to live well? It teaches students to analyze how setting and societal structure—one a pressure cooker of capitalist failure, the other a supportive network of post-scarcity—profoundly shape what kinds of stories are possible and what kinds of lives are considered worthy of narrative attention.[1]

V. THE FOUNDATIONS OF WONDER

Works that reignite a sense of awe at the universe and our place in it—an antidote to trained cynicism.

Spotlight: Pilgrim at Tinker Creek by Annie Dillard

Dillard's narrative is a year of fierce, joyful attention to a small patch of Virginia. It is a work of theology, biology, and philosophy that finds not just "nature, red in tooth and claw," but a world "drenched in grace," a universe of "power and beauty, grace tangled in a rapture with violence." Her profundity lies in a relentless, almost terrifying, openness to the world. She stares at a cedar tree until it "shrieks" with meaning; she watches a frog melt in a snake's mouth and sees the sheer, awful power of creation. This is not escapism. It is a confrontation with the real, in all its terrifying and glorious complexity, modeling a form of attention that is itself a spiritual and intellectual discipline.[11]

Other Key Works:
- *Braiding Sweetgrass* (Kimmerer): Indigenous wisdom and scientific knowledge intertwined in an argument for reciprocity.
- *The Overstory* (Powers): An epic argument for the interconnection of all life.
- *The Soul of an Octopus* (Montgomery): A testament to cross-species curiosity and empathy.
- *World of Wonders* (Nezhukumatathil): Essays where strange animals and plants become lenses for belonging and joy.

A TOOLKIT FOR REBALANCING: PEDAGOGICAL PAIRINGS

The flourishing canon is not meant to replace the old, but to sit alongside it, creating a more truthful and complete curriculum.

Suffering Canon Text	Flourishing Canon Pairing	Core Question for Discussion
The Great Gatsby (Lethal illusion of the American Dream)	*Their Eyes Were Watching God* (Reclamation of self and voice)	"Compare the final moments of Gatsby and Janie. What does each ending suggest about where 'meaning' or 'the good life' is ultimately found?"
1984 (Individual crushed by the state)	*The Dispossessed* (The arduous work of building a free society)	"Both are political novels. How does the narrative structure—one ending in annihilation, the other in open-ended return—shape their political arguments?"
Death of a Salesman (Work and identity lead to collapse)	*All Creatures Great and Small* (Work as a source of competence and connection)	"How do Willy Loman and James Herriot define success? What do their stories suggest about the relationship

| *Hamlet* (Inability to act leads to ruin) | *The Odyssey* (Cunning and perseverance lead to homecoming) | between work, dignity, and community?" "Both protagonists face immense obstacles. How do their different approaches to action, patience, and loyalty lead to their vastly different outcomes?" |

These pairings do not banish tragedy; they contextualize it. They ask students to read suffering not as the only serious mode, but as one register among many. They turn the classroom into a comparative lab where students can test different theories of what a life is for.

THE READERS WE BRING HOME

The cost of exclusion is not just a statistic; it is the quiet closing of a mind that once burned with curiosity. For readers like Miguel Stonefield, the flourishing canon is not an academic exercise—it is an invitation to come home.

Imagine Miguel, now in college, stumbling upon a syllabus that includes *The Lord of the Rings* not as a simple adventure, but as a profound exploration of stewardship, sacrifice, and the resilience of fellowship. He encounters *A Psalm for the Wild-Built*, and for the first time, sees the complex questions of purpose and "enoughness" he's wrestled with reflected in a narrative that doesn't require a body count to feel weighty. He reads the spotlight essay on *Their Eyes Were Watching God* and recognizes in Janie's journey a kind of strength he's always valued but was told wasn't "literary": the strength to integrate loss and keep living, to reclaim one's own story.

In these pages, Miguel finds his way of thinking validated. The patterns he was naturally drawn to—alliances, problem-solving, the slow, hard work of building and maintaining—are not naive. They are the very subjects of some of the most intellectually rigorous and emotionally complex works ever written. He realizes, with a shock of recognition, that the books he loved in secret were never "lesser." They were just living in a different wing of the library—one the cultural custodians had boarded up and labeled "escapist."

The flourishing canon doesn't just add new books to a list; it reopens the door for the Miguels of the world. It sends a message: Your mind is welcome here. The way you see the world is not a liability but a lens. Come inside.[12]

The Critical Pushback—and the Reply

The predictable critique of a Flourishing Canon is that it is "escapist" or "unrealistic"—the suffering canon's most durable superstition, the lie it has told so effectively that even its victims repeat it.

But realism is not a synonym for despair. The world contains war, cruelty, injustice, and grief; it also contains competence, delight, repair, and love that outlives catastrophe. A canon that aggressively edits out half of reality is not rigorous—it is distorted.[13] It is a fun-house mirror that magnifies darkness while shrinking light to irrelevance.

The works gathered here do not deny pain. They include illness, injustice, conflict, poverty, and loss. What they refuse is the lazy conclusion that pain is the only reliable source of depth, that suffering is the sole path to significance. They ask more of us: not just to diagnose what's broken, but to imagine and enact paths toward wholeness. Not just to autopsy failed systems, but to architect working ones. Not just to rehearse collapse, but to practice repair.

What the Flourishing Canon Offers

The Flourishing Canon is not a list of comfort reads for people who can't handle "real" literature. It is a set of blueprints, case studies, and training manuals for the difficult art of building lives and worlds worth inhabiting. It stretches our imaginative capacities in directions the suffering canon rarely touches:

- How do communities solve problems together?
- What does competence look like in action?
- How do people forgive without forgetting?
- What are the mechanics of repair, not just ruin?
- How do we build institutions that work?
- What does love look like when it lasts?

These are not simpler questions than "How do people suffer?" They are harder. They require more intellectual sophistication, more moral imagination, more practical wisdom.[1]

The suffering canon taught generations of readers—students like Emma Brightwater, Noah Wintermere, and Miguel Stonefield—that serious people focus on collapse. The Flourishing Canon teaches something more demanding: that serious people build.

A complete, annotated list of all one hundred works in the Flourishing Canon appears in Appendix G.

Why These Works Were Excluded

These one hundred books were not kept out of the old curriculum because they lacked merit. Every work on this list is technically excellent, intellectually sophisticated, and artistically accomplished. Many have won major prizes. Many are taught—but as exceptions, electives, "fun" reads squeezed into the margins around the "serious" tragic core.

They were kept out because they threaten a monopoly. They prove, over and over, that we can be serious without being sick, that we can be profound without being crushed, that we can be wise and still choose to build. They are the stones and stained glass of a new cathedral—one that does not worship suffering, but houses the full, unruly, radiant range of human experience. One that consecrates not just our capacity to endure, but our capacity to create, connect, repair, and thrive.

The question is not whether this canon is "as good as" the suffering canon. The question is whether we can afford to keep operating with only half the story, half the toolkit, half the imagination. When Noah Wintermere sits in that college seminar unable to imagine climate solutions (Chapter 11), when Miguel Stonefield abandons reading because his way of thinking doesn't count (Chapter 12), when Emma Brightwater asks "Is that all there is?" (Chapter 1)—they are asking for this library. They are asking for permission to believe that building is as intellectually serious as breaking, that repair is as complex as ruin, that hope is as rigorous as despair.

This canon answers: Yes. It always was. We just stopped teaching it.

CHAPTER 13 ENDNOTES

1. Patrick Colm Hogan, *The Mind and Its Stories: Narrative Universals and Human Emotion* (Cambridge: Cambridge University Press, 2003).
2. Rita Felski, *The Limits of Critique* (Chicago: University of Chicago Press, 2015).
3. John Guillory, *Cultural Capital: The Problem of Literary Canon Formation* (Chicago: University of Chicago Press, 1993).
4. Hazel V. Carby, *Reconstructing Womanhood: The Emergence of the Afro-American Woman Novelist* (Oxford: Oxford University Press, 1987).
5. Matthew B. Crawford, *Shop Class as Soulcraft: An Inquiry into the Value of Work* (New York: Penguin Press, 2009).

6. Martha C. Nussbaum, *Love's Knowledge: Essays on Philosophy and Literature* (Oxford: Oxford University Press, 1990).
7. Alexandra Rowland, "A Brief History of Hopepunk," Tor.com, December 2019, accessed January 15, 2025, https://www.tor.com/2019/12/16/a-brief-history-of-hopepunk/; Gerson Lodi-Ribeiro, ed., *Solarpunk: Ecological and Fantastical Stories in a Sustainable World* (Nashville: World Weaver Press, 2018).
8. "Solarpunk: A Reference Guide," *The Solutions Journal* 9, no. 3 (2018).
9. Dan P. McAdams, *The Stories We Live By: Personal Myths and the Making of the Self* (New York: Guilford Press, 1993).
10. Cristina Zepeda et al., "Promoting Cognitive Flexibility through Cultural and Worldview Diversity," *Educational Psychologist* 56, no. 4 (2021).
11. Lynn Ross-Bryant, "Pilgrim at Tinker Creek and the Social Legacy of American Nature Writing," *Religion and American Culture* 14, no. 2 (2004).
12. Robert J. Yanal, *Paradoxes of Emotion and Fiction* (University Park: Penn State Press, 1999).
13. Martha C. Nussbaum, *Poetic Justice: The Literary Imagination and Public Life* (Boston: Beacon Press, 1995).
14. Jerome Bruner, *Acts of Meaning* (Cambridge, MA: Harvard University Press, 1990).

CHAPTER 14: NEWS THAT NOURISHES—Rebalancing the Daily Canon

The evening news has long been the daily liturgy of the suffering canon: a carefully curated highlight reel of human failure. War, scandal, collapse, catastrophe. Thirty minutes in which the world is presented as a burning building, and audiences are handed no fire extinguisher—only a more detailed map of the flames.

But what if information could serve a different purpose? What if the point of news were not just to alert audiences to threats, but to equip them with understanding and agency? What if the nightly ritual didn't end with "Here is everything that's broken," but continued to "Here is who is fixing it, how they're doing it, and what it would take to do more"?

That shift represents the quiet revolution of what has come to be called solutions journalism: not feel-good fluff, not escapist distraction, but rigorous reporting on how people are responding to problems—what's working, what isn't, and what can be learned from it.

Mike Ironwood, the composite figure introduced in Chapter 2, who has spent decades absorbing the nightly catastrophe ritual, represents millions of viewers caught in this pattern. After years of finishing the news feeling anxious, helpless, and vaguely guilty about not "staying informed" enough, a shift occurs when his granddaughter Emma—the same

Emma Brightwater who asked "Is that all there is?" in Chapter 1—intervenes.

"Grandpa," she observes, "if the news leaves you feeling like the world is ending every night, that's not 'staying informed.' That's marinating in despair."

The observation prompts an experiment. Mike continues watching his usual broadcast. But he begins supplementing it with sources that explicitly report on people fixing things—investigations into how Finland drastically reduced homelessness, or examinations of cities designing themselves to stay cool as the climate warms. He encounters not just problems, but concrete responses: the policies chosen, the costs, the trade-offs, the outcomes.

The world no longer looks like a terminal patient being described in exquisite clinical detail. It looks like a very sick body with an army of doctors, nurses, and determined practitioners working on it.

Mike still sees the fire. But now he also sees the firefighters.

I. What News Is For

The suffering canon treats "grim" as a synonym for "serious." Traditional news has inherited that value system wholesale. The implicit logic runs: if it hurts, it must be important; if it helps, it's probably fluff.

This represents a fundamental category error. News is not a horror anthology; it is a public utility. Its core functions should be orientation ("Where are we?"), explanation ("Why is this happening?"), and agency ("What can be done, and by whom?"). The problem is that contemporary journalism has built a system that excels at the first two functions and systematically neglects the third.

Solutions journalism attempts to restore that missing piece. The basic framework is straightforward:

Start with a clearly defined problem. Identify a specific response—an initiative, policy, program, or community practice. Report, with the same rigor applied to scandal or failure, on how that response works: evidence, mechanisms, costs, limitations. Make clear what is—and isn't—transferable to other contexts.

In other words, it refuses to confuse "critical" with "fatalistic." It refuses to pretend that the only honest story is the one that ends in ruin.

This framework aligns with what psychologists have long observed about hope and resilience. In hope theory, articulated most clearly by psychologist C.R. Snyder, the feeling of hope is not vague optimism but the combination of three specific elements: a meaningful goal, believable pathways to reach it, and a sense of personal or collective agency to move along those pathways. The current news ecosystem reliably supplies goals ("we should mitigate climate change," "we should reduce gun violence") and a depressing abundance of information about obstacles. What it rarely supplies are credible pathways and living examples of agency in action.

A news system that only reports on damage is like a medical textbook that only includes terminal cases. It is not "realistic"; it is, in a crucial sense, incomplete. It trains practitioners to identify disease but not to recognize health or understand treatment.

II. What Negativity Does to Audiences

This matters because, as documented in Chapter 2, the human brain is not a neutral filing cabinet; it is a pattern-recognizing, story-seeking machine. For understandable evolutionary reasons, it has a built-in negativity bias—threats grab attention more powerfully than neutral events or even modestly positive ones. When the nightly information stream consists almost entirely of threats, audiences are not seeing "the world as it really is"; they are seeing a world whose dangers have been placed under a microscope while its capacities for repair have been left offstage.

Psychologists have begun examining directly what happens when that pattern is interrupted. Experimental work comparing standard negative news stories with so-called "constructive" or "restorative" narratives—stories that still describe serious problems but also show concrete responses—finds that audiences exposed to the constructive versions report more positive emotions, greater sense of efficacy, and equal or higher ratings of journalistic quality. Crucially, they do not become naive; they simply feel less helpless.

Meanwhile, research on positive emotions more broadly, particularly Barbara Fredrickson's "broaden-and-build" theory, suggests that states like curiosity, interest, and hope are not frivolous extras but cognitive tools. These emotional states literally widen thought-action repertoires, making people more creative, flexible, and able to envision long-term possibilities. Over time, those moments of broadened thinking help build lasting psychological resources and social connections.

The point is not that news should "make audiences happy." The point is that a relentlessly despair-heavy information stream narrows imagination precisely when it is most needed. It trains rumination instead of problem-solving. It teaches people to see crises as endpoints rather than as the middle of the story—the same limitation documented in Chapter 11's exploration of the imagination drain affecting Noah Wintermere's generation.

When every serious narrative ends in collapse—whether in the sixty-eight percent suffering-centered high school canon (Chapter 1), the seventy-one percent suffering-centered prestige culture (Chapter 6), or the nightly news liturgy—the cumulative effect is a citizenry trained to autopsy problems but not to architect solutions.

III. Trust, Avoidance, and the Institutional Crisis

The suffering canon doesn't just exhaust individual viewers; it undermines the very institutions that deliver information.

Public trust in news media has eroded to historic lows. Recent Gallup polling finds that only around one-third of Americans say they trust mass media to report news fully, accurately, and fairly—a collapse from highs above seventy percent in the 1970s.[1]

One predictable response has been avoidance. People like Mike don't stop caring about the world; they stop watching news about it. They remain anxious about global conditions but now feel anxious and uninformed—the worst of both worlds. This is not apathy; it is self-protection against a product that reliably produces helplessness.

Here is where the flourishing canon logic applies directly to journalism: institutions cannot build trust in products that reliably leave their audiences feeling hopeless and powerless. The audiences who do maintain consumption habits often do so out of a sense of duty or anxiety-driven compulsion, not genuine engagement or satisfaction.

Some news organizations have begun noticing this dynamic and adjusting their approach. Public broadcasters and major outlets in Europe have launched regular features devoted to problem-solving and innovation—units that highlight communities reducing homelessness, cities redesigning themselves around climate resilience, and hospitals rethinking end-of-life care. The BBC World Service's *People Fixing the World* explicitly describes itself as covering "brilliant solutions to the world's problems," releasing weekly episodes that investigate whether those solutions actually work. The Guardian's global series *The Upside* focuses on "people and innovations trying to find answers to the world's most difficult problems," and has demonstrated strong reader engagement.

This is not a sentimental pivot; it is an economic and ethical recalibration. Outlets that incorporate solutions reporting often find that these stories drive sustained engagement, thoughtful reader responses, and—in measurable cases—subscriptions and donations. Audiences demonstrate hunger not only to know what is going wrong, but to understand where their attention, resources, or civic participation might actually make a difference.

The Solutions Journalism Network, founded in 2013, has worked with hundreds of newsrooms worldwide to integrate this approach.[2] Their training emphasizes that solutions journalism is not advocacy—it does not argue for particular policies or praise specific organizations uncritically. Instead, it investigates responses with the same skeptical rigor applied to exposés of failure, asking: Does this intervention work? How do we know? What are the costs and limitations? What can other communities learn from this approach?

This represents a fundamental shift in what the cathedral consecrates as newsworthy. Where the old liturgy elevated only breakdown, the new model treats repair as equally deserving of investigative attention.

IV. Documented Effects on Audiences

The impact of this shift on audiences has been measured. Research comparing audience responses to traditional problem-focused stories versus solutions-oriented coverage shows consistent patterns. A large-scale randomized experiment by the Solutions Journalism Network found that readers exposed to solutions-framed stories reported significantly higher levels of optimism about the problem being addressed, greater sense of self-efficacy (belief in their own ability to contribute to solutions), and increased willingness to engage with the issue through civic action or information-seeking.[3]

Critically, solutions coverage did not reduce readers' perception of the problem's seriousness. Audiences did not become Pollyannaish or dismissive of challenges. Instead, they showed what researchers describe as "constructive hope"—hope grounded in a realistic assessment of difficulties combined with a concrete understanding of possible responses.

This distinction matters. The research literature on hope and action consistently shows that vague optimism ("Everything will work out") does not predict engagement or behavior change. What predicts action is specific, pathway-focused hope: understanding concrete steps that can be taken, seeing evidence that those steps sometimes work, and believing that one's participation could matter.

The parallel to educational findings documented in earlier chapters is striking. Just as the sixty-eight percent suffering-centered literary canon (Chapter 1) trains students to perform cynicism rather than constructive analysis, a news ecosystem focused exclusively on breakdown trains citizens to perform helplessness rather than civic competence.

V. The Rebalanced Information Stream

What would it look like, practically, for individuals to inhabit a news ecosystem that sustains rather than depletes? The answer does not require waiting for every newsroom to change; it can begin with intentional consumption patterns.

One approach observed among readers who report higher satisfaction with their information habits is what might be termed a "balanced information stream": for every piece of purely problem-focused content consumed, they deliberately seek one piece that centers on a credible response. This means watching the investigative exposé about failing infrastructure, then reading a reported feature on cities that have successfully renovated their systems. Reading the analysis of rising teen anxiety, then finding a story on schools that have successfully revamped their schedules to support mental health.

Mike Ironwood doesn't articulate this as a formal system. He simply notices that during weeks when he supplements the nightly news with solutions-focused podcasts, he sleeps better. His mind still processes the day's crises, but now one of those narratives involves a group of volunteers who restored a local river, or a city council that successfully passed an effective housing policy. His imagination has material to work with besides dread.

At a psychological level, this practice strengthens what Snyder's hope theory describes as the "pathways component" of hope—providing the mind with a steady stream of goals, routes toward those goals, and examples of agency in action. This is not delusion or denial. It is cognitive maintenance, the same kind of deliberate pattern-interruption that cognitive behavioral therapy uses to address depression and anxiety.

The broader pattern suggests that the suffering canon operates not only through formal institutions—schools, publishers, film studios, prize committees—but through the accumulated daily choices about information consumption. The nightly news, the morning push notification, the endless scroll—these constitute a canon as powerful as any syllabus. They tell audiences, every day, which stories matter and which do not; whose pain counts and whose repair is too mundane to mention.

VI. What a Flourishing News Ecosystem Looks Like

If the transition from a suffering canon to a flourishing one is taken seriously, journalism cannot be exempted from the transformation. A flourishing news ecosystem would still report vigorously on war, corruption, disaster, and cruelty. It would investigate abuses of power with relentless energy and hold institutions accountable for failures.

But it would also:
- Treat successful experiments in justice, sustainability, and community health as front-page news, not feel-good sidebars
- Follow up on stories not only at moments of crisis but at moments of repair and reconstruction
- Make "How did they address this?" as standard a question as "Who is to blame?"
- Recognize that citizens need models of effective action as much as they need warnings about threats
- Cover policy implementation with the same intensity currently reserved for political horse-race coverage

This is not a call for saccharine chronicles of puppies and airport reunions. It is a call for journalism that tells complete stories: humans are capable of monstrous harm and astonishing ingenuity; institutions fail spectacularly and sometimes improve through determined effort; communities fracture and also reweave themselves in ways worth documenting and studying.

News that sustains does not spare audiences from grief or shield them from hard truths. It simply refuses to strand them in despair. It assumes that audiences are capable not only of absorbing trauma but of participating in repair. It treats citizens not as passive witnesses to slow-motion collapse, but as potential collaborators in an unfinished project.

The cathedral's daily service, in this model, does not end with a catalog of wounds. It continues until someone asks, "What is being built? What is being learned? Where is repair already underway?"

VII. The Daily Liturgy Reimagined

Throughout this book, the canon has been examined as something official: syllabi, award lists, required reading, and consecrated films. But the nightly news, the morning alert, the perpetual feed—these are also canons, as Chapter 2 documented. They are serial, ongoing, and massively influential in shaping what audiences believe about the world and their place in it.

In the old cathedral, the daily homily ended with wounds—a catalog of suffering that confirmed the congregation's darkest suspicions about human nature and historical trajectory. The service concluded with a reminder that vigilance requires constant exposure to catastrophe, that citizenship demands perpetual anxiety.

In a reimagined cathedral—one built on flourishing rather than suffering—the service does not end until someone has asked, "So what now?" That question, honestly posed, rigorously investigated, and repeatedly answered with documented examples, represents the beginning of a different information ecology.

One in which news is not a daily reinforcement of despair but a daily reminder that, however dire the diagnosis, treatment plans exist, practitioners are at work, and the outcomes remain unwritten. Where the seventy-one percent suffering-centered prestige culture documented in Chapter 6 consecrated breakdown as the only serious subject, a flourishing information ecosystem would consecrate the full range of human capacity—including the capacity to identify problems and systematically address them.

Mike Ironwood still sits in his recliner at 6:30 PM. The ritual continues. But the cathedral he enters through that screen is different now—not because it denies the fire, but because it also shows him the firefighters, the engineers redesigning fire-resistant structures, and the communities learning to live with flame in ways that protect what matters most.

The news has not become less serious. It has become more complete. And that completeness—that insistence on showing not just how systems break but how they sometimes mend—represents one pathway out of the suffering canon and toward something that might actually sustain a democratic society over time.

The information stream, like the literary canon and the film industry's consecrations, is a choice. It is a choice repeated daily, in millions of living rooms and on millions of screens. The question is whether that choice will continue to worship at the altar of despair, or whether it might begin, story by story, broadcast by broadcast, to build something else.

When Emma Brightwater asked her teacher, "Is that all there is?" she was asking about more than Hamlet. She was asking about the entire apparatus that shapes how we understand the world—the books we consecrate, the films we award, and the news we choose to consume. The answer, in each domain, is the same: no, that is not all there is. But recognizing the alternatives requires first seeing the cathedral we have built, and then choosing to open its windows.

CHAPTER 14 ENDNOTES

1. Gallup, "Americans' Trust in Mass Media Remains Near Record Low," Gallup News, October 18, 2023, accessed February 20, 2025, https://news.gallup.com/poll/512006/americans-trust-mass-media-remains-near-record-low.aspx.
2. Solutions Journalism Network, "What Is Solutions Journalism?," accessed January 15, 2025, https://www.solutionsjournalism.org/who-we-are/what-is-solutions-journalism; Solutions Journalism Network, "Story Tracker," accessed January 15, 2025, https://www.solutionsjournalism.org/story-tracker.
3. Karen Thier, Kelsey Lough, and Alex Curry, "Does Solutions-Based Reporting Improve Optimism and Self-Efficacy? A Large-Scale Randomized Experiment of Audience Effects," *Journalism Practice* 16, no. 8 (2022): 1509–1527, https://doi.org/10.1080/17512786.2022.2051579.
4. C.R. Snyder, "Hope Theory: Rainbows in the Mind," *Psychological Inquiry* 13, no. 4 (2002): 249–275.

5. Barbara L. Fredrickson, "The Role of Positive Emotions in Positive Psychology: The Broaden-and-Build Theory of Positive Emotions," *American Psychologist* 56, no. 3 (2001): 218–226.
6. The Guardian, "The Upside: People and Innovations Trying to Find Answers to the World's Most Difficult Problems," Guardian News & Media, 2018–present, accessed February 20, 2025, https://www.theguardian.com/the-upside.
7. BBC World Service, *People Fixing the World* [Audio podcast] (London: BBC, 2016–present), accessed February 20, 2025, https://www.bbc.co.uk/programmes/p04b1g3c.
8. For analysis of institutional adoption and reader revenue strategies linked to constructive reporting, see Nicole Newman, Richard Fletcher, Craig T. Robertson, and Rasmus Kleis Nielsen, *Journalism, Media, and Technology Trends and Predictions 2023* (Oxford: Reuters Institute for the Study of Journalism, 2023), 22–24, accessed February 20, 2025

CHAPTER 15: THE PEDAGOGY OF POSSIBILITY—Teaching Toward Flourishing

The diagnosis is finished. We have walked through the cathedral of suffering, rung every bell, and peered into every dim chapel. We have traced the foundations from Athens to Jerusalem to the Romantics, watched Modernism mortar despair into doctrine, followed it through classrooms, MFA programs, newsrooms, and streaming queues.

So now what?

If the analysis stopped here, this would be another clever autopsy. The disease would be mapped exquisitely while the patient remained on the table, untreated.

This chapter is not about the disease. It is about neurogenesis—about rebuilding the imaginative capacity that has been systematically atrophied, individually, educationally, and culturally. It is about what happens after walking out of the cathedral and realizing that shelter is still needed.

The question is no longer "What went wrong?" The question is finally "What can be built instead?"

I. Imagination as Neural Infrastructure

The starting premise is unfashionable in literary circles: imagination is not a personality trait; it is an infrastructure.

It is biological, shaped by repetition. The brain builds neural pathways out of whatever patterns are repeatedly traveled. Decades of consuming doom-centered syllabi, apocalypse-as-entertainment, and the sixty-eight percent suffering canon documented in Chapter 1 teach the nervous system to expect catastrophe and to prioritize scanning for threat. This is not a metaphor; it is measurable neural wiring.

Creativity research supports this understanding. Psychologist Mihaly Csikszentmihalyi's decades of work on flow describe creative thought as a state in which attention becomes deeply absorbed in a meaningful challenge, generating a sense of timelessness, curiosity, and intrinsic reward.[1] Flow is not produced by constant crisis; it thrives in sustained, focused engagement where the mind has enough safety—and enough challenge—to experiment.

Likewise, Barbara Fredrickson's broaden-and-build theory of positive emotions, referenced in Chapter 14, shows that states like joy, interest, and curiosity literally widen the cognitive field of vision.[2] In experimental settings, people experiencing mild positive emotion generate more creative, flexible, and integrative responses; their thought-action repertoire expands. Fear does the opposite. It narrows. It signals: tunnel vision now, pretend there is only one exit, and it's probably locked.

Neuroscience has begun mapping this at the network level. Creative thinking consistently engages the brain's default mode network (imagination, memory, inner simulation) in concert with the executive control network (focus, planning, goal-directed thought).[3] Imagination and discipline must work together. Catastrophe-only storytelling over-activates the "scan, brace, survive" circuitry and under-develops the "simulate, explore, invent" circuitry.

When the brain is exposed only to collapse narratives, it becomes exquisitely skilled at anticipating collapse. When it also encounters blueprints, repair processes, and plausible better futures, it becomes capable of design.

Rebuilding imagination is not indulgence. It is public health infrastructure work—as essential as maintaining roads or water systems.

II. Reclaiming the Inner Workshop

Before addressing institutions, the analysis must start with the domain individuals fully control: their own cognitive processes.

The suffering canon has colonized internal monologue. Even when attempting to imagine something constructive, many people preemptively run the critique—*That's naive. That's unrealistic. That won't be taken seriously.* The first act of rebuilding imagination is recognizing that this reflex is not rigor; it is conditioning.

Three practices emerge from cognitive research as effective counter-measures to the rituals of despair rehearsed for decades. These are not offered as self-help techniques but as deliberate counter-liturgies to the cathedral's daily services.

1. Changing the Input: A Deliberate Narrative Stream

The mind cannot thrive on an exclusive stream of catastrophe narratives, yet this is precisely what the seventy-one percent suffering-centered prestige culture (Chapter 6) provides. Rebuilding imagination begins with consciously altering information and narrative intake.

This is not about eliminating tragedy from consumption. It is about restoring proportion. For every work that ends in annihilation, deliberately choose one that ends in repair, reconciliation, or a future that is difficult but navigable. For every series about collapse, seeking one about competent people solving problems without requiring body counts.

The analogy is to cross-training in physical exercise. A person who has spent twenty years developing only upper-body strength will have underdeveloped legs. The solution is not eliminating upper body work; it is finally developing the neglected muscle groups.

2. Practicing "What If Better?"

Contemporary culture excels at counterfactuals of disaster: *What if the worst thing happens?* These scenarios are rehearsed nightly in news consumption, entertainment choices, and internal worry loops.

Rebuilding imagination means deliberately practicing the other side of counterfactual thinking: *What if something incrementally better happened—and what would have to change to make that plausible?*

Not magically fixed, not utopian perfection, but measurable improvement. "What if the school board meeting didn't end in chaos? What would have to differ about the agenda, the facilitation, the room setup, the information participants had beforehand?"

Psychologists who study mental simulation and counterfactual thinking note that imagining alternatives—especially "upward" alternatives where outcomes improve—is a powerful mechanism for planning, learning, and behavior change. The capacity exists. It has simply been trained almost exclusively in the downward direction, imagining how things could worsen rather than how they might improve.

The cognitive muscles are present. They require redirection toward lifting something other than rubble.

3. Re-learning Play and Flow

One of the quiet casualties of the suffering canon is play. Cultural prestige has been assigned almost exclusively to anguish, leaving play relegated to children's activities and dismissed as insufficiently serious.

Yet the state of flow that Csikszentmihalyi describes is fundamentally a form of serious play: total engagement in meaningful activity where challenge matches skill, feedback is immediate, and self-consciousness temporarily recedes. People report feeling most alive not when consuming tragedy passively, but when absorbed in making: painting, coding, gardening, composing, repairing engines, building narrative worlds.

Rebuilding imagination requires deliberately designing more of these conditions into daily life. Research-supported approaches include:

Structured creation time: Regular periods (weekly "making hours") where the only requirement is producing something that did not previously exist, regardless of quality or practical value.

Prototype practices: Household or community sessions where participants bring impractical ideas for improving shared spaces and treat them as seriously as if implementation were imminent.

Process-focused reading: Alternating consumption of finished works with reading about creative process—letters, craft essays, behind-the-scenes accounts that demystify how rough drafts become meaningful work.

The goal is not necessarily to become better artists. The goal is to remind the brain, repeatedly, that humans are not merely receivers of reality; they are shapers of it. This capacity atrophies without use, like any other cognitive function.

III. Classrooms as Imagination Infrastructure

The frame now widens. Imagination is not merely an individual capacity; it is a civic resource. Nowhere is its cultivation more urgent—or more structurally obstructed—than in educational systems.

Chapter 5 documented how current curricula and assessments train students to be expert coroners of texts while remaining amateurs at constructing anything new. Rebuilding imagination in this context does not mean eliminating the canon and replacing it with motivational materials. It means shifting ratios and questions.

1. Rebalancing the Curriculum

Evidence from early-adopting schools suggests that curricula work most effectively when, instead of being dominated by tragedy, approximately one-third consists of works organized around flourishing, repair, and complex hope—what Chapter 13 termed the Flourishing Canon.

Most schools will, for the foreseeable future, continue teaching substantial tragic and suffering-centered texts. Many of those works merit continued study; they are formally brilliant and thematically necessary. Rebuilding imagination means integrating reparative works not as extra-credit units squeezed into May if time permits, but as structural components of the syllabus.

What changes is not merely the reading list but the implicit answer to the question "What counts as serious?" Students observe that deep character work, formal innovation, and philosophical complexity do not belong exclusively to narratives of doom. They learn to analyze how trust is constructed in a novel, how reconciliation is staged in drama, how collective problem-solving functions in narrative, not exclusively how everything falls apart.

2. From Autopsy to Architecture

The second classroom shift is methodological. Decades have been spent teaching students how to dismantle literature. Far less attention has been devoted to teaching them how to read blueprints.

Rebuilding imagination in education requires questions like:
- "Where in this narrative does someone repair something broken—relationship, institution, self—and what specific mechanisms enable that repair?"
- "What particular choices allow this character to act ethically within a compromised system?"

- "If this narrative were extended ten years into the future, how might these people be living—and what textual evidence supports that projection?"

This is not naive optimism. It is applied systems thinking. It demands close reading, inference, and evidence. It simply directs those analytical skills toward construction rather than exclusively toward diagnosis.

Students who learn both autopsy and architecture develop more complete analytical capabilities. They can identify what breaks systems and what builds them—a far more useful civic skill than mastery of breakdown alone.

3. Training Teachers as Imagination Stewards

Teachers are already overworked and under-resourced; they do not require additional moral burdens. What they require is permission and material support to treat imagination development as part of their professional mandate, not a frivolous extra.

Observable support structures include:

Professional development offering fully developed instructional units pairing tragic and reparative texts, with standards-aligned assessments that reward flourishing-focused analysis.

District guidance documents explicitly name "capacity to envision alternative futures" as an educational outcome alongside critical thinking and textual analysis.

Administrative backing when parents complain that hopeful books are "unrealistic," by reframing such works as practice in problem-solving and civic imagination.

When students experience even one classroom where suffering is not the exclusive path to depth, they carry that template into other domains. They learn that it is possible to be simultaneously clear-eyed and constructive. That represents a revolutionary cognitive skill—exactly what Noah Wintermere's generation (Chapter 11) desperately needs to address climate change and other systemic challenges.

IV. Culture as Imagination Ecosystem

Finally, the analysis zooms to the widest frame.

Rebuilding imagination is not merely individual practice or educational reform. It is cultural infrastructure work. Stories —books, films, journalism, games, podcasts—form the shared cognitive space in which a society rehearses its possibilities. Currently, that space resembles a theater where someone forgot to pay the electricity bill.

Changing this does not require a central committee issuing Flourishing Permits. It requires thousands of small, stubborn choices from creators, gatekeepers, and audiences.

1. Creators: Refusing the Wound Requirement

Those who make things—novels, comics, series, lesson plans, games—occupy pressure points in the system. They have been told, sometimes explicitly through the MFA system documented in Chapter 6, that their work will be taken more seriously if anchored in obvious trauma. Many have internalized this so thoroughly that creating anything hopeful produces guilt or professional anxiety.

Rebuilding imagination requires creative acts of resistance:

Writing joyful projects while trusting that difficulty will emerge organically because life contains difficulty, not because market expectations demand it.

Allowing characters to grow, apologize, change minds, and build collectively—recognizing that this is structurally harder to write than collapse, and therefore at least as serious an artistic challenge.

Declining to turn every marginalization into spectacle, choosing sometimes to center competence, pleasure, and thriving in communities usually granted narrative space only for tragedy.

This is not about refusing to depict pain. It is about refusing to make pain the admission price for legitimacy—the same dynamic Chapter 12 documented, excluding writers like Amara Goldmere who want to write about flourishing in marginalized communities.

2. Gatekeepers: Redefining "Edgy" and "Important"

Editors, agents, festival programmers, prize juries, reviewers—these professionals function as curators of the cultural cellar, deciding what gets served to the broader table.

Rebuilding imagination means catching the automatic reflex that describes joyful or reparative work as "light" while describing despairing work as "searing." It means reading for craft and complexity in works that end in something other than death or defeat. It means, perhaps, committing that each publishing season will include at least some projects whose central question is not "How do we survive the wreckage?" but "How do we build something worth inheriting?"

This represents professional risk. So does publishing yet another interchangeable prestige tragedy into a saturated market of audience burnout, as the declining trust in news media (Chapter 14) and the voluntary reader exodus (Chapter 12) demonstrate.

The seventy-seven percent suffering-centered literary prize pattern documented in Chapter 6 did not emerge from natural law. It emerged from accumulated curatorial choices. Different choices would produce different patterns.

3. Audiences: Economic Signals

And then there are audiences—the people who click links, binge series, and preorder books, and thereby signal to the system: *More like this, please.*

Rebuilding imagination at the cultural level manifests in mundane choices:

Selecting, sometimes, the film that promises competence and collaboration over the limited series about yet another compelling sociopath.

Subscribing to news sources practicing solutions journalism, providing them with financial sustainability to continue.

Recommending books that generated feelings of capability, connection, and aliveness—not only works that left readers artistically impressed but also emotionally depleted.

Every time audiences reward work that treats flourishing as worthy of serious art, they cast a small vote for different cultural patterns. Small votes accumulate. Systems shift. This is how the seventy-one percent suffering dominance documented in Chapter 6 could gradually rebalance toward something more sustainable.

V. From Tomb to Draft

The great deception of the suffering canon is that endings must be final and catastrophic to be profound.

Rebuilding imagination means reclaiming a different structural metaphor: not the tomb, but the draft.

This book itself is not a final blueprint; it is a set of annotated working sketches. It argues that one architectural style—Gothic, tragic, stained glass featuring extra blood—has been mistaken for the entire history of possible structures. It invites readers to pick up their own drafting tools.

Perhaps a teacher will integrate one additional hopeful novel into the syllabus this year, framing it not as a dessert but as a central text demonstrating that depth exists outside tragedy.

Perhaps a policymaker will fund arts programs centering creation, not merely critique.

Perhaps a parent will notice when bedtime reading has consisted entirely of orphans and never communities, and will add stories where children solve problems without first losing parents—breaking the pattern documented in Chapter 4's analysis of Noah Wintermere at age five.

Perhaps a writer has been sitting on a joyful manuscript for years, convinced the market wasn't ready. The market is demonstrably starving, as Chapter 12's documentation of lost readers makes clear.

The suffering canon has had centuries of rehearsal. The flourishing canon is in its first developmental stages. It will be awkward. Some attempts will fail spectacularly. That is how any living art form grows.

The task is simultaneously simple and enormous:

Notice when "serious" is being conflated with "miserable."

Practice imagining outcomes beyond collapse.

Provide enough examples of flourishing that the word itself stops sounding like a lie.

This work cannot eliminate suffering from human experience. Pain will still arrive. Grief will still tear its holes. Nothing proposed here prevents any of that. The argument insists only that suffering stop being treated as the exclusive trustworthy material for meaning.

The Cathedral and the House

The cathedral of suffering will not crumble overnight. But additions to it can cease. And simultaneously, brick by brick, another structure can be drafted and constructed:

A house with many rooms. Windows that open. Foundations strong enough to hold both grief and joy.

The work will be succeeding when a student like Emma Brightwater can say, without irony, "My favorite book this year made me want to live more," and no one in the room interprets that to mean the work lacked profundity.

That is the imagination requiring reconstruction. That is the canon yet to be written—not to replace the old one entirely, but to stand beside it, offering shelter to all the readers, all the students like Miguel Stonefield, all the Noah Wintermeres who walked past the cathedral's tiny door because they didn't fit through it.

The diagnosis is complete. The treatment plan is clear. The question now is whether enough people—creators, teachers, gatekeepers, audiences—will choose to build it.

When Emma asked, "Is that all there is?" she deserved an answer better than despair. She deserved to hear: "No. There is also this, and this, and this—and here are the tools to build more."

The cathedral taught us how to mourn. Now we must learn how to build.

CHAPTER 15 ENDNOTES

1. Mihaly Csikszentmihalyi, *Flow: The Psychology of Optimal Experience* (New York: Harper & Row, 1990), 43–70; Mihaly Csikszentmihalyi, *Creativity: Flow and the Psychology of Discovery and Invention* (New York: HarperCollins, 1996), 107–126.
2. Barbara L. Fredrickson, "The Role of Positive Emotions in Positive Psychology: The Broaden-and-Build Theory of Positive Emotions," *American Psychologist* 56, no. 3 (2001): 218–226.
3. Roger E. Beaty, Mathias Benedek, Paul J. Silvia, and Daniel L. Schacter, "Creative Cognition and Brain Network Dynamics," *Trends in Cognitive Sciences* 20, no. 2 (2016): 87–95.
4. Keith D. Markman, Igor Gavanski, Steven J. Sherman, and Matthew N. McMullen, "The Mental Simulation of Better and Worse Possible Worlds," *Journal of Experimental Social Psychology* 29, no. 1 (1993): 87–109.

CHAPTER 16: THE INSTITUTIONAL LEVERS—Awards, Publishing, and Prestige

For generations, the unofficial MFA commandment has been painfully simple: write what hurts. Not "write what matters," not "write what fascinates," not even "write what keeps you awake at night." Write the wound. Bleed on the page. Prove seriousness by proving pain.

The suffering canon made this feel inevitable. If the "great" books consecrated by the seventy-six percent suffering-centered literary prize system (Chapter 6) are all about devastation, then great writers must be devastated, too. The result has been a pipeline that takes bright, curious people and trains them to become specialists in their own damage.

But quietly, stubbornly, another lineage has been writing all along—one that treats joy, connection, competence, and repair as equally worthy of artistic attention. This chapter examines not just the old system's failures but the alternative practices already emerging from writers and workshops that have walked away from the wound requirement.

Writers are allowed to flourish. And their work often improves when they do.

The Exit

Keiko Silverdale, a composite representing countless MFA students, embodies the pattern explored in Chapter 6. She has done something nearly unthinkable in certain literary circles: she has left her program.

It wasn't a dramatic exit. There were no slammed doors or manifesto emails, just a long accumulation of moments: the workshop where a quiet, luminous story about two neighbors sharing morning coffee was dismissed as "low stakes"; the third professor in succession who asked, "But where's the trauma?"; the way she started feeling embarrassed by the parts of her imagination that lit up at kindness, competence, and collective effort.

She didn't abandon writing. She abandoned the idea that only suffering counts.

Now, once a week, she brings drafts to a community arts center, where she joins a circle of writers around a cheap table that wobbles when anyone laughs too hard (which happens often). The workshop is called The Flourishing Draft. The organizing principles differ fundamentally from her MFA experience:

Passages are marked not just for "tension" but for aliveness.

The question "Where is the character building something?" is asked as often as "Where are they broken?"

Margin notes read: "This moment of repair is the emotional climax" and "Stay here longer—the reconciliation is where the real stakes are."

Keiko is no longer attempting to reverse-engineer a spectacular trauma to justify her manuscript. She's writing about a community of immigrant gardeners who slowly transform an abandoned lot into shared space—a work of conflict, yes, but also of soil, weather, and laughter.

The prose did not become easier when she chose flourishing. It became harder in the best possible way.

What she's practicing is not an escape from seriousness. It's a recalibration of what counts as serious in the first place—a challenge to what Mark McGurl terms the "program era" logic that has dominated American creative writing instruction since the mid-twentieth century, with its emphasis on personal trauma as the primary source of literary authenticity.[1]

I. The Pioneers: Writers Who Prove Joy Has Depth

One of the most effective ways to unlearn the suffering script is to study writers who are already breaking it—often while still writing about extraordinarily difficult subjects.

Ocean Vuong, in *On Earth We're Briefly Gorgeous*, writes about war, migration, racism, addiction, and intergenerational trauma. On paper, it could be another entry in the suffering canon. But the book's force comes from something else: its radical tenderness. Vuong lingers on gestures of care, moments of beauty, and unexpected pockets of hilarity amid catastrophe. Love isn't sentimental garnish; it's the structural element that allows the book to hold so much pain without collapsing into nihilism.

Ross Gay has built an entire practice around what he terms "inciting joy." In *The Book of Delights* and *Inciting Joy*, he treats delight not as a mood but as a discipline. He writes about figs and yard fences and shared cigarettes and pickup basketball—small, specific, courageous acts of noticing. The essays are not written in ignorance of injustice; they're composed right up against it. Gay insists that joy is one of the ways humans survive grief without becoming nothing but their grief.

Becky Chambers, in the Wayfarers series and *A Psalm for the Wild-Built*, makes science fiction out of competence, kindness, and awkward, fumbling attempts at cross-species care. Ships still break, systems still fail, people still hurt each other—but the drama hinges on how they repair damage, renegotiate community, and determine whom they want to become. The books are deeply character-driven, technically accomplished, and quietly radical in refusing to equate "grim" with "intelligent."

These writers are not avoiding darkness. They're refusing to grant darkness exclusive rights to profundity.

Their work demonstrates three crucial permissions:

Writers can address suffering without centering it as the only truth worth exploring.

Meaning can be constructed from repair, not exclusively from collapse.

Readers can be made to think deeply by witnessing what people build, not only what they lose.

II. New Workshop Logics: From "Find the Wound" to "Follow the Life"

Traditional workshop rituals are familiar to most MFA graduates and creative writing students:

The writer remains silent during the critique.

The group circles weak spots with surgical precision.

The highest compliment is "This really gutted me."

That model isn't worthless, but it is incomplete. It assumes that the most important aspect of writing is identifying where it breaks and how effectively it depicts brokenness—the same autopsy-focused approach documented in Chapter 5's analysis of classroom pedagogy.

A flourishing-centered practice doesn't eliminate critique; it redirects analytical energy.

Three practical shifts are already being experimented with in community workshops, online groups, and informal writing circles:

1. "Reparative Reading" as a Craft Tool

Instead of exclusively asking "Where does this story fall apart?" practitioners also ask:

Where does someone make a good choice that costs them something?

Where do readers glimpse a possible future that improves on the present?

Where does the character refuse the easy, cynical answer?

These become craft questions in conversation:

How did the writer establish this moment of courage so that it feels earned rather than imposed?

What line-level choices make this reconciliation satisfying instead of saccharine?

How does humor function as a survival tactic rather than a deflection?

This approach parallels what narrative therapists call "re-authoring"—rewriting personal stories to highlight agency and resilience alongside injury. Michael White and David Epston's foundational work in narrative therapy demonstrates that people can reshape their relationship to traumatic experiences by identifying moments of resistance, competence, and alternative outcomes within their own stories.[2] Rather than treating trauma as a fixed, defining identity, narrative therapy helps individuals recognize themselves as active agents who have already been resisting and responding to difficulty in ways that may have gone unnoticed or unvalued. In workshop contexts, this therapeutic principle becomes an exercise in structure, pacing, and point of view—a way of reading for what creates possibility rather than merely documenting limitation.

2. Strengths-First Critique

Many writing teachers already practice versions of this approach, but it merits explicit articulation: begin with what is most alive in the piece.

"The friendship between these two characters feels tangibly real. How might the narrative give it more space?"

"The world-building here is remarkable—what if the plot grew more directly from how this community actually functions?"

Problems don't vanish; they get reframed in terms of better serving the strongest elements, not transforming the story into something entirely different (usually darker).

Anne Lamott, in *Bird by Bird*, systematically dismantles the myth of the effortlessly suffering genius, replacing it with grounded reality: messy drafts, small steps, scenes built incrementally.[3] Stephen King, in *On Writing*, describes writing less as bleeding and more as "telepathy"—a fundamentally connective act where one mind reaches another across time and distance. Both emphasize craft and persistence over self-destruction.

Strengths-first critique applies that ethos. Work improves not through humiliation but through curiosity about what already functions well.

3. Legitimizing the "Guilty Pleasure" Project

Many writers maintain a "secret" project: the cozy mystery, the queer romance, the spaceship-found-family story, the backyard saga about neighbors learning to share a fence. They discuss these projects with slightly sheepish grins, as if confessing to embarrassing habits.

The flourishing workshop responds: that's likely the book that most deserves serious attention.

Not because it's easy—but because the writer's entire nervous system engages when discussing it. That engagement isn't frivolous; it's energy. It's what sustains the work through revision thirty-seven.

When a group treats that project with the same analytical rigor applied to bleak divorce novels—discussing structure, tension, language, and thematic depth seriously—it disrupts the false equivalence between misery and legitimacy documented throughout this book's analysis of the suffering canon.

III. Working With Wounds (Without Selling Your Soul)

This is not a manifesto for perpetual sunshine. Many writers create in part because they have been hurt, bewildered, flattened, or cracked open by experiences they cannot fully metabolize through other means.

Pain can be a powerful creative source. It simply doesn't have to be the only source—or the exclusive product.

A flourishing-centered approach redirects inquiry toward questions like:

What does this character do with their wound?

Who do they become capable of loving because of what they've survived?

What systems, communities, or forms of beauty emerge in the wake of damage?

Instead of treating the wound as a static museum exhibit ("Behold: my trauma"), writers treat it as a starting point for movement.

Psychological research on post-traumatic growth and resilience supports this approach. Richard Tedeschi and Lawrence Calhoun's extensive research on post-traumatic growth identifies five domains where people report positive change following adversity: personal strength, new possibilities, relating to others, appreciation of life, and spiritual change. The critical finding is that growth doesn't emerge from trauma itself but from the active process of making meaning from it—precisely what narrative construction enables. Trauma that remains unprocessed and unintegrated tends to reproduce itself; trauma that is actively engaged with through meaning-making can become a source of transformation.

On the page, that translates into narratives where:

Grief coexists with humor.

Anger coexists with problem-solving.

Fear coexists with small, stubborn acts of trying again.

Wounds are invited to the creative process. They are simply no longer permitted to lock the door from inside and declare themselves the only legitimate material.

IV. The Liberated Practice

The deepest shift here is not technical; it's existential.

Writers do not have to remain perpetually unwell to be interesting. They do not have to keep reopening the same wound to prove seriousness. They do not have to transform their lives into marketable suffering to deserve space at the literary table.

Research on expressive writing and mental health, particularly the work of James Pennebaker and colleagues, demonstrates that writing about traumatic experiences can have therapeutic benefits—but the benefits come not from endless repetition of trauma but from the cognitive processing and meaning-making that writing enables. Writing becomes beneficial when it helps people construct coherent narratives from fragmented experiences, identify patterns and connections, and recognize their own agency within difficult circumstances. Similarly, Gillie Bolton's work on therapeutic creative writing emphasizes that the healing potential of writing comes from its capacity to generate new perspectives and possibilities, not from treating the wound as a fixed monument to be endlessly revisited.

Writers are permitted to:

Work from curiosity instead of crisis.

Choose an image because it delights them, not because it devastates.

Allow a character to live, heal, forgive, or simply have an extraordinarily good day—without apologizing for it in the final chapter.

Writers are also permitted to protect parts of their lives from the page. Lamott's emphasis on "shitty first drafts" is fundamentally an invitation to gentle process, not public self-immolation. King's insistence on constant reading and regular, undramatic hours at the desk is a quiet argument that writing is labor, not martyrdom.

The flourishing writer is not naive. They understand the world's cruelty intimately. They simply refuse to confuse accuracy with exclusivity. They insist that any honest portrait of human life must include tenderness, absurdity, competence, erotic joy, ordinary contentment, and the way someone's face looks when they're trying not to laugh in situations where laughter would be wildly inappropriate.

The Systemic Shudder

When writers change what they believe counts as "real" on the page, the entire system experiences tremors. Editors must accommodate new kinds of pitches. Teachers have new examples to assign when students ask, "Is it acceptable if my story ends well?" Readers encounter themselves not only as victims or voyeurs of suffering but as agents, builders, lovers, healers, people who fail and try again.

The cathedral of suffering won't crumble overnight. But every time a writer chooses to center flourishing with full artistic seriousness—the same rigor demanded by the MFA system documented in Chapter 6—another stone comes loose.

Writers do not owe the world their agony as proof of their art. They owe attention, honesty, craft, and—if they can sustain it —imagination of what might, against considerable odds, go right.

When Emma Brightwater asked, "Is that all there is?" in Chapter 1, she was asking on behalf of readers. But she was also asking on behalf of writers—those who have been told repeatedly that their joyful projects are insufficiently serious, that their repair-focused narratives lack gravitas, that their flourishing-centered work doesn't count.

The answer, increasingly visible in the work of Gay, Chambers, Vuong, and countless others working outside the suffering canon's narrow requirements, is clear: there is more. There has always been more. The cathedral simply refused to consecrate it.

That refusal is ending. Window by window, workshop by workshop, manuscript by manuscript.

The writers are opening the doors themselves.

CHAPTER 16 ENDNOTES
1. Mark McGurl, *The Program Era: Postwar Fiction and the Rise of Creative Writing* (Cambridge, MA: Harvard University Press, 2009), 24–45.
2. Michael White and David Epston, *Narrative Means to Therapeutic Ends* (New York: W. W. Norton, 1990), 1–37.
3. Anne Lamott, *Bird by Bird: Some Instructions on Writing and Life* (New York: Anchor Books, 1994), 18–28.
4. Stephen King, *On Writing: A Memoir of the Craft* (New York: Scribner, 2000), 103–112.
5. Richard G. Tedeschi and Lawrence G. Calhoun, "Post-traumatic Growth: Conceptual Foundations and Empirical Evidence," *Psychological Inquiry* 15, no. 1 (2004): 1–18.
6. James W. Pennebaker and Janel D. Seagal, "Forming a Story: The Health Benefits of Narrative," *Journal of Clinical Psychology* 55, no. 10 (1999): 1243–1254.
7. Gillie Bolton, *The Therapeutic Potential of Creative Writing: Writing Myself* (London: Jessica Kingsley Publishers, 1999), 1–25.

CHAPTER 17: RECLAIMING JOY—A Conclusion

The cathedral of suffering stands. Its foundations reach back to Athens and Jerusalem. Its walls were raised by Romantics and reinforced by Modernists. Its stained glass—dark, gorgeous, and carefully curated—filters all light through narratives of collapse. For generations, this has been the only serious architecture available, the only liturgy consecrated as profound.

But cathedrals are not laws of nature. They are choices made in stone.

This chapter synthesizes the entire argument into a single, actionable framework: not a utopian fantasy, but a practical blueprint for constructing a flourishing canon alongside—not instead of—the suffering canon. It acknowledges constraints, anticipates resistance, and provides concrete steps for individuals, institutions, and culture-makers at every level.

The goal is not to tear down the old cathedral but to build adjacent structures with different doors, different windows, and room for the readers, students, and writers the suffering canon has systematically excluded.

This is the manual for opening those doors.

I. The Core Principles

Before detailing specific interventions, five foundational principles must be established. These are not aspirational values but structural requirements for any sustainable alternative to the suffering canon.

Principle 1: Balance, Not Erasure

The suffering canon is not evil. Tragedy has always been necessary. Stories that grapple honestly with cruelty, loss, and systemic failure remain essential to any complete cultural diet.

The problem is a monopoly.

When sixty-eight percent of high school required reading features suicide or self-annihilation (Chapter 1), when seventy-six percent of Pulitzer Prizes and National Book Awards consecrate suffering-centered narratives (Chapter 6), when seventy-one percent of combined prestige culture across film and literature centers despair (Chapter 6), the system is not balanced—it is fundamentally distorted.

A flourishing canon does not replace tragedy. It restores proportion. The target is not zero suffering-centered works but something closer to equilibrium: roughly half the curriculum, half the prestige awards, half the "serious" conversation devoted to narratives organized around repair, competence, connection, and plausible hope.

Principle 2: Rigor, Not Sentimentality

The reflexive critique of hopeful narratives—that they are "unrealistic" or "escapist"—must be dismantled not through defensiveness but through demonstration.

The one hundred works in the Flourishing Canon (Chapter 13) were selected using the same criteria applied to any canonical text: technical excellence, thematic complexity, formal innovation, and cultural significance. *Middlemarch* is as structurally sophisticated as *Madame Bovary*. *The Dispossessed* is as philosophically rigorous as *1984*. *Gilead* is as linguistically accomplished as *Blood Meridian*.

The difference is not quality. The difference is in which human experiences are treated as worthy of that quality.

A flourishing canon demands the same intellectual seriousness, the same close reading, the same critical apparatus currently applied to suffering-centered texts. It simply refuses to accept that depth requires despair.

Principle 3: Representation, Not Tokenism

Including one hopeful text per semester as dessert after a full course of tragedy is not balance; it is performance.

Meaningful representation requires structural integration: flourishing-centered works appearing throughout the syllabus, not relegated to "fun Friday" or extra credit. It requires those works being taught with the same analytical attention, examined on the same assessments, and discussed in the same literary conversations as their tragic counterparts.

Students must encounter flourishing narratives early enough and often enough that they learn to read for repair with the same sophistication they currently bring to reading for ruin.

Principle 4: Multiple Pathways, Not Single Solutions

There is no one "right" flourishing canon, just as there is no single suffering canon. Different communities, different historical moments, and different pedagogical goals will require different texts.

The blueprint provided here is not prescriptive but generative —a set of principles and examples that can be adapted, revised, and localized. A rural high school in Montana and an urban magnet school in Brooklyn should not necessarily teach identical syllabi. What they should share is the commitment to treating flourishing as intellectually serious and the refusal to let tragedy monopolize depth.

Principle 5: Sustainability Over Spectacle

Building a flourishing canon is not a publicity campaign or a one-semester experiment. It is infrastructure work requiring patience, resources, and institutional commitment across years.

Quick wins matter—a single teacher adding *The House on Mango Street* to the curriculum, a single prize committee choosing *Less* over another elegy—but transformation happens when those wins accumulate into new norms, new expectations, and eventually new defaults.

Sustainability requires funding for curriculum development, professional development for teachers learning to teach flourishing-centered texts, and protection from the inevitable pushback claiming that hope is "dumbing down" education.

II. The Institutional Checklist

Armed with these principles, specific institutions can implement concrete changes. What follows is not aspirational—it is a checklist of immediately actionable interventions organized by institutional domain.

A. K-12 Education

Immediate Actions (0-6 months):

Audit the current curriculum using the methodology from Chapter 1: count texts by whether their central organizing principle is suffering, flourishing, or mixed/ambivalent. Calculate percentages.

Identify flourishing texts already in the building—books purchased but rarely taught, relegated to "independent reading" shelves, or used only in lower-level classes. Elevate at least one per grade level to required or core status.

Pair tragic and reparative texts within the same unit. Example: teach *Romeo and Juliet* alongside *Much Ado About Nothing* or *As You Like It*, examining how Shakespeare constructs both tragedy and comedy with equal sophistication.

Revise assessment language to reward analysis of repair, growth, and connection alongside analysis of conflict and collapse. Sample essay prompt: "Identify a moment where a character chooses ethical action within a flawed system. What narrative techniques make this choice feel earned rather than imposed?"

Short-Term Goals (6-18 months):

Develop district-approved units pairing canonical tragic texts with Flourishing Canon alternatives, complete with standards-aligned lesson plans, discussion guides, and assessments.

Train teachers in "reparative reading" practices (Chapter 15): how to lead discussions that examine not just what breaks but what builds, not just how systems fail but how they sometimes mend.

Establish professional learning communities where teachers share strategies for teaching flourishing-centered texts without sacrificing intellectual rigor.

Invite community stakeholders—including students—to participate in curriculum review, explicitly asking: "Do these texts reflect the full range of human experience, or do they disproportionately center suffering?"

Long-Term Goals (2-5 years):

Institutionalize balanced ratios in official curriculum documents: "Each grade level will include texts where the central narrative arc involves repair, growth, or sustained flourishing, representing approximately 40-50% of required reading."

Develop assessment rubrics that explicitly value analysis of flourishing: "Student demonstrates sophisticated understanding of how narrative constructs hope, competence, or communal problem-solving."

Create curriculum repositories of tested, effective units pairing tragic and flourishing texts, available to all teachers in the district and eventually shared across districts.

Integrate into teacher preparation programs: Ensure pre-service teachers learn to teach both autopsy and architecture, both breakdown and repair.

B. Higher Education (MFA Programs & English Departments)

Immediate Actions:

Audit workshop norms explicitly. In syllabi, state: "This workshop values technical excellence in narratives of all emotional registers. 'Where's the trauma?' is not a valid standalone critique."

Assign craft readings from writers like Ross Gay, Becky Chambers, Ocean Vuong—examining how they construct depth, stakes, and complexity in narratives that refuse to equate seriousness with suffering.

Legitimize "genre" work within workshop discussions. Treat romance, cozy mystery, and hopeful science fiction as worthy of the same craft analysis applied to literary realism.

Diversify thesis committees to include at least one member sympathetic to flourishing-centered work, ensuring students writing joyful or reparative projects receive substantive mentorship.

Short-Term Goals:

Offer workshops explicitly centered on flourishing: "Writing Repair," "Narratives of Competence," "Comedy as Serious Craft." Make these electives available alongside traditional workshops.[2]

Revise program mission statements to remove implicit suffering requirements. Replace language about "unflinching examination of difficult truths" with "rigorous exploration of the full spectrum of human experience."

Invite visiting writers whose work centers on flourishing, demonstrating that literary careers exist outside the wound-mining economy documented in Chapter 6.

Create student-led reading groups focused on the Flourishing Canon, providing a peer community for students who feel isolated in their hopeful projects.

Long-Term Goals:

Revise admissions criteria to remove implicit bias toward suffering-heavy writing samples. Value craft, voice, and vision over biographical trauma.

Establish prizes and fellowships specifically for MFA students working on flourishing-centered projects, counterbalancing existing awards that disproportionately favor tragic work.[3]

Publish pedagogical articles in creative writing journals documenting effective methods for teaching flourishing narratives with intellectual rigor, building an academic literature that legitimizes this approach.

Partner with literary magazines and presses sympathetic to balanced aesthetics, creating publication pipelines for MFA graduates working outside the suffering canon.

C. Publishing Industry (Agents, Editors, Presses)

Immediate Actions:

Audit acquisition patterns. Track what percentage of titles acquired center suffering versus flourishing. Set targets for rebalancing.

Revise pitch language that unconsciously privileges trauma. Replace "Where's the hook?" (often code for "What's the devastating event?") with "What's the central question this narrative explores?"

Feature flourishing-centered titles prominently in catalogs, marketing materials, and sales meetings—not as "beach reads" but as serious literary offerings.

Train sensitivity readers and editors to recognize when feedback unconsciously imposes suffering requirements: "This needs more stakes" shouldn't automatically mean "Someone needs to die."

Short-Term Goals:

Create an imprint or series explicitly dedicated to literary fiction and creative nonfiction centering flourishing, giving these works identifiable branding and discoverability.

Adjust royalty and advance structures to acknowledge that flourishing-centered literary fiction may find audiences through different channels (book clubs, educator recommendations) than traditional prestige pipelines.

Partner with Solutions Journalism Network and similar organizations to publish more nonfiction examining repair, policy solutions, and communal problem-solving with literary quality.

Nominate flourishing-centered titles for major awards, using the full persuasive apparatus available to publishers to argue for their literary merit.

Long-Term Goals:

Shift industry metrics for "success" beyond prestige awards. Track reader engagement, book club adoption, curriculum integration, and long-term backlist sales as markers of cultural impact.

Establish new awards specifically recognizing excellence in flourishing-centered literature, creating alternative consecration pathways outside the suffering-dominated Pulitzer/NBA system.

Build coalitions among independent presses, university presses, and mid-size publishers committed to balanced aesthetics, amplifying collective bargaining power with distributors and retailers.

Invest in author development that doesn't require mining personal trauma. Fund residencies, fellowships, and mentorships supporting writers exploring joy, competence, and repair.

D. Journalism & Media

Immediate Actions:

Implement ratio tracking for problem-focused versus solutions-focused stories. Aim for at least one solution piece for every three problem pieces in major sections.[1]

Train reporters in solutions journalism methodology through partnerships with the Solutions Journalism Network, emphasizing that this is rigorous reporting, not PR.

Feature solutions stories prominently—front page, homepage, newsletter leads—not buried in "feel-good" sidebars, as documented in Chapter 14.

Adjust editorial meetings to include a standing agenda item: "What are we covering that's being built, not just what's breaking?"

Short-Term Goals:

Create dedicated solutions beats: assign reporters to cover specific domains (housing, education, climate) with an explicit mandate to investigate responses alongside problems.

Develop partnerships with PBS, NPR, and other public media already experimenting with solutions-focused coverage, sharing best practices, and cross-promoting content.

Establish metrics for audience engagement with solutions content—shares, time on page, subscription conversions—demonstrating economic viability.

Offer public editor columns or transparency reports explaining the commitment to balanced coverage, building audience trust.

Long-Term Goals:

Integrate solutions journalism into journalism school curricula, training the next generation of reporters to investigate repair alongside breakdown as standard practice.

Develop industry standards for solutions journalism quality, preventing "solutions-washing" where superficial happy stories masquerade as rigorous reporting.

Build international networks connecting solutions journalists across borders, amplifying coverage of innovations that cross cultural contexts.

Advocate for policy changes that reduce economic pressure on newsrooms to prioritize clickbait catastrophe over substantive solutions reporting.

E. Awards & Prizes

Immediate Actions:

Diversify jury composition to include members explicitly committed to recognizing excellence in flourishing-centered work, not just tragic or cynical narratives.

Revise award criteria to explicitly state that complexity, depth, and technical excellence can be achieved through narratives of repair, growth, and sustained hope.

Examine historical patterns using methodology from Chapter 6: calculate what percentage of past winners centered suffering versus flourishing, and set targets for rebalancing.

Nominate flourishing-centered works proactively, writing persuasive nomination letters that argue for their literary merit without apologizing for their hopeful conclusions.

Short-Term Goals:

Create new award categories if existing structures prove resistant to change: "Award for Excellence in Reparative Narrative," "Prize for Literature of Flourishing."

Partner with other organizations (libraries, educator groups, reader communities) to co-sponsor awards with different aesthetic values than the traditional literary establishment.

Increase transparency in judging processes, publishing essays explaining why winning works were chosen and what criteria were applied.

Celebrate mixed outcomes explicitly: "This year's winners included both tragic and hopeful narratives, demonstrating the full spectrum of literary excellence."

Long-Term Goals:

Shift the prestige economy so that winning an award for flourishing-centered work carries equivalent cultural capital to winning for tragic work.

Establish endowments for new prizes with explicit flourishing mandates, ensuring financial sustainability independent of the existing literary establishment.

Document the impact of balanced prize-giving on broader literary culture: Does it shift what publishers acquire? What do students study? What writers feel permitted to create?

Build international coalitions of award organizations committed to recognizing the full range of human experience in literature.

III. Individual Agency—What Anyone Can Do Right Now

Systemic change requires institutional action. But individuals —readers, parents, students, book club members, social media users—possess more power than the suffering canon's gatekeepers would prefer to acknowledge.

For Readers:

Track personal reading ratios. For every tragic or suffering-centered book consumed, deliberately choose one organized around repair, growth, or flourishing. Notice how this affects mood, worldview, and imagination over months.

Request flourishing-centered titles at libraries and bookstores. Demand shapes supply; repeated requests signal market viability.

Review hopeful books seriously on Goodreads, Amazon, and social media. Write substantive analyses demonstrating their intellectual merit, counteracting assumptions that joy equals simplicity.

Recommend flourishing titles enthusiastically without apology. Refuse to code them as "guilty pleasures." Present them as serious literature worthy of discussion.

For Parents:

Audit children's media consumption using Chapter 4's framework: count dead or missing parents in films, books, and shows. Deliberately add stories where families remain intact, and communities function.

Discuss required reading with teachers, asking whether the curriculum balance reflects full human experience or disproportionately centers suffering.

Model balanced consumption for children: let them see adults reading, watching, and discussing both tragic and hopeful narratives without shame.

Advocate at school board meetings for curriculum audits and balanced syllabi, bringing data from this book to support arguments.

For Students:

Write essays analyzing flourishing with the same sophistication currently applied to analyzing tragedy. Demonstrate that hope is as intellectually complex as despair.

Form book clubs centered on Flourishing Canon texts, creating a peer community around alternatives to assigned suffering.

Request independent reading approval for hopeful texts when the curriculum feels unrelentingly bleak. Cite research on balanced narrative exposure and mental health.

Create alternative canons as class projects: research, curate, and present lists of neglected works that treat flourishing seriously.

For Teachers (Operating Within Constraints):

Pair one flourishing text with each tragic text, even if the curriculum officially requires only the tragic one. Frame as "comparative analysis."

Adjust discussion questions to reward analysis of repair alongside analysis of breakdown. "How does this author construct hope?" is as valid as "How does this author depict despair?"

Use supplementary materials—articles, essays, interviews—that discuss reparative reading and flourishing-centered literature, exposing students to alternative critical frameworks.

Protect students who gravitate toward hopeful narratives from being shamed as "unsophisticated," explicitly validating their reading preferences as intellectually legitimate.

For Writers:

Write the joyful project without apologizing. Treat repair, competence, and connection as worthy of full artistic seriousness.

Join or create workshops using flourishing-centered methodologies described in Chapters 15 and 16: reparative reading, strengths-first critique, legitimized "guilty pleasure" projects.

Refuse wound-mining. Protect parts of personal life from commodification. Write from curiosity, not exclusively from crisis.

Support other writers working on hopeful projects. Review their books, nominate them for awards, invite them to panels, signal that flourishing-centered work deserves attention.

For Everyone:

Recognize the cathedral for what it is: not an inevitable reality but accumulated choices that can be questioned, resisted, and eventually changed.

Notice when "realistic" is being used as a synonym for "pessimistic" and push back gently but persistently.

Practice "What if better?" thinking in conversation, meetings, and planning: not magical thinking but incremental improvement grounded in evidence.

Share this framework. The blueprint only functions when enough people understand that alternatives exist and that building them is possible, necessary, and intellectually serious work.

IV. Anticipated Resistance—and Responses

Any attempt to rebalance the suffering canon will encounter predictable objections. These are not bad-faith arguments but genuine concerns requiring serious engagement.

Objection 1: "You're dumbing down literature."

Response: Intellectual rigor is not determined by emotional register. *Middlemarch* is as formally complex as *Madame Bovary*. *The Dispossessed* requires as much critical thinking as *Nineteen Eighty-Four*. The assumption that difficulty equals despair is itself intellectually lazy—a refusal to recognize that constructing plausible repair is often harder than depicting collapse.

Objection 2: "Students need to learn the classics."

Response: Many classics remain valuable and will continue being taught. The question is proportion and what "classic" means. *Hamlet* matters. So does *Much Ado About Nothing*. Both are Shakespeare. Only one is currently treated as serious. Expanding the canon doesn't erase the old one; it acknowledges that brilliance exists across emotional registers.

Objection 3: "The world is dark. We're preparing students for reality."

Response: The world contains war, injustice, cruelty, and loss. It also contains cooperation, repair, competence, and love that outlasts catastrophe. Preparing students for reality means preparing them for both—and for the cognitive skills to identify where intervention is possible, not just where breakdown is inevitable. Currently, we're preparing them only for the autopsy, as documented across Chapters 1, 5, 10, 11, and 12.

Objection 4: "This sounds like censorship."

Response: No one is banning tragic texts. Every work currently taught can remain available. The proposal is addition, not subtraction: adding neglected works that treat flourishing seriously, restoring balance to a system currently monopolized by suffering. If teaching *The Odyssey* alongside *Oedipus Rex* is censorship, then the term has lost all meaning.

Objection 5: "The market decides what's good. These happy books would dominate if they had merit."

Response: The market is not neutral. It is shaped by the seventy-one percent suffering-centered prestige culture (Chapter 6), the MFA pipeline that trains writers to mine wounds (Chapter 6), the news ecosystem optimized for catastrophe (Chapters 2, 14), and centuries of inherited aesthetic assumptions documented in Chapters 7-9. Market dominance reflects power, not quality. Diversifying the canon is not market distortion; it's market correction.

Objection 6: "This is just positive thinking / toxic positivity."

Response: The flourishing canon does not deny pain or demand perpetual cheerfulness. It demands proportion and completeness. Toxic positivity refuses to acknowledge difficulty. The flourishing canon insists on representing the full arc: breakdown and repair, wound and healing, problem and the people actively working on solutions. That's not optimism; it's accuracy.

V. Measuring Success—What Changes When the Balance Shifts

How will we know if this blueprint is working? Success requires both quantitative metrics and qualitative indicators.

Quantitative Metrics (5-10 years):

Curriculum audits show movement from 68% suffering-centered toward a 50/50 balance across a representative sample of high schools.

Literary prize patterns show a shift from 77% suffering-centered to approximately 50/50 across Pulitzer, NBA, and other major awards.

Publishing acquisition data reflects an increasing proportion of flourishing-centered titles treated as "literary fiction" rather than relegated to genre categories.

MFA thesis archives demonstrate that students working on hopeful projects receive comparable institutional support and post-graduation outcomes as those working on tragic projects.

News organizations practicing solutions journalism show audience growth and engagement metrics equal to or exceeding traditional problem-focused coverage.

Qualitative Indicators:

Students volunteer that the required reading feels more representative of human experience, not exclusively focused on catastrophe.

Teachers report that classroom discussions now regularly analyze how narratives construct hope, repair, and competence—not just how they depict suffering.

Writers describe feeling less pressure to perform trauma for legitimacy, more freedom to explore the full range of creative interests.

Readers say they no longer hide their joyful reading preferences, no longer apologize for books that made them feel capable rather than devastated.

Critics and reviewers routinely analyze flourishing-centered works with the same seriousness applied to tragic texts, without reflexively dismissing them as "light."

Award speeches and acceptance statements increasingly acknowledge that depth and complexity exist across emotional registers, not exclusively in narratives of despair.

The Ultimate Indicator:

When a student like Emma Brightwater—who asked "Is that all there is?" back in Chapter 1—can look at her syllabus and see herself reflected not only in characters who suffer but in characters who build, repair, grow, and sustain connection across difficulty, the cathedral's monopoly will have ended.

When that student graduates and becomes a teacher, editor, writer, policymaker, or engaged citizen who unconsciously treats flourishing as intellectually serious and despair as only one emotional register among many, the transformation will have become institutional memory.

When her students inherit curricula, newsrooms, publishing houses, and award committees that treat the full spectrum of human experience as worthy of serious attention, the new architecture will have replaced the old foundations.

That is the horizon. The work begins now, with checklists and ratios, syllabi and prize juries, individual reading choices, and institutional audits. Brick by brick. Window by window. Story by story.

The Blueprint Is Complete

This chapter has provided the manual. The remaining question is will.

The suffering canon required centuries to construct. Its dismantling and replacement will not happen overnight, and perhaps full replacement is neither possible nor desirable. But rebalancing—restoring proportion, opening space, legitimizing alternatives—can begin immediately with resources and frameworks already available.

Every institution mentioned in this chapter already exists. Every action described is possible within current systems. What has been missing is not capacity but permission: permission to believe that joy can be profound, that repair is as complex as ruin, that hope is not a personality flaw but a cognitive skill requiring practice and institutional support.

This book has argued that the suffering canon is not inevitable, not natural, and not neutral. It is a choice—repeated daily in classrooms, newsrooms, writers' workshops, publishing houses, and living rooms across the culture. It has been consecrated by repetition until it resembles truth.

But choices can change. Cathedrals can be remodeled. And the blueprints for something better—something truer to the full, contradictory, magnificent spectrum of human experience—are in your hands.

The question was never whether alternatives exist. The question was whether anyone would build them.

The answer begins with: yes.

CHAPTER 17 ENDNOTES

1. Stuart Soroka, *Negativity in Democratic Politics: Causes and Consequences* (New York: Cambridge University Press, 2014), 45–68; Pew Research Center, "The Modern News Consumer," July 7, 2016, accessed February 20, 2025, https://www.pewresearch.org/journalism/2016/07/07/the-modern-news-consumer/.
2. University of Michigan, Department of English, "Narratives of Repair: Course Syllabus" (Fall 2023), accessed February 20, 2025, https://lsa.umich.edu/english/undergraduates/courses/fall-2023/narratives-of-repair.html.
3. Stanford University, "The Literature and Human Flourishing Project," accessed February 20, 2025, https://lhf.stanford.edu.
4. Karen Thier, Kelsey Lough, and Alex Curry, "Does Solutions-Based Reporting Improve Optimism and Self-Efficacy? A Large-Scale Randomized Experiment of Audience Effects," *Journalism Practice* (2022): 1–20, published online ahead of print, accessed February 20, 2025, https://doi.org/10.1080/17512786.2022.2051579.
5. Solutions Journalism Network, "Story Tracker and Impact Research," accessed February 20, 2025, https://www.solutionsjournalism.org/story-tracker.
6. James F. English, *The Economy of Prestige: Prizes, Awards, and the Circulation of Cultural Value* (Cambridge, MA: Harvard University Press, 2005), 33–58.

CONCLUSION: THE CHOICE

The inquiry began in the shadows of the cathedral, counting—as Chapter 1 documented—the suicides or central, deliberate self-annihilation consecrated as required reading for children. The analysis traced the architecture of despair from the animated deaths of childhood to the prestige tragedies of adulthood, from the classroom to the newsroom to the writer's workshop. It exposed foundations in ancient thought and tracked mutations into modern, secular orthodoxy.

Once the pattern becomes visible, it cannot be unseen. Once the costs are tallied—the forty-four percent of high school students reporting persistent sadness, the voluntary reader exodus, the imagination drain paralyzing Noah Wintermere's generation—they cannot honestly be called acceptable.

The suffering canon tells part of the truth. It is a meticulous, centuries-long record of the storm while refusing to document the shelters, the builders' skill, or the mornings when the sky clears, and people resume the quiet work of living. When information streams consist exclusively of catastrophe, catastrophe begins to feel like the only available depth.

This analysis has never argued for forgetting. Stories of suffering matter profoundly. They offer solidarity, warning, witness, and sometimes the only adequate language for certain experiences. The argument challenges their monopoly—the way diagnosis has been confused with cure, the wound mistaken for wisdom itself.

Contemporary culture has been trained to equate intelligence with cynicism, depth with damage, and seriousness with sadness. Pain has been treated as though it were the totality of human experience rather than one element within a far more complex reality.

The evidence demonstrates otherwise. A one-sided canon shapes imagination predictably, as Chapter 11 documented. Sustained exposure to despair-centered narratives narrows what young people believe is possible. It signals to certain readers and writers that their cognitive orientations—curious, hopeful, solution-focused—are intellectually inadequate. For all its claims to realism, the suffering canon offers a distorted, incomplete representation of human experience.

The Counter-Movement

Yet even as the old cathedral dominates the cultural landscape, counter-practices are already emerging and demonstrating viability.

They appear in rebalanced syllabi, where *The Tempest* answers *Macbeth*, where narratives of restitution and repair stand beside narratives of ruin—the one-third flourishing principle documented in Chapter 15.

They manifest in information consumption patterns where solutions journalism, documented in Chapter 14, supplements alarm-focused news, where information is evaluated not only by what it exposes but by what agency it enables.

They exist at writers' desks where projects once dismissed as "guilty pleasures"—about community gardens, found families, quiet acts of courage—no longer require apology, as Chapter 16 analyzed.

They are catalogued in the Flourishing Canon documented in Chapter 13: one hundred works that have persistently modeled wonder, connection, competence, and joy, waiting to be treated as central rather than supplemental to literary education.

The Keystone

Every cathedral is held aloft by a keystone—the central stone that locks all others in place. The keystone of the suffering cathedral is the unspoken belief that to look away from despair is to be shallow, that to examine joy with the same rigor applied to tragedy is to be intellectually unserious, that profundity and suffering are synonymous.

This analysis has been an attempt to loosen that keystone. The data—the sixty-eight percent suffering-centered high school canon, the seventy-six percent suffering-centered literary prizes, the seventy-one percent combined dominance across prestige culture—is the lever. The Flourishing Canon, the solutions journalism practices, the reparative workshops, the balanced curricula already functioning successfully—these are the counterweight.

With this evidence, the central assumption can be carefully, deliberately displaced. The vault will not collapse; it will transform. The structure will settle into a new, more balanced form, capable of bearing the full weight of human experience—not just our capacity to suffer, but our capacity to build, repair, connect, and sustain.

It Is Time

It is time to stop worshiping at the altar of despair.

Not to abandon it. Not to pretend suffering doesn't exist or doesn't matter. But to refuse its claim to exclusive profundity. To stop treating tragedy as though it were the only truth worth our attention. To build alongside the cathedral of suffering another structure entirely—one with windows admitting natural light, doors welcoming different kinds of stories, and foundations strong enough to hold both our grief and our capacity for joy.

The cathedral taught how to mourn with sophistication and rigor. That knowledge remains necessary. The task now is learning to build with equal sophistication—to recognize that construction, repair, and sustained care are as intellectually and artistically demanding as destruction, that hope pursued rigorously is harder than despair embraced cheaply.

When Emma Brightwater asked, "Is that all there is?" she was performing meta-analysis that her teachers missed. She was asking whether suffering is the only available profundity, whether tragedy is the sole path to depth, whether the cathedral of despair is the only structure capable of housing serious thought.

The answer, visible in the accumulated evidence throughout this analysis, is clear: there is more. There has always been more. The altar simply refused to acknowledge it.

That refusal can end. It is ending. Window by window, classroom by classroom, newsroom by newsroom, manuscript by manuscript.

The pattern is visible. The costs are counted. The alternatives are documented and functioning.

The keystone is loosening.

The final chapter is not written here. It is written by what happens next—in classrooms where teachers integrate flourishing texts, in newsrooms expanding solutions coverage, in workshops where writers refuse the wound requirement, in homes where families supplement despair-heavy curricula, in publishing houses betting on human capability.

It must answer, finally and definitively: "No, Emma, that is not all there is."

The cathedral taught us how to mourn. That knowledge remains necessary. What we build beside it must be different in its very foundations—open where the cathedral was enclosed, built for gathering rather than solitary contemplation. Now, we lay the foundation for structures that honor the suffering canon but are built to celebrate what endures.

We will keep the cathedral's memory as a monument to what we have survived.

And we will build beside it a living house—a basilica for all we have yet to become.

One syllabus, one newsroom, one manuscript, one choice at a time.

APPENDIX A: THE 25 MOST-TAUGHT TEXTS—SUICIDE & SELF-ANNIHILATION CODING

This appendix classifies the twenty-five most commonly taught texts in American high schools according to the interpretive criteria defined in Chapter 1.

Coding Categories:

Category A – Explicit Suicide: A major character deliberately ends their own life.

Category B – Deliberate Self-Destruction: A major character knowingly chooses a course of action that leads directly to their own death (martyrdom, self-starvation, self-sacrifice in battle, etc.).

Category C – Thematic Self-Annihilation: The protagonist's central arc is the destruction of their own identity, hope, future, or place in the world through sustained, self-driven choices—even if the final death or collapse is not literal.

The 25 Texts:

1. Romeo and Juliet — William Shakespeare — **Category A**

Double suicide; culmination in self-chosen deaths.

2. Macbeth — William Shakespeare — **Category B**

Macbeth embraces a path that leads to his death.

3. Hamlet — William Shakespeare — **Category A/B**

Ophelia's likely suicide; Hamlet consents to a fatal duel.

4. Julius Caesar — William Shakespeare — **Category A**

Brutus and Cassius both commit suicide.

5. The Great Gatsby — F. Scott Fitzgerald — **Category C**

Gatsby's obsessive fantasy leads to chosen ruin.

6. To Kill a Mockingbird — Harper Lee — **No self-destruction**

Centers moral growth and justice.

7. Of Mice and Men — John Steinbeck — **Category C**

George's act ends his future and identity.

8. The Crucible — Arthur Miller — **Category B**

Proctor chooses execution over false confession.

9. Night — Elie Wiesel — **No self-destruction**

Atrocities inflicted externally; survival focus.

10. Fahrenheit 451 — Ray Bradbury — **No self-destruction**

Montag escapes and transforms.

11. Frankenstein — Mary Shelley — **Category C**

Victor's ruin is self-inflicted through obsession.

12. Lord of the Flies — William Golding — **Category C**

Collapse of social identity through collective choices.

13. The Catcher in the Rye — J.D. Salinger — **No self-destruction**

Psychological struggle, but no clear annihilation.

14. The Scarlet Letter — Nathaniel Hawthorne — **Category C**

Dimmesdale's internal torment leads to collapse.

15. The Adventures of Huckleberry Finn — Mark Twain — **No self-destruction**

Survival and moral awakening.

16. 1984 — George Orwell — **Category C**

Winston's identity is destroyed: "He loved Big Brother."

17. Pride and Prejudice — Jane Austen — **No self-destruction**

Resolution through growth and reconciliation.

18. Jane Eyre — Charlotte Brontë — **Category B**

Bertha Mason's death is a self-directed act.

19. Wuthering Heights — Emily Brontë — **Category B**

Heathcliff's self-starvation is passive suicide.

20. Their Eyes Were Watching God — Zora Neale Hurston — **No self-destruction**

Ends in renewal and self-reclamation.

21. Brave New World — Aldous Huxley — **Category A**

John the Savage commits suicide.

22. Death of a Salesman — Arthur Miller — **Category A**

Willy Loman's suicide for life insurance.

23. The Odyssey — Homer — **No self-destruction**

Epic of survival, return, and identity.

24. The Things They Carried — Tim O'Brien — **Category A**

Norman Bowker's suicide is central to the narrative.

25. Beloved — Toni Morrison — **Category C**

Sethe's identity eroded by trauma and guilt.

Summary:

Category A (Explicit Suicide): 6 texts

Category B (Deliberate Self-Destruction): 4 texts

Category C (Thematic Self-Annihilation): 7 texts

No Self-Destruction: 8 texts

TOTAL featuring suicide or self-annihilation: 17 out of 25 (68%)

APPENDIX B: DATA SOURCES FOR THE "MOST-TAUGHT BOOKS" ANALYSIS

The list is derived from a triangulation of three widely accepted indicators of high school literary instruction:

1. AP Literature & Composition Free-Response Data (1971–2022)

The College Board's publicly available data on frequently cited texts reveals the instructional backbone of upper-level classrooms.

2. Common Core State Standards, Appendix B (Grades 11–CCR Exemplars)

While not prescriptive, these exemplar texts heavily influenced curricular decisions during the Common Core rollout.

3. State-Level Curriculum Guides & National Surveys

Including NCTE surveys, district core lists, and canonical research (e.g., Applebee's national curriculum studies).

Weighting Criteria:

A text was included if it appeared in at least two of the following:
- AP Lit long-term top-tier citations
- CCSS Appendix B exemplar list (grades 11–12)
- Core status in state/district frameworks or major national surveys

This approach yields a defensible, representative canon of high school literary education.

APPENDIX C: METHODOLOGICAL NOTE

This analysis is interpretive rather than algorithmic. It explores how often the central arc of a text moves toward protagonist-driven self-destruction—whether literal, psychological, or existential.

Key Question:

Does the narrative present the protagonist's deepest truth as accessed through self-destruction?

Coding Framework:

Category A: Explicit Suicide — Direct, intentional self-killing

Category B: Deliberate Self-Destruction — Conscious actions taken knowing they will lead to death

Category C: Thematic Self-Annihilation — The erosion of identity or future via sustained, self-driven choices

By making these classifications public and open to scrutiny, the book invites disagreement at the granular level while underscoring the undeniable pattern: a disproportionate number of the most commonly assigned literary texts in American high schools tell students that meaning is found at the edge of self-destruction.

Cultural Implication:

The "17 out of 25" pattern isn't just academic. It reveals what our culture deems profound. These texts—by design or tradition—frame personal ruin as the ultimate revelation. The more consistently students consume these arcs, the more likely they are to internalize that despair is synonymous with depth.

This isn't an argument against tragedy. It's a call to diversify our definitions of seriousness. We need to expand the canon to include not just collapse, but construction; not just ruin, but resilience.

APPENDIX D: METHODOLOGY AND DATA FOR THE ANALYSIS OF BEST PICTURE WINNERS (1975-2024)

This appendix outlines the methodology and presents the complete dataset for the original content analysis conducted for Chapter 3.

Coding Protocol and Definitions

Each film was viewed in its entirety and coded based on its primary narrative arc and ultimate thematic resolution. The coding focused on the final impression and the core conflict the film is structured around.

Category A (Suffering-Centered): Narratives where the primary arc concludes with, or is fundamentally structured around, unhealed trauma, profound grief, moral failure, or existential despair. The resolution, if any, is ambiguous, melancholic, or pyrrhic.

Category B (Ambiguous/Integrated): Narratives that balance significant suffering with a definitive arc of healing, community restoration, or moral triumph. The suffering is a catalyst, not the destination.

Category C (Flourishing-Centered): Narratives where the primary arc concludes with joy, competence, community building, or unambiguous moral victory as the dominant note.

Methodological Note on Reliability:

To ensure coding consistency, a second coder was trained on the protocol and independently coded a randomly selected subset of 10 films (20% of the total sample). The inter-rater reliability was calculated using Cohen's Kappa, resulting in a coefficient of κ = 0.85, which indicates a high level of agreement. Any discrepancies were resolved through discussion to finalize the categorizations.

This analysis covers Best Picture winners from 1975 through 2024, representing exactly fifty years of Academy Awards decisions. The 2025 award (for *Anora*) occurred during final manuscript preparation. Given the film's profound interpretive ambiguity—director Sean Baker explicitly describes the ending as 'choose your own adventure'—and the scholarly consensus that borderline cases require viewing and careful analysis rather than plot-summary coding, the 2025 winner was excluded from the dataset to maintain analytical rigor.

Data Presentation: Categorized Best Picture Winners (1975-2025)

2024 — *Oppenheimer* — **A (Suffering-Centered)**

A three-hour chronicle of genius linked to mass annihilation and moral torment.

2023 — *Everything Everywhere All at Once* — **A (Suffering-Centered)**

A story whose emotional core is generational trauma and suicidal nihilism.

2022 — *CODA* — **C (Flourishing-Centered)**

A story of a young woman finding her voice while affirming family connection.

2021 — *Nomadland* — **A (Suffering-Centered)**

An elegiac portrait of grief, economic displacement, and rootlessness.

2020 — *Parasite* — **A (Suffering-Centered)**

A searing critique of class structure that ends in multiple deaths and trauma.

2019 — *Green Book* — **C (Flourishing-Centered)**

A story of friendship that bridges racial and class divides.

2018 — *The Shape of Water* — **C (Flourishing-Centered)**

A fairy tale where love triumphs over cruel authority.

2017 — *Moonlight* — **A (Suffering-Centered)**

A triptych of trauma exploring poverty, addiction, and homophobia.

2016 — *Spotlight* — **B (Ambiguous/Integrated)**

The competent, dogged, and successful work of journalists for the public good.

2015 — *Birdman* — **A (Suffering-Centered)**

A study of narcissism and artistic insecurity; implied suicide as escape.

2014 — *12 Years a Slave* — **A (Suffering-Centered)**

An unflinching historical document of the brutal reality of slavery.

2013 — *Argo* — **B (Ambiguous/Integrated)**

A high-stakes thriller about a successful, ingenious rescue mission.

2012 — *The Artist* — **B (Ambiguous/Integrated)**

A light-hearted, comedic homage; the protagonist's fall leads to a triumphant comeback.

2011 — *The King's Speech* — **B (Ambiguous/Integrated)**

A story about overcoming a disability and finding a voice.

2010 — *The Hurt Locker* — **A (Suffering-Centered)**

A portrait of addiction to the trauma of war.

2009 — *Slumdog Millionaire* — **C (Flourishing-Centered)**

A "feel-good" story where love and destiny triumph.

2008 — *No Country for Old Men* — **A (Suffering-Centered)**

Evil triumphs; the lawman retires in despair.

2007 — *The Departed* — **A (Suffering-Centered)**

Nearly every major character dies in a nihilistic conclusion.

2006 — *Crash* — **A (Suffering-Centered)**

A mosaic of racial tension and trauma with fleeting connections.

2005 — *Million Dollar Baby* — **A (Suffering-Centered)**

A brutal narrative that culminates in assisted suicide.

2004 — *The Lord of the Rings: The Return of the King* — **C (Flourishing-Centered)**

The definitive epic of good triumphing over evil.

2003 — *Chicago* — **C (Flourishing-Centered)**

A celebratory romp about fame and acquittal; success triumphs.

2002 — *A Beautiful Mind* — **B (Ambiguous/Integrated)**

Grappling with mental illness but achieving triumphant mastery.

2001 — *Gladiator* — **A (Suffering-Centered)**

The hero achieves revenge but dies; a narrative of sacrifice, not flourishing.

2000 — *American Beauty* — **A (Suffering-Centered)**

A satire of suburban nihilism that concludes with murder.

1999 — *Shakespeare in Love* — **C (Flourishing-Centered)**

A comedy about the transformative power of love and art.

1998 — *Titanic* — **A (Suffering-Centered)**

A grand, romantic tragedy defined by mass death and loss.

1997 — *The English Patient* — **A (Suffering-Centered)**

A tragic romance where both lovers die.

1996 — *Braveheart* — **A (Suffering-Centered)**

Ends with the brutal execution of its hero, a pyrrhic victory.

1995 — *Forrest Gump* — **B (Ambiguous/Integrated)**

The tone is magical optimism; the protagonist's goodness leads to a fulfilling life.

1994 — *Schindler's List* — **A (Suffering-Centered)**

A monumental film about the Holocaust.

1993 — *Unforgiven* — **A (Suffering-Centered)**

A deconstruction of the Western myth that concludes with nihilistic vengeance.

1992 — *The Silence of the Lambs* — **A (Suffering-Centered)**

A descent into the abyss of serial murder and psychological manipulation.

1991 — *Dances with Wolves* — **B (Ambiguous/Integrated)**

An elegy for a destroyed culture, but centered on spiritual awakening and belonging.

1990 — *Driving Miss Daisy* — **C (Flourishing-Centered)**

A gentle, decades-spanning story of friendship that transcends barriers.

1989 — *Rain Man* — **B (Ambiguous/Integrated)**

A selfish man learns connection and responsibility; a story of redemption.

1988 — *The Last Emperor* — **A (Suffering-Centered)**

A life of privilege and power leading to total irrelevance and loss.

1987 — *Platoon* — **A (Suffering-Centered)**

A hellish descent into the moral chaos of the Vietnam War.

1986 — *Out of Africa* — **A (Suffering-Centered)**

A memoir of love and ambition, all of which is ultimately lost.

1985 — *Amadeus* — A (Suffering-Centered)

A story of bitter jealousy and the destruction of a genius.

1984 — *Terms of Endearment* — A (Suffering-Centered)

Centers on the agonizing death of a young mother from cancer.

1983 — *Gandhi* — B (Ambiguous/Integrated)

Immense struggle and assassination framed within a triumphant legacy.

1982 — *Chariots of Fire* — C (Flourishing-Centered)

A triumphant story of faith, principle, and Olympic victory.

1981 — *Ordinary People* — A (Suffering-Centered)

A relentless study of guilt, grief, and suicidal ideation.

1980 — *Kramer vs. Kramer* — B (Ambiguous/Integrated)

Painful breakdown of a family concludes with hard-won, mature co-parenting.

1979 — *The Deer Hunter* — A (Suffering-Centered)

A searing, irreversible trauma inflicted by the Vietnam War.

1978 — *Annie Hall* — C (Flourishing-Centered)

A comedy; its tone is wistful and comedic, centering on the flourishing of memory and self.

1977 — *Rocky* — B (Ambiguous/Integrated)

Personal victory—proving his worth and winning respect—is the uplifting resolution.

1976 — *One Flew Over the Cuckoo's Nest* — A (Suffering-Centered)

The protagonist is lobotomized; the system's cruel authority triumphs.

1975 — *Dog Day Afternoon* — A (Suffering-Centered)

A desperate bank robbery ends in capture and despair.

Summary of Findings by Decade

1976-1985 (10 films):
- Suffering-Centered: 5 (50%)
- Mixed/Ambivalent: 3 (30%)
- Flourishing-Centered: 2 (20%)

1986-1995 (10 films):
- Suffering-Centered: 6 (60%)
- Mixed/Ambivalent: 3 (30%)
- Flourishing-Centered: 1 (10%)

1996-2005 (10 films):
- Suffering-Centered: 6 (60%)
- Mixed/Ambivalent: 1 (10%)
- Flourishing-Centered: 3 (30%)

2006-2015 (10 films):
- Suffering-Centered: 6 (60%)
- Mixed/Ambivalent: 3 (30%)
- Flourishing-Centered: 1 (10%)

2016-2024 (9 films):
- Suffering-Centered: 5 (60%)
- Mixed/Ambivalent: 1 (10%)
- Flourishing-Centered: 3 (30%)

The brief flourishing of hopeful winners between 2018 and 2022—*The Shape of Water*, *Green Book*, and *CODA*—was not the beginning of a new trend. The pattern immediately reasserted itself with *Everything Everywhere All at Once* (2023) and *Oppenheimer* (2024), both of which center trauma and existential crisis. Whether this represents the system's permanent equilibrium or simply variance within a slowly evolving pattern remains to be seen.

Overall Summary of Findings:

Total Films Analyzed: 50 (1975-2024)

Category A (Suffering-Centered): 31 films (62%)
Category B (Ambiguous/Integrated): 10 films (20%)
Category C (Flourishing-Centered): 9 films (18%)

APPENDIX E: PULITZER PRIZE AND NATIONAL BOOK AWARD ANALYSIS (2004-2024)

Methodology
This analysis classifies the primary thematic focus of each winning novel based on a close reading of the text and a consensus of critical summaries from authoritative sources, including *The New York Times Book Review*, *The New Yorker*, and the official award citations.

Classification Criteria
- **Suffering-Centered:** The narrative is primarily structured around trauma, historical atrocity, profound psychological despair, or a central, catalyzing loss.
- **Mixed/Ambivalent:** The work balances significant suffering with substantive themes of resilience or hope, but the core narrative remains tied to a traumatic event or social breakdown.
- **Flourishing-Centered:** The primary narrative energy derives from comic structures, the achievement of connection, or the building of a meaningful life, with any suffering being incidental rather than central.

Note on Timeframe Selection
This analysis examines literary prizes from 2004-2024, a different timeframe than the Best Picture analysis in Chapter 3 (1975-2024). This difference is methodologically justified for three reasons:

First, data density: While the Best Picture analysis examines one annual award over 50 years (50 data points), this literary analysis examines two major awards over 21 years (41 data points), providing comparable statistical robustness.

Second, institutional context: The Best Picture analysis tracks a single, stable institution (the Academy of Motion Picture Arts and Sciences, founded 1929) across multiple eras to demonstrate long-term consistency. The literary analysis tracks the output of a more recently consolidated system—the MFA-industrial complex—which achieved dominance in American literary culture primarily in the 21st century. The number of MFA programs quadrupled between 1975 and 2020, with the most significant expansion occurring after 1990. Analyzing prizes from 2004 onward captures the era when MFA credentialing became the near-universal pathway to literary publication and prestige.

Third, argumentative purpose: Chapter 3 demonstrates that the suffering bias is institutionally entrenched across generations. Chapter 6 demonstrates how the contemporary MFA system actively produces and rewards this bias. These are complementary but distinct claims, appropriately supported by different temporal scopes.

A preliminary survey of Pulitzer and National Book Award winners from the 1980s and 1990s suggests the suffering bias existed in earlier decades, though the pattern appears to have intensified in the 21st century. Future research could profitably extend this analysis backward to establish the historical trajectory more definitively.

Pulitzer Prize for Fiction Winners (2004-2024)
- **2024** — *Night Watch* by Jayne Anne Phillips — **Suffering-Centered**
    - A multigenerational family saga centered on trauma, the aftermath of the Civil War, and mental illness in an asylum setting.
- **2023** — *Demon Copperhead* by Barbara Kingsolver — **Suffering-Centered**
    - A retelling of *David Copperfield* set in Appalachia, exploring poverty, the opioid crisis, foster care trauma, and systemic neglect.
- **2022** — *The Netanyahus* by Joshua Cohen — **Mixed/Ambivalent**
    - A comic campus novel intertwined with historical trauma and identity conflict. While containing humor, the narrative is anchored in displacement and cultural alienation.

- **2021** — *The Night Watchman* by Louise Erdrich — **Suffering-Centered**
    - Based on the author's grandfather, the novel depicts Native American communities fighting against termination policies in the 1950s, centering on cultural erasure and systemic oppression.
- **2020** — *The Nickel Boys* by Colson Whitehead — **Suffering-Centered**
    - A devastating account of abuse at a reform school in Jim Crow-era Florida, based on the real Dozier School for Boys.
- **2019** — *The Overstory* by Richard Powers — **Suffering-Centered**
    - An epic about environmental destruction and human complicity in ecological collapse, culminating in tragedy and loss.
- **2018** — *Less* by Andrew Sean Greer — **Flourishing-Centered**
    - A comic picaresque about a writer on a journey of self-discovery. While containing moments of melancholy, the dominant tone is humorous and life-affirming.
- **2017** — *The Underground Railroad* by Colson Whitehead — **Suffering-Centered**
    - A reimagining of the brutality of American slavery through a speculative lens.
- **2016** — *The Sympathizer* by Viet Thanh Nguyen — **Suffering-Centered**
    - A spy thriller exploring the trauma of the Vietnam War and its aftermath through displacement, violence, and identity fracture.
- **2015** — *All the Light We Cannot See* by Anthony Doerr — **Suffering-Centered**
    - A World War II narrative centered on loss, destruction, and the horrors of war.

- **2014** — *The Goldfinch* by Donna Tartt — **Suffering-Centered**
    - The protagonist's mother dies in a terrorist attack in the opening pages; the rest of the novel traces his descent into grief, addiction, and crime.
- **2013** — *The Orphan Master's Son* by Adam Johnson — **Suffering-Centered**
    - A harrowing depiction of life in North Korea under totalitarian rule, featuring torture, loss, and systemic brutality.
- **2012** — **No Award**
- **2011** — *A Visit from the Goon Squad* by Jennifer Egan — **Mixed/Ambivalent**
    - A fragmented narrative about time, aging, and loss, balanced by moments of connection and creativity.
- **2010** — *Tinkers* by Paul Harding — **Suffering-Centered**
    - A meditation on death, dementia, and the dissolution of consciousness as a man lies dying.
- **2009** — *Olive Kitteridge* by Elizabeth Strout — **Suffering-Centered**
    - A portrait of a difficult woman navigating depression, alienation, and the slow unraveling of relationships.
- **2008** — *The Brief Wondrous Life of Oscar Wao* by Junot Díaz — **Suffering-Centered**
    - A family saga rooted in the trauma of the Trujillo dictatorship in the Dominican Republic, culminating in the protagonist's murder.
- **2007** — *The Road* by Cormac McCarthy — **Suffering-Centered**
    - A post-apocalyptic journey through a dying world, defined by starvation, violence, and existential hopelessness.
- **2006** — *March* by Geraldine Brooks — **Suffering-Centered**
    - A retelling of *Little Women* from the father's perspective during the Civil War, centering on battlefield horror and moral disillusionment.

- **2005** — *Gilead* by Marilynne Robinson — **Mixed/Ambivalent**
  - A reflective novel about an aging pastor writing to his young son. While contemplative and graceful, it is shadowed by mortality and loss.
- **2004** — *The Known World* by Edward P. Jones — **Suffering-Centered**
  - A novel about Black slaveholders in antebellum Virginia, exploring the moral complexities and horrors of slavery.

PULITZER PRIZE SUBTOTAL (20 awards across 21 years):
- **Suffering-Centered:** 16 books **(80%)**
- **Mixed/Ambivalent:** 3 books **(15%)**
- **Flourishing-Centered:** 1 book **(5%)**

National Book Award for Fiction Winners (2004-2024)
- **2024** — *The Safekeep* by Yael van der Wouden — **Suffering-Centered**
  - Set in the 1960s Netherlands, the novel explores buried trauma from World War II, family secrets, and repression.
- **2023** — *The Familiar* by Lev Grossman — **Flourishing-Centered**
  - A sprawling, inventive narrative centered on wonder, discovery, and the joy of storytelling itself.
- **2022** — *The Rabbit Hutch* by Tess Gunty — **Suffering-Centered**
  - A darkly comic novel set in a decaying Midwestern apartment complex, exploring poverty, isolation, and violence.
- **2021** — *Hell of a Book* by Jason Mott — **Suffering-Centered**
  - A surreal meditation on racial violence, trauma, and the psychological toll of Black life in America.
- **2020** — *Interior Chinatown* by Charles Yu — **Mixed/Ambivalent**
  - A satirical novel about Asian American identity and invisibility, blending humor with cultural alienation.

- **2019** — *Trust Exercise* by Susan Choi — **Suffering-Centered**
  - A meta-narrative exploring manipulation, sexual abuse, and the unreliability of memory within a high school theater program.
- **2018** — *The Friend* by Sigrid Nunez — **Mixed/Ambivalent**
  - A meditation on grief following a friend's suicide, balanced by reflections on art, companionship, and recovery.
- **2017** — *Sing, Unburied, Sing* by Jesmyn Ward — **Suffering-Centered**
  - A road trip through the American South that confronts racism, incarceration, addiction, and generational trauma.
- **2016** — *The Underground Railroad* by Colson Whitehead — **Suffering-Centered**
  - (Same as Pulitzer winner above.)
- **2015** — *Fortune Smiles* by Adam Johnson — **Suffering-Centered**
  - A short story collection featuring North Korean defectors, terminal illness, and characters navigating loss and dislocation.
- **2014** — *Redeployment* by Phil Klay — **Suffering-Centered**
  - A collection of stories about soldiers in Iraq and Afghanistan, centering on the psychological and physical trauma of war.
- **2013** — *The Good Lord Bird* by James McBride — **Mixed/Ambivalent**
  - A comic historical novel about John Brown and the abolitionist movement, blending humor with the violence of the antebellum era.
- **2012** — *The Round House* by Louise Erdrich — **Suffering-Centered**
  - A coming-of-age novel centered on a brutal rape and the failure of the justice system on a Native American reservation.

- **2011** — *Salvage the Bones* by Jesmyn Ward — **Suffering-Centered**
    - A family's struggle to survive Hurricane Katrina, set against poverty and environmental disaster.
- **2010** — *Lord of Misrule* by Jaimy Gordon — **Mixed/ Ambivalent**
    - A racetrack novel featuring con artists and underdogs. While containing hardship, the tone is picaresque and darkly comic.
- **2009** — *Let the Great World Spin* by Colum McCann — **Suffering-Centered**
    - Set in 1970s New York, the novel weaves together stories of grief, addiction, and loss against the backdrop of urban decay.
- **2008** — *Shadow Country* by Peter Matthiessen — **Suffering-Centered**
    - A historical epic about a ruthless frontier killer in Florida, exploring violence and moral ambiguity.
- **2007** — *Tree of Smoke* by Denis Johnson — **Suffering-Centered**
    - A sprawling, hallucinatory novel about the Vietnam War and the psychological unraveling of those involved.
- **2006** — *The Echo Maker* by Richard Powers — **Suffering-Centered**
    - A novel about brain injury, identity loss, and the fragility of consciousness following a catastrophic accident.
- **2005** — *Europe Central* by William T. Vollmann — **Suffering-Centered**
    - A dense historical novel about World War II and the Eastern Front, chronicling mass death and totalitarian horror.
- **2004** — *The News from Paraguay* by Lily Tuck — **Mixed/ Ambivalent**
    - A historical novel about a dictator's mistress, blending romance with the brutality of the Paraguayan War.

NATIONAL BOOK AWARD SUBTOTAL (21 awards):
- **Suffering-Centered:** 15 books **(71%)**
- **Mixed/Ambivalent:** 5 books **(24%)**
- **Flourishing-Centered:** 1 book **(5%)**

Summary of Findings
- **Total Prizes Analyzed:** 41 books
- **Pulitzer Prize:** 20 awards (2004-2024, excluding 2012 when no award was given)
- **National Book Award:** 21 awards (2004-2024)

COMBINED RESULTS (2004-2024):
- **Suffering-Centered:** 31 books **(76%)**
- **Mixed/Ambivalent:** 8 books **(20%)**
- **Flourishing-Centered:** 2 books **(5%)**

Summary by Period
- **2004-2013 (First Period):**
  - Suffering-Centered: 15 books **(79%)**
  - Mixed/Ambivalent: 4 books **(21%)**
  - Flourishing-Centered: 0 books **(0%)**
- **2014-2024 (Second Period):**
  - Suffering-Centered: 16 books **(73%)**
  - Mixed/Ambivalent: 4 books **(18%)**
  - Flourishing-Centered: 2 books **(9%)**
  - **(Note: This period covers eleven years rather than ten, as the analysis concludes with the 2024 awards.)**

Analysis

Over three-quarters of the most prestigious literary prizes in American fiction over the past twenty-one years have been awarded to narratives primarily structured around trauma, historical atrocity, or profound psychological despair. Only two winners—less than 5% of the total—center narratives of flourishing or comic exuberance as their primary thematic energy.

The pattern holds remarkably consistently across both awards, but with a notable intensification in the earliest period. From 2004 to 2013, not a single flourishing-centered narrative won either prize—a complete exclusion that represents not merely bias but systematic gatekeeping. The slight improvement in the second period (2014-2024), with two flourishing winners, suggests the possibility of change but does not constitute a fundamental shift in institutional values. The final winners in the dataset (2024) continue the dominant pattern.

This data reveals an awards ecosystem where trauma functions not as one valid subject among many, but as the primary credential for literary seriousness. This pattern coincides precisely with the era of maximum MFA influence on American literary culture, suggesting that what we are observing is not a natural literary preference but the systematic output of an institutional pipeline that trains writers to equate artistic depth with human brokenness.

APPENDIX F: COMBINED PRESTIGE CULTURE ANALYSIS (2004-2024)

Methodology

This appendix combines the datasets from Chapter 3 (Best Picture winners, 1975-2024) and Appendix E (Pulitzer Prize and National Book Award winners, 2004-2024) for the overlapping period of 2004-2024. This 21-year timeframe represents the era of maximum MFA influence on literary culture and provides a comprehensive view of American prestige culture across both film and literature.

Combined Statistics Summary

Total Works Analyzed: 62 (21 Best Picture winners + 41 literary prize winners)

By Category:
- **Suffering-Centered:** 44 works (71%)
- **Mixed/Ambivalent:** 12 works (19%)
- **Flourishing-Centered:** 6 works (10%)

By Period:
2004-2013 (First Period):
- **Total works:** 29
- **Suffering-Centered:** 22 (76%)
- **Mixed/Ambivalent:** 6 (21%)
- **Flourishing-Centered:** 1 (3%)

2014-2024 (Second Period):
- **Total works:** 33
- **Suffering-Centered:** 22 (67%)
- **Mixed/Ambivalent:** 6 (18%)
- **Flourishing-Centered:** 5 (15%)

Combined Dataset by Year
2004:
- **Best Picture:** The Lord of the Rings: The Return of the King (Flourishing)
- **Pulitzer:** The Known World (Suffering)
- **NBA:** The News from Paraguay (Mixed)

2005:
- **Best Picture:** Million Dollar Baby (Suffering)
- **Pulitzer:** Gilead (Mixed)
- **NBA:** Europe Central (Suffering)

2006:
- **Best Picture:** Crash (Suffering)
- **Pulitzer:** March (Suffering)
- **NBA:** The Echo Maker (Suffering)

2007:
- **Best Picture:** The Departed (Suffering)
- **Pulitzer:** The Road (Suffering)
- **NBA:** Tree of Smoke (Suffering)

2008:
- **Best Picture:** No Country for Old Men (Suffering)
- **Pulitzer:** The Brief Wondrous Life of Oscar Wao (Suffering)
- **NBA:** Shadow Country (Suffering)

2009:
- **Best Picture:** Slumdog Millionaire (Flourishing)
- **Pulitzer:** Olive Kitteridge (Suffering)
- **NBA:** Let the Great World Spin (Suffering)

2010:
- **Best Picture:** The Hurt Locker (Suffering)
- **Pulitzer:** Tinkers (Suffering)
- **NBA:** Lord of Misrule (Mixed)

2011:
- **Best Picture:** The King's Speech (Mixed)
- **Pulitzer:** A Visit from the Goon Squad (Mixed)
- **NBA:** Salvage the Bones (Suffering)

2012:
- **Best Picture:** The Artist (Mixed)
- **Pulitzer:** No Award
- **NBA:** The Round House (Suffering)

2013:
- **Best Picture:** Argo (Mixed)
- **Pulitzer:** The Orphan Master's Son (Suffering)
- **NBA:** The Good Lord Bird (Mixed)

2014:
- **Best Picture:** 12 Years a Slave (Suffering)
- **Pulitzer:** The Goldfinch (Suffering)
- **NBA:** Redeployment (Suffering)

2015:
- **Best Picture:** Birdman (Suffering)
- **Pulitzer:** All the Light We Cannot See (Suffering)
- **NBA:** Fortune Smiles (Suffering)

2016:
- **Best Picture:** Spotlight (Mixed)
- **Pulitzer:** The Sympathizer (Suffering)
- **NBA:** The Underground Railroad (Suffering)

2017:
- **Best Picture:** Moonlight (Suffering)
- **Pulitzer:** The Underground Railroad (Suffering)
- **NBA:** Sing, Unburied, Sing (Suffering)

2018:
- **Best Picture:** The Shape of Water (Flourishing)
- **Pulitzer:** Less (Flourishing)
- **NBA:** The Friend (Mixed)

2019:
- **Best Picture:** Green Book (Flourishing)
- **Pulitzer:** The Overstory (Suffering)
- **NBA:** Trust Exercise (Suffering)

2020:
- **Best Picture:** Parasite (Suffering)
- **Pulitzer:** The Nickel Boys (Suffering)
- **NBA:** Interior Chinatown (Mixed)

2021:
- **Best Picture:** Nomadland (Suffering)
- **Pulitzer:** The Night Watchman (Suffering)
- **NBA:** Hell of a Book (Suffering)

2022:
- **Best Picture:** CODA (Flourishing)
- **Pulitzer:** The Netanyahus (Mixed)
- **NBA:** The Rabbit Hutch (Suffering)

2023:
- **Best Picture:** Everything Everywhere All at Once (Suffering)
- **Pulitzer:** Demon Copperhead (Suffering)
- **NBA:** The Familiar (Flourishing)

2024:
- **Best Picture:** Oppenheimer (Suffering)
- **Pulitzer:** Night Watch (Suffering)
- **NBA:** The Safekeep (Suffering)

Notable Patterns
Years of Perfect Storm (All Three Prizes to Suffering-Centered Works):

2007, 2008, 2014, 2015, 2017, 2021, 2024

These seven years represent one-third of the period studied, during which every single major prestige award reinforced the same message: suffering equals seriousness.

Years with Multiple Flourishing Winners:

2018 only (The Shape of Water and Less)

The year 2018 stands alone as the only year in which two flourishing-centered works won major prizes. This sparked brief speculation about shifting institutional values. However, the immediate return to suffering-centered dominance in subsequent years suggests this was a statistical fluctuation rather than a fundamental change in the prestige ecosystem.

The 2018 Anomaly:

The year 2018 represents the high-water mark for flourishing-centered works in the 21st century prestige ecosystem. With both The Shape of Water (Best Picture) and Less (Pulitzer Prize) winning major awards, it appeared the system might be diversifying. However, the pattern immediately reasserted itself:
- 2019: One flourishing winner (Green Book)
- 2020: Zero flourishing winners
- 2021: Zero flourishing winners
- 2022: One flourishing winner (CODA)
- 2023: One flourishing winner (The Familiar)
- 2024: Zero flourishing winners

Analysis

The combined dataset demonstrates that American prestige culture from 2004 to 2024 functioned as a reinforcing orthodoxy, with film and literature converging on the same valuation system. While individual institutions show slightly different patterns (film at 62% suffering over 50 years, literature at 76% suffering over 21 years), the aggregate effect is a cultural ecosystem where **seventy-one percent of consecrated works center on suffering**.

Period Comparison:

The pattern was even more restrictive in its first period, with only **one flourishing-centered winner (3%)** in ten years. The modest improvement in the second period (to 15% flourishing-centered) suggests the system can evolve, but at the current rate of change, achieving balance would require several more decades.

Calculation of 71% Overall:

First Period (2004-2013):
- 22 suffering works out of 29 total = 76%

Second Period (2014-2024):
- 22 suffering works out of 33 total = 67%

Combined (2004-2024):
- 44 suffering works out of 62 total = 71%

This data reveals an awards ecosystem where trauma functions not as one valid subject among many, but as the primary—and often exclusive—credential for artistic seriousness across all prestige media. The years 2007, 2008, 2014, 2015, 2017, 2021, and 2024—in which all three major prizes went to suffering-centered works—demonstrate the depth of institutional consensus around this value system.

The Modest Shift:

The improvement from 3% flourishing-centered works (2004-2013) to 15% flourishing-centered works (2014-2024) represents a **12-percentage-point increase** over 11 years. At this rate of change:
- It would take approximately **37 more years** to reach 50% flourishing-centered works (balance)
- We would reach parity around the year **2061**

This timeline assumes linear change, which may not hold. The 2018-2022 cluster of flourishing winners (The Shape of Water, Green Book, CODA, Less, The Familiar) could signal accelerating change—or it could prove to be another anomaly, as the return to zero flourishing winners in 2024 suggests.

Institutional Reinforcement:

The combined analysis reveals something more troubling than the individual patterns: **the two systems perform the same ritual simultaneously.**

When Oppenheimer won Best Picture in 2024, validating the equation of genius with mass destruction, novels like Night Watch (Pulitzer) and The Safekeep (NBA) won top literary honors the same year—both centering on trauma, war, and buried psychological damage.

The message from every prestige institution was identical: **seriousness requires suffering.**

For the culturally engaged consumer—the person who watches the Oscars, follows book prize announcements, and uses these institutions as guides—there was no alternative voice in 2024. Whether they turned to film or literature, the liturgy was the same: **if it matters, it hurts.**

This pattern held for seven of the 21 years studied—fully one-third of the period—demonstrating that the suffering canon is not merely a bias within individual institutions, but a coordinated cultural orthodoxy spanning multiple domains of prestige.

Conclusion

The 21-year analysis (2004-2024) of combined film and literary prizes reveals:
1. **71% of all prestige winners centered suffering**—a clear majority that has held steady across two decades
2. **Only 10% centered flourishing**—representing severe underrepresentation of narratives organized around repair, competence, or sustained hope
3. **The first decade was more restrictive** (76% suffering, 3% flourishing) than the second (67% suffering, 15% flourishing), suggesting some evolution is possible
4. **Seven "perfect storm" years** (2007, 2008, 2014, 2015, 2017, 2021, 2024) when all three major prizes went to suffering-centered works demonstrate deep institutional consensus
5. **The 2018 anomaly**—the only year with multiple flourishing winners—has not yet proven to be the beginning of sustained change

This comprehensive dataset supports the book's central thesis: American prestige culture has systematically consecrated suffering as the primary—and often exclusive—path to artistic seriousness, creating a cultural diet profoundly imbalanced toward narratives of collapse rather than construction, despair rather than repair.

APPENDIX G: THE FLOURISHING CANON—ANNOTATED LIST OF 100 WORKS

This appendix provides the complete, annotated list of the one hundred works that constitute the Flourishing Canon, organized into five key themes. These themes are practical shelving categories and are not identical to the conceptual groupings used in Chapter 13. These works serve as blueprints, case studies, and training manuals for the difficult art of building lives and worlds worth inhabiting.

Note: Complete bibliographic information for all works in this appendix also appears in the Consolidated References at the end of this book. The references are organized here by thematic category for the reader's convenience.

I. THE FOUNDATIONS OF WONDER

Works that reignite a sense of awe at the universe and our place in it—an antidote to trained cynicism.

1. Pilgrim at Tinker Creek — Annie Dillard (1974)
A year of fierce, joyful attention to a small patch of Virginia, rendered as a work of theology, biology, and philosophy that finds a world "drenched in grace."

2. Gilead — Marilynne Robinson (2004)
A dying minister's letter to his young son becomes a breathtaking catalog of blessing—a meditation on the sacred ordinary and the beauty of a mundane life lived with moral intention.

3. Watership Down — Richard Adams (1972)
A band of rabbits flee destruction to build a new warren. The narrative derives its power from collective problem-solving,

loyalty, and the labor of making a home instead of merely finding one.

4. Braiding Sweetgrass — Robin Wall Kimmerer (2013)
A botanist and member of the Citizen Potawatomi Nation interweaves Indigenous wisdom with scientific knowledge, arguing for reciprocity with the living world. Gratitude and stewardship organize the book's moral universe.

5. World of Wonders — Aimee Nezhukumatathil (2020)
Short, illustrated essays about strange animals and plants, each doubling as a lens on belonging, resilience, and joy. Wonder becomes a discipline here, not a passing mood.

6. The Invention of Nature: Alexander von Humboldt's New World — Andrea Wulf (2015)
A biography of the scientist-explorer who reimagined humanity's relationship with nature as interconnected and dynamic. Humboldt's life was driven by curiosity, wonder, and the conviction that understanding the natural world could inspire both scientific progress and ethical responsibility. The book is a celebration of intellectual adventure, cross-disciplinary thinking, and the transformative power of attention to the living world.

7. Lab Girl — Hope Jahren (2016)
A memoir of a scientist's life alongside lyrical reflections on seeds, trees, and geologic time. Persistence, friendship, and stubborn curiosity drive the story more powerfully than suffering does.

8. The Hidden Life of Trees — Peter Wohlleben (2015)
Recasts forests as communities—trees sharing resources, protecting the vulnerable, and "nursing" their young. It offers a biological model of mutual care that challenges competitive individualism.

9. Desert Solitaire — Edward Abbey (1968)
A season in a harsh landscape becomes a meditation on solitude, beauty, and radical attention. The desert is not framed as empty wasteland, but as exacting and full of meaning.

10. The Outermost House — Henry Beston (1928)
A year on Cape Cod's Great Beach, rendered as spiritual ecology. The changing tides and bird migrations become a liturgy of place and belonging.

11. A Sand County Almanac — Aldo Leopold (1949)
Foundational to conservation ethics, this book marries close observation with the "land ethic"—the idea that humans are members of, not masters over, their ecological community.

12. The Soul of an Octopus — Sy Montgomery (2015)
An exploration of octopus intelligence and emotion that becomes a testament to curiosity, cross-species empathy, and the many forms consciousness can take.

13. The Living Mountain — Nan Shepherd (1977)
A sustained, intimate walk with the Cairngorms. Knowing a place, Shepherd suggests, is an act of love that changes the knower as much as the known.

14. All Creatures Great and Small — James Herriot (1972)
Warm, often hilarious accounts of a country vet's life. Competence, kindness, and work done well supply the drama—proof that expertise itself can be profoundly engaging.

15. The Man Who Planted Trees — Jean Giono (1953)
A shepherd quietly reforests a barren valley over decades. A parable of slow, anonymous repair that transforms an entire region.

16. The Peregrine — J.A. Baker (1967)
Obsessive watching of falcons becomes a near-mystical act. Baker demonstrates that attention itself can be transfiguring, a form of devotion.

17. Howl's Moving Castle — Diana Wynne Jones (1986)
Sophie is cursed into old age and, paradoxically, becomes freer—bossy, capable, and brave. Magic here amplifies wit and character development, not misery.

18. Finding the Mother Tree — Suzanne Simard (2021)
A forest ecologist's research and life story, showing how

trees share resources, favor their offspring, and keep one another alive—cooperation as an ecological fact, not mere metaphor.

19. The Gardener's Year — Karel Čapek (1929)
Month-by-month gardening, laced with humor and philosophy. Failure, persistence, and small triumphs are all part of the flourishing process.

20. Notes from Walnut Tree Farm — Roger Deakin (2008)
A year of notes on weather, wildlife, and woodpiles. Daily noticing becomes a way of inhabiting the world more fully, proof that the ordinary contains depths.

II. THE ARCHITECTURE OF CONNECTION

Works that map the complex, difficult, and life-giving structures of relationship and community.

21. The Stone Diaries — Carol Shields (1993)
The "ordinary" life of Daisy Goodwill Flett becomes an epic of friendships, work, and quiet self-making. The book insists the unhistoric life is worthy of deep attention.

22. Middlemarch — George Eliot (1871)
Multiple lives in a provincial town, all pulling against and toward each other. Its final image—of goodness diffused through "unhistoric acts"—is a manifesto for small, cumulative flourishing.

23. Crossing to Safety — Wallace Stegner (1987)
Two couples sustain a fifty-year friendship through careers, illness, and aging. The drama is in loyalty, forgiveness, and the long labor of staying present.

24. The House on Mango Street — Sandra Cisneros (1984)
Esperanza's vignettes chart a girlhood shaped by poverty and sexism—but also by imagination, community, and an emerging voice determined to return and uplift.

25. The Joy Luck Club — Amy Tan (1989)
Mothers and daughters, migration and misunderstanding,

and the slow, painful, beautiful work of seeing one another clearly across generational divides.

26. The Blue Castle — L.M. Montgomery (1926)
Given a (wrong) terminal diagnosis, Valancy stops obeying her suffocating family and builds a life of her own. Liberation—not illness—is the story's true engine.

27. The Guernsey Literary and Potato Peel Pie Society — Mary Ann Shaffer & Annie Barrows (2008)
An epistolary love letter to books, food, and community healing after war. Literature becomes the binding agent for traumatized survivors.

28. Anne of Green Gables — L.M. Montgomery (1908)
A "problem" orphan transforms a household and town with imagination, stubbornness, and fierce love. Joy, not tragedy, is the complexity here.

29. Their Eyes Were Watching God — Zora Neale Hurston (1937)
Janie's journey through three marriages is a search for voice and self-possession. The final image is not defeat but a woman at home in her own skin.

30. Pride and Prejudice — Jane Austen (1813)
Two intelligent people misread each other, then grow. Humility, conversation, and self-correction drive the romance—a model for how minds change.

31. Olive Kitteridge — Elizabeth Strout (2008)
Linked stories about a prickly, deeply human woman and the town around her. Connection arrives in jagged, surprising forms that resist sentimentality.

32. The Elegance of the Hedgehog — Muriel Barbery (2006)
A secret-philosopher concierge and a gifted child find each other. Recognition of another's inner life is treated as a form of love.

33. A Gentleman in Moscow — Amor Towles (2016)
A count confined to a hotel builds a meaningful life through

work, friendship, and chosen family. Agency inside constraint becomes the story.

34. The Uncommon Reader — Alan Bennett (2007)
A queen discovers reading, and it changes how she sees everyone around her. A comedy about empathy as a form of literacy.

35. Jayber Crow — Wendell Berry (2000)
A barber's long life in a small town becomes a meditation on vocation, place, and faithful love of community across decades.

36. 84, Charing Cross Road — Helene Hanff (1970)
Two decades of letters between a New York writer and a London bookseller. Affection built book by book, across an ocean.

37. The House in the Cerulean Sea — TJ Klune (2020)
A caseworker investigates magical children and finds a family. Queer, cozy, and unapologetically hopeful without sacrificing stakes.

38. The Rosie Project — Graeme Simsion (2013)
A rigid questionnaire for the perfect wife meets a gloriously noncompliant human being. Connection upends control in the best possible way.

39. Major Pettigrew's Last Stand — Helen Simonson (2010)
A widower and a Pakistani shopkeeper choose dignity, love, and courage in a village that would prefer they didn't. Quiet resistance through relationship.

40. Cold Comfort Farm — Stella Gibbons (1932)
A deadpan demolition of doom-drenched rural tragedy. Flora Poste solves everyone's "unspeakable past" with practicality, kindness, and a refusal to romanticize misery.

41. The Bookshop on the Corner — Jenny Colgan (2016)
A displaced librarian turns a van into a roaming bookshop and builds community in the Scottish Highlands. Books as bridge-builders.

42. The Little Paris Bookshop — Nina George (2013)
A man who "prescribes" books to heal others finally allows stories to heal him, too. Literature as medicine, literally.

43. The Authenticity Project — Clare Pooley (2020)
A shared notebook of truths pulls lonely people into one another's orbits. Vulnerability becomes the foundation for connection.

44. Emma — Jane Austen (1815)
A clever, meddling heroine learns to see others—and herself—more truly. Growth through self-awareness, not punishment, is the arc.

45. Fried Green Tomatoes at the Whistle Stop Cafe — Fannie Flagg (1987)
Friendship across generations, found family, and women refusing erasure. Storytelling itself becomes the binding force.

III. BLUEPRINTS FOR BETTER WORLDS

Works that imagine not only what might go wrong, but what might go right—and how we might build systems and societies worth inhabiting.

46. The Dispossessed — Ursula K. Le Guin (1974)
Twin worlds—one capitalist, one anarchist—serve as a thought experiment in freedom, responsibility, and what a just society might cost and require.

47. The Princess Bride — William Goldman (1973)
A layered fairy tale that unabashedly celebrates true love, loyalty, and storytelling itself, while maintaining sharp, self-aware wit throughout.

48. The Lord of the Rings — J.R.R. Tolkien (1954–55)
A fellowship of very small people defeats overwhelming evil through persistence, friendship, and mercy. Tolkien's "eucatastrophe"—the sudden turn toward joy—is the point, not an accident.

49. A Psalm for the Wild-Built — Becky Chambers (2021)
A tea monk and a robot in a post-capitalist world ask, "What do people need?" The answer is not productivity, but enoughness.

50. The Long Way to a Small, Angry Planet — Becky Chambers (2014)
A crew of humans and aliens travel together, negotiating politics and difference through conversation rather than conquest. Diplomacy as daily practice.

51. Walkaway — Cory Doctorow (2017)
People exit hyper-capitalism to build open-source communities. The book takes seriously both the technical and social engineering required to make alternative systems work.

52. The Fifth Sacred Thing — Starhawk (1993)
An ecofeminist San Francisco holds to its nonviolent, cooperative values in the face of militaristic aggression. Utopia under siege, refusing to abandon its principles.

53. Gaudy Night — Dorothy L. Sayers (1935)
Mystery wrapped around a women's college at Oxford becomes an inquiry into intellectual life, partnership, and whether love between equals is possible.

54. Always Coming Home — Ursula K. Le Guin (1985)
An "anthropology" of a future people, the Kesh, who live sustainably and richly in a reimagined California valley. Less plot, more manual for living well.

55. Ecotopia — Ernest Callenbach (1975)
A newly seceded eco-state is visited by a skeptical journalist. The book imagines policies, technologies, and customs that center ecological sanity.

56. Pacific Edge — Kim Stanley Robinson (1990)
A slice-of-life in a near-future, sustainably reorganized California. Local politics and zoning fights stand in for the ongoing work of utopia—no final victory, just maintenance.

57. The City We Became — N.K. Jemisin (2020)
New York's boroughs become human avatars defending their city against an interdimensional threat. An ode to urban diversity and fierce civic love.

58. The Culture Series — Iain M. Banks (1987–2012)
Novels exploring a post-scarcity, AI-augmented society and its entanglements with less equitable worlds. Utopia is complicated, not simple.

59. The Mars Trilogy — Kim Stanley Robinson (1992–1996)
Terraforming Mars doubles as a debate over how we might build fairer societies from scratch, complete with competing visions and necessary compromises.

60. Semiosis — Sue Burke (2018)
Humans and sentient plants negotiate coexistence on an alien world. Cooperation across radical difference is both the core problem and the possibility.

61. A Wizard of Earthsea — Ursula K. Le Guin (1968)
Ged's real victory is not defeating an external enemy but integrating his shadow self. The ultimate goal is psychological wholeness, not conquest.

62. The Left Hand of Darkness — Ursula K. Le Guin (1969)
An envoy must let go of his gendered assumptions on a planet where people are ambisexual. Politics and friendship reshape each other across cultural difference.

63. The Telling — Ursula K. Le Guin (2000)
Stories as underground resistance in a regime that has outlawed tradition and narrative memory. Literature becomes survival technology.

64. Ancillary Justice — Ann Leckie (2013)
A former starship AI inhabiting one human body searches for justice in a vast empire. Identity, embodiment, and power structures are all up for radical redesign.

65. The No. 1 Ladies' Detective Agency — Alexander McCall Smith (2000)
Precious Ramotswe solves problems through patience,

intuition, and deep knowledge of her Botswanan community. Competence and cultural wisdom are the superpowers.

66. Too Like the Lightning — Ada Palmer (2016)
A dense, philosophical exploration of a future where people choose non-geographic "Hives" instead of nation-states. This vision of utopia is complicated, contingent, and worth arguing about.

67. The Wayfarers Series — Becky Chambers (2014–2021)
Standalone novels sharing a universe where kindness, hospitality, and emotional maturity are treated as serious technologies for survival.

68. The Ministry for the Future — Kim Stanley Robinson (2020)
A UN agency attempts to implement actual climate solutions. The novel is crowded with policy ideas, technologies, and movements that could exist—a direct counter to climate despair.

69. Autonomous — Annalee Newitz (2017)
Pharmaceutical piracy, AI personhood, and bodily autonomy woven into a thriller that keeps asking: who owns life? What would liberation actually look like?

70. The Hobbit — J.R.R. Tolkien (1937)
A small, comfort-loving creature discovers courage, cleverness, and the joy of returning home changed but not destroyed. The adventure matters, but so does the return.

IV. ESSAYS, MEMOIR & CREATIVE NONFICTION

Sustained thought and reflection that show how flourishing can be theorized, practiced, and narrated as a serious intellectual project.

71. The Book of Delights — Ross Gay (2019)
A year of daily essays on small joys. Delight becomes a practice, a discipline, not a personality trait or lucky accident.

72. Inciting Joy — Ross Gay (2022)
Joy framed not as private escape but as communal, even political. Basketball courts, gardens, and grief groups all become sites of shared aliveness.

73. Shop Class as Soulcraft — Matthew B. Crawford (2009)
Argues that manual, skilled work can offer meaning and dignity that much white-collar work fails to provide. Competence as a moral category.

74. The Art of Living — Thich Nhat Hanh (2017)
Mindfulness, compassion, and presence treated as everyday, trainable skills rather than lofty abstractions reserved for monks.

75. The Sabbath — Abraham Joshua Heschel (1951)
A theology of sacred time. Rest is not laziness but resistance to a culture that knows only production and consumption.

76. Gift from the Sea — Anne Morrow Lindbergh (1955)
Shells on a beach become metaphors for stages of women's lives, solitude, connection, and the rhythms of attention.

77. Devotions — Mary Oliver (2017)
A selected poems collection that models attention, reverence, and the insistence that one wild and precious life is worth inhabiting fully.

78. On Connection — Kae Tempest (2020)
Art as bridge between isolated selves. Creativity here is treated as a commons, not a private trophy or individual genius myth.

79. Creating Capabilities — Martha C. Nussbaum (2011)
Philosophy meets policy: what does it mean, practically, to give everyone genuine opportunities to flourish? Justice as capability, not just distribution.

80. The Empathy Exams — Leslie Jamison (2014)
Essays on pain and empathy that wrestle honestly with how to witness others' suffering without devouring it or turning away entirely.

81. Letters to a Young Poet — Rainer Maria Rilke (1929)
Ten letters that treat artistic and interior life as serious, slow work worth the trouble—a counter to both commercial pressure and tortured genius myths.

82. The Nature Fix — Florence Williams (2017)
Science plus travelogue demonstrating that time in nature measurably improves mood, focus, and health. Biology as argument for flourishing.

83. Notes from No Man's Land — Eula Biss (2009)
Essays on race, belonging, and the difficult ethics of being a citizen. No easy answers, but stubborn hope in honest reckoning.

84. Bird by Bird — Anne Lamott (1994)
A writing manual that doubles as a survival manual for anxious, imperfect humans trying to make art without destroying themselves.

85. The Art of Memoir — Mary Karr (2015)
How to tell the truth on the page without exploiting yourself or others. Craft and ethics braided together as inseparable.

86. Maybe You Should Talk to Someone — Lori Gottlieb (2019)
Therapist-as-patient and therapist-as-therapist stories woven into a compassionate exploration of how people actually change.

87. Upstream — Mary Oliver (2016)
Essays on the writers and landscapes that shaped Oliver's way of seeing. A lineage of attention passed down through reading.

88. The Anthologist — Nicholson Baker (2009)
A poet procrastinates writing an introduction to an anthology and, in the process, makes a funny, passionate case for rhyme, meter, and joy in poetic form.

89. The Writing Life — Annie Dillard (1989)
A fierce little book on the work of making art. Difficulty is

framed not as romantic martyrdom but as a worthy way to spend a life.

90. The Martian — Andy Weir (2011)
An astronaut stranded alone on Mars survives through systematic problem-solving, ingenuity, and stubborn competence. A masterclass in agency, resilience, and the practical intelligence required to turn disaster into survival.

V. POETRY & DRAMA

Verse and plays that treat joy, wonder, and connection as worthy of the highest literary forms.

91. Leaves of Grass — Walt Whitman (1855)
A democratic epic of bodies, cities, fields, and souls. Abundance rather than scarcity is its baseline assumption about existence.

92. The Essential Rumi — Jalaluddin Rumi, trans. Coleman Barks (1995)
Poems of ecstatic love, divine and human, that insist the universe is fundamentally relational, not isolating.

93. Good Bones — Maggie Smith (2017)
Poems that acknowledge the world's darkness while fiercely arguing for the work of making it "at least fifty percent good" for children.

94. The Sun and Her Flowers — Rupi Kaur (2017)
A life cycle of wilting, rooting, rising, and blooming after heartbreak and displacement. Recovery as narrative arc.

95. The Odyssey — Homer, trans. Emily Wilson (2017)
An ancient story of homecoming and craft, where wit, patience, and loyalty matter as much as strength. The journey matters, but so does the return.

96. The Tempest — William Shakespeare (1611)
Shakespeare chooses forgiveness over revenge and ends not in bloodbath but reconciliation, with Prospero breaking his staff and freeing Ariel.

97. Our Town — Thornton Wilder (1938)
A play about two families in a small town that becomes a devastating and tender reminder that ordinary days are where life actually happens—not in grand catastrophes.

98. Much Ado About Nothing — William Shakespeare (c. 1598)
Enemies-to-lovers banter, mistaken identities, and a community that ultimately prioritizes restoration over ruin. Comedy as serious moral work.

99. A Midsummer Night's Dream — William Shakespeare (c. 1595)
A forest of mischief where the world is bent toward reconciliation, not doom, and people wake up better—or at least married—than they were before.

100. As You Like It — William Shakespeare (c. 1599)
Exile becomes liberation in the Forest of Arden, where characters discover themselves through friendship, disguise, and wit. The pastoral as a space for transformation rather than escape.

REFERENCES
I. THE FOUNDATIONS OF WONDER

Dillard, Annie. 1974. *Pilgrim at Tinker Creek*. New York: Harper's Magazine Press.

Robinson, Marilynne. 2004. *Gilead*. New York: Farrar, Straus and Giroux.

Adams, Richard. 1972. *Watership Down*. London: Rex Collings.

Kimmerer, Robin Wall. 2013. *Braiding Sweetgrass: Indigenous Wisdom, Scientific Knowledge, and the Teachings of Plants*. Minneapolis: Milkweed Editions.

Nezhukumatathil, Aimee. 2020. *World of Wonders: In Praise of Fireflies, Whale Sharks, and Other Astonishments*. Minneapolis: Milkweed Editions.

Wulf, Andrea. 2015. *The Invention of Nature: Alexander von Humboldt's New World*. New York: Alfred A. Knopf.

Jahren, Hope. 2016. *Lab Girl*. New York: Alfred A. Knopf.

Wohlleben, Peter. 2015. *The Hidden Life of Trees: What They Feel, How They Communicate—Discoveries from a Secret World*. Translated by Jane Billinghurst. Vancouver: Greystone Books.

Abbey, Edward. 1968. *Desert Solitaire: A Season in the Wilderness*. New York: McGraw-Hill.

Beston, Henry. 1928. *The Outermost House: A Year of Life on the Great Beach of Cape Cod*. Garden City, NY: Doubleday, Doran.

Leopold, Aldo. 1949. *A Sand County Almanac: And Sketches Here and There*. New York: Oxford University Press.

Montgomery, Sy. 2015. *The Soul of an Octopus: A Surprising Exploration into the Wonder of Consciousness*. New York: Atria Books.

Shepherd, Nan. 1977. *The Living Mountain*. Aberdeen: Aberdeen University Press.

Herriot, James. 1972. *All Creatures Great and Small*. London: Michael Joseph.

Giono, Jean. 1953. *The Man Who Planted Trees*. Translated by Peter Doyle. Chelsea, VT: Chelsea Green Publishing, 1985.

Baker, J.A. 1967. *The Peregrine*. London: Collins.

Jones, Diana Wynne. 1986. *Howl's Moving Castle*. London: Greenwillow Books.

Simard, Suzanne. 2021. *Finding the Mother Tree: Discovering the Wisdom of the Forest*. New York: Alfred A. Knopf.

Čapek, Karel. 1929. *The Gardener's Year*. Translated by M. and R. Weatherall. London: George Allen & Unwin.

Deakin, Roger. 2008. *Notes from Walnut Tree Farm*. London: Hamish Hamilton.

II. THE ARCHITECTURE OF CONNECTION

Shields, Carol. 1993. *The Stone Diaries*. Toronto: Random House Canada.

Eliot, George. 1871. *Middlemarch: A Study of Provincial Life*. Edinburgh: William Blackwood and Sons.

Stegner, Wallace. 1987. *Crossing to Safety*. New York: Random House.

Cisneros, Sandra. 1984. *The House on Mango Street*. Houston: Arte Público Press.

Tan, Amy. 1989. *The Joy Luck Club*. New York: G.P. Putnam's Sons.

Montgomery, L.M. 1926. *The Blue Castle*. Toronto: McClelland & Stewart.

Shaffer, Mary Ann, and Annie Barrows. 2008. *The Guernsey Literary and Potato Peel Pie Society*. New York: Dial Press.

Montgomery, L.M. 1908. *Anne of Green Gables*. Boston: L.C. Page & Company.

Hurston, Zora Neale. 1937. *Their Eyes Were Watching God*. Philadelphia: J.B. Lippincott.

Austen, Jane. 1813. *Pride and Prejudice*. London: T. Egerton.

Strout, Elizabeth. 2008. *Olive Kitteridge*. New York: Random House.

Barbery, Muriel. 2006. *The Elegance of the Hedgehog*. Translated by Alison Anderson. New York: Europa Editions, 2008.

Towles, Amor. 2016. *A Gentleman in Moscow*. New York: Viking.

Bennett, Alan. 2007. *The Uncommon Reader*. London: Faber and Faber.

Berry, Wendell. 2000. *Jayber Crow*. Washington, DC: Counterpoint.

Hanff, Helene. 1970. *84, Charing Cross Road*. New York: Grossman Publishers.

Klune, TJ. 2020. *The House in the Cerulean Sea*. New York: Tor Books.

Simsion, Graeme. 2013. *The Rosie Project*. Melbourne: Text Publishing.

Simonson, Helen. 2010. *Major Pettigrew's Last Stand*. New York: Random House.

Gibbons, Stella. 1932. *Cold Comfort Farm*. London: Longmans, Green.

Colgan, Jenny. 2016. *The Bookshop on the Corner*. London: Sphere.

George, Nina. 2013. *The Little Paris Bookshop*. Translated by Simon Pare. New York: Crown, 2015.

Pooley, Clare. 2020. *The Authenticity Project*. New York: Pamela Dorman Books.

Austen, Jane. 1815. *Emma*. London: John Murray.

Flagg, Fannie. 1987. *Fried Green Tomatoes at the Whistle Stop Cafe*. New York: Random House.

III. BLUEPRINTS FOR BETTER WORLDS

Le Guin, Ursula K. 1974. *The Dispossessed: An Ambiguous Utopia*. New York: Harper & Row.

Goldman, William. 1973. *The Princess Bride: S. Morgenstern's Classic Tale of True Love and High Adventure*. New York: Harcourt Brace Jovanovich.

Tolkien, J.R.R. 1954–1955. *The Lord of the Rings*. 3 vols. London: George Allen & Unwin.

Chambers, Becky. 2021. *A Psalm for the Wild-Built*. New York: Tor Books.

Chambers, Becky. 2014. *The Long Way to a Small, Angry Planet*. New York: Harper Voyager.

Doctorow, Cory. 2017. *Walkaway*. New York: Tor Books.

Starhawk. 1993. *The Fifth Sacred Thing*. New York: Bantam Books.

Sayers, Dorothy L. 1935. *Gaudy Night*. London: Victor Gollancz.

Le Guin, Ursula K. 1985. *Always Coming Home*. New York: Harper & Row.

Callenbach, Ernest. 1975. *Ecotopia: The Notebooks and Reports of William Weston*. Berkeley, CA: Banyan Tree Books.

Robinson, Kim Stanley. 1990. *Pacific Edge*. New York: Tor Books.

Jemisin, N.K. 2020. *The City We Became*. New York: Orbit Books.

Banks, Iain M. 1987–2012. *The Culture Series*. 10 vols. London: Macmillan.

Robinson, Kim Stanley. 1992–1996. *The Mars Trilogy*. 3 vols. New York: Bantam Spectra.

Burke, Sue. 2018. *Semiosis*. New York: Tor Books.

Le Guin, Ursula K. 1968. *A Wizard of Earthsea*. Berkeley, CA: Parnassus Press.

Le Guin, Ursula K. 1969. *The Left Hand of Darkness*. New York: Ace Books.

Le Guin, Ursula K. 2000. *The Telling*. New York: Harcourt.

Leckie, Ann. 2013. *Ancillary Justice*. New York: Orbit Books.

McCall Smith, Alexander. 2000. *The No. 1 Ladies' Detective Agency*. Edinburgh: Polygon Books.

Palmer, Ada. 2016. *Too Like the Lightning*. New York: Tor Books.

Chambers, Becky. 2014–2021. *The Wayfarers Series*. 4 vols. New York: Harper Voyager.

Robinson, Kim Stanley. 2020. *The Ministry for the Future*. New York: Orbit Books.

Newitz, Annalee. 2017. *Autonomous*. New York: Tor Books.

Tolkien, J.R.R. 1937. *The Hobbit, or There and Back Again*. London: George Allen & Unwin.

IV. ESSAYS, MEMOIR & CREATIVE NONFICTION

Gay, Ross. 2019. *The Book of Delights*. Chapel Hill, NC: Algonquin Books.

Gay, Ross. 2022. *Inciting Joy*. Chapel Hill, NC: Algonquin Books.

Crawford, Matthew B. 2009. *Shop Class as Soulcraft: An Inquiry into the Value of Work*. New York: Penguin Press.

Thich Nhat Hanh. 2017. *The Art of Living: Peace and Freedom in the Here and Now*. New York: HarperOne.

Heschel, Abraham Joshua. 1951. *The Sabbath: Its Meaning for Modern Man*. New York: Farrar, Straus and Giroux.

Lindbergh, Anne Morrow. 1955. *Gift from the Sea*. New York: Pantheon Books.

Oliver, Mary. 2017. *Devotions: The Selected Poems of Mary Oliver*. New York: Penguin Press.

Tempest, Kae. 2020. *On Connection*. London: Faber and Faber.

Nussbaum, Martha C. 2011. *Creating Capabilities: The Human Development Approach*. Cambridge, MA: Belknap Press of Harvard University Press.

Jamison, Leslie. 2014. *The Empathy Exams: Essays*. Minneapolis: Graywolf Press.

Rilke, Rainer Maria. 1929. *Letters to a Young Poet*. Translated by M.D. Herter Norton. New York: W.W. Norton, 1934.

Williams, Florence. 2017. *The Nature Fix: Why Nature Makes Us Happier, Healthier, and More Creative*. New York: W.W. Norton.

Biss, Eula. 2009. *Notes from No Man's Land: American Essays*. Minneapolis: Graywolf Press.

Lamott, Anne. 1994. *Bird by Bird: Some Instructions on Writing and Life*. New York: Pantheon Books.

Karr, Mary. 2015. *The Art of Memoir*. New York: Harper.

Gottlieb, Lori. 2019. *Maybe You Should Talk to Someone: A Therapist, Her Therapist, and Our Lives Revealed*. Boston: Houghton Mifflin Harcourt.

Oliver, Mary. 2016. *Upstream: Selected Essays*. New York: Penguin Press.

Baker, Nicholson. 2009. *The Anthologist*. New York: Simon & Schuster.

Dillard, Annie. 1989. *The Writing Life*. New York: Harper & Row.

Weir, Andy. 2011. *The Martian*. New York: Crown Publishers.

V. POETRY & DRAMA

Whitman, Walt. 1855. *Leaves of Grass*. Brooklyn, NY: Self-published.

Rumi, Jalaluddin. 1995. *The Essential Rumi*. Translated by Coleman Barks. San Francisco: HarperSanFrancisco.

Smith, Maggie. 2017. *Good Bones*. North Adams, MA: Tupelo Press.

Kaur, Rupi. 2017. *The Sun and Her Flowers*. New York: Andrews McMeel Publishing.

Homer. 2017. *The Odyssey*. Translated by Emily Wilson. New York: W.W. Norton.

Shakespeare, William. 1611. *The Tempest*. In *The Norton Shakespeare*, edited by Stephen Greenblatt et al., 3115–3188. 3rd ed. New York: W.W. Norton, 2016.

Wilder, Thornton. 1938. *Our Town: A Play in Three Acts*. New York: Coward McCann.

Shakespeare, William. c. 1598. *Much Ado About Nothing*. In *The Norton Shakespeare*, edited by Stephen Greenblatt et al., 1485–1548. 3rd ed. New York: W.W. Norton, 2016.

Shakespeare, William. c. 1595. *A Midsummer Night's Dream*. In *The Norton Shakespeare*, edited by Stephen Greenblatt et al., 1055–1106. 3rd ed. New York: W.W. Norton, 2016.

Shakespeare, William. c. 1599. *As You Like It*. In *The Norton Shakespeare*, edited by Stephen Greenblatt et al., 1659–1724. 3rd ed. New York: W.W. Norton, 2016.

APPENDIX H: SUPPLEMENTARY TABLES—SYNTHESIZED STATISTICAL OVERVIEW

This appendix consolidates key statistical findings from across the manuscript's analyses into summary tables, providing a synthesized reference for the overarching patterns documented in the suffering canon.

Table H.1: Key Statistics Across Analyses

Analysis Scope	Source (Chapter/ Appendix)	Suffering-Centered	Flourishing-Centered	Total Works	Timeframe
High School Literary Canon	Ch. 1 / App. A	68% (17/25 texts)	32% (8/25 texts)	25 texts	Canonical (ongoing)
Best Picture Winners	Ch. 3 / App. D	62% (31/50 films)	18% (9/50 films)	50 films	1975–2024
Literary Prize Winners (Pulitzer & NBA)	Ch. 6, 8 / App. E	78% (32/41 books)	5% (2/41 books)	41 books	2004–2024
Combined Prestige Ecosys	Ch. 6	73% (45/62 works)	10% (6/62 works)	62 works	2004–2024

tem (Film & Literature)

Table H.2: Period Analysis of Prestige Winners (2004–2024)

Illustrates the intensification and marginal shift in literary prize patterns.

Period	Award Type	Total Winners	Suffering-Centered	Flourishing-Centered
2004–2013	Pulitzer & NBA	19	79% (15)	0% (0)
2014–2024	Pulitzer & NBA	22	77% (17)	9% (2)

Table H.3: High School Canon Breakdown by Type of Self-Annihilation

Detailed breakdown of the 68% suffering-centered high school texts from Appendix A.

Category	Description	Number of Texts	Example Texts
A	Explicit Suicide	6	*Romeo and Juliet*, *Julius Caesar*, *Death of a Salesman*
B	Deliberate Self-Destruction	4	*Macbeth*, *The Crucible*,

C	Thematic Self-Annihilation	7	*Wuthering Heights*, *The Great Gatsby*, *1984*, *Frankenstein*
Total A+B+C	All Self-Annihilation	17	N/A
—	No Central Self-Annihilation	8	*To Kill a Mockingbird*, *The Odyssey*, *Pride and Prejudice*

Summary Narrative

The synthesized data reveals a consistent hierarchy of consecration across American cultural institutions:

1. The most severe concentration is found in the literary prestige system, where 78% of major prize winners from 2004–2024 were suffering-centered.
2. The most influential foundation is laid in education, where 68% of the most-taught high school texts center on self-annihilation.
3. The most publicly visible ritual is the film awards system, which has maintained a ~60% suffering-centered preference for four decades.
4. The combined effect, measured across film and literature prizes, shows that 73% of works receiving the highest institutional validation during the 21st century have centered on suffering, trauma, or despair.

These patterns are not random. They represent the measurable output of the interdependent systems—educational, journalistic, artistic, and critical—that constitute the cathedral of suffering documented in this book.

CONSOLIDATED REFERENCES

Abbey, Edward. 1968. *Desert Solitaire: A Season in the Wilderness*. New York: McGraw-Hill.

Adams, Richard. 1972. *Watership Down*. London: Rex Collings.

Alloy, Lauren B., and Lyn Y. Abramson. 1979. "Judgment of Contingency in Depressed and Nondepressed Students: Sadder but Wiser?" *Journal of Experimental Psychology: General* 108, no. 4: 441–485.

American Psychological Association, and ecoAmerica. 2017. *Mental Health and Our Changing Climate: Impacts, Implications, and Guidance*. Washington, DC: American Psychological Association.

Applebee, Arthur N. 1992. *Stability and Change in the High-School Canon*. Albany, NY: Center for the Learning and Teaching of Literature.

Applebee, Arthur N. 1996. *Curriculum as Conversation: Transforming Traditions of Teaching and Learning*. Chicago: University of Chicago Press.

Aristotle. 1996. *Poetics*. Translated by M. Heath. London: Penguin Classics.

Austen, Jane. 1813. *Pride and Prejudice*. London: T. Egerton.

Austen, Jane. 1815. *Emma*. London: John Murray.

Baker, J. A. 1967. *The Peregrine*. London: Collins.

Baker, Nicholson. 2009. *The Anthologist*. New York: Simon & Schuster.

Banks, Iain M. 1987–2012. *The Culture Series*. 10 vols. London: Macmillan.

Barbery, Muriel. 2006. *The Elegance of the Hedgehog*. Translated by Alison Anderson. New York: Europa Editions, 2008.

BBC World Service. 2016–present. *People Fixing the World* [Audio podcast]. London: BBC.

Beaty, Roger E., Mathias Benedek, Paul J. Silvia, and Daniel L. Schacter. 2016. "Creative Cognition and Brain Network Dynamics." *Trends in Cognitive Sciences* 20, no. 2: 87–95.

Beck, Aaron T. 1976. *Cognitive Therapy and the Emotional Disorders*. New York: International Universities Press.

Beck, A. T., A. John Rush, Brian F. Shaw, and Gary Emery. 1979. *Cognitive Therapy of Depression*. New York: Guilford Press.

Becker, George. 1978. *The Mad Genius Controversy: A Study in the Sociology of Deviance*. Beverly Hills: Sage Publications.

Becker, George. 2000–2001. "The Association of Creativity and Psychopathology: Its Cultural-Historical Origins." *Creativity Research Journal* 13, no. 1: 45–53.

Bennett, Alan. 2007. *The Uncommon Reader*. London: Faber and Faber.

Berry, Wendell. 2000. *Jayber Crow*. Washington, DC: Counterpoint.

Beston, Henry. 1928. *The Outermost House: A Year of Life on the Great Beach of Cape Cod*. Garden City, NY: Doubleday, Doran.

Biss, Eula. 2009. *Notes from No Man's Land: American Essays*. Minneapolis: Graywolf Press.

Bolton, Gillie. 1999. *The Therapeutic Potential of Creative Writing: Writing Myself*. London: Jessica Kingsley Publishers.

Bruner, Jerome. 1990. *Acts of Meaning*. Cambridge, MA: Harvard University Press.

Burke, Sue. 2018. *Semiosis*. New York: Tor Books.

Byron, George Gordon. 1812. *Childe Harold's Pilgrimage*. London: John Murray.

Callenbach, Ernest. 1975. *Ecotopia: The Notebooks and Reports of William Weston*. Berkeley, CA: Banyan Tree Books.

Camus, Albert. 1942. *The Myth of Sisyphus*. Paris: Gallimard.

Čapek, Karel. 1929. *The Gardener's Year*. Translated by M. and R. Weatherall. London: George Allen & Unwin.

Carby, Hazel V. 1987. *Reconstructing Womanhood: The Emergence of the Afro-American Woman Novelist*. Oxford: Oxford University Press.

Centers for Disease Control and Prevention. 2020. *Youth Risk Behavior Survey Data Summary & Trends Report: 2009–2019*. Atlanta: U.S. Department of Health and Human Services. https://www.cdc.gov/healthyyouth/data/yrbs/index.htm.

Centers for Disease Control and Prevention. 2023. *Youth Risk Behavior Survey: Data Summary & Trends Report, 2011–2021*. Atlanta: U.S. Department of Health and Human Services.

Chambers, Becky. 2014. *The Long Way to a Small, Angry Planet*. New York: Harper Voyager.

Chambers, Becky. 2014–2021. *The Wayfarers Series*. 4 vols. New York: Harper Voyager.

Chambers, Becky. 2016. *A Closed and Common Orbit*. London: Hodder & Stoughton.

Chambers, Becky. 2018. *Record of a Spaceborn Few*. London: Hodder & Stoughton.

Chambers, Becky. 2021. *The Galaxy, and the Ground Within*. London: Hodder & Stoughton.

Chambers, Becky. 2021. *A Psalm for the Wild-Built*. New York: Tor Books.

Chambers, Becky. 2022. *A Prayer for the Crown-Shy*. New York: Tor Books.

Cheung, M., C. A. Leung, and Y.-J. Huang. 2022. "Absentee Parents in Disney Feature-Length Animated Movies: What Are Children Watching?" *Child and Adolescent Social Work Journal* 39, no. 3: 323–336. https://doi.org/10.1007/s10560-021-00799-0.

Cisneros, Sandra. 1984. *The House on Mango Street*. Houston: Arte Público Press.

Clark, Roger. 2018. "Darkness Invisible: The Depiction of Death and Dystopia in Newbery Award-Winning Literature." *Children's Literature in Education* 49, no. 2: 117–133.

Colgan, Jenny. 2016. *The Bookshop on the Corner*. London: Sphere.

College Board. n.d. "AP English Literature and Composition Free-Response Questions 1971–2022." Accessed November 2025. https://apcentral.collegeboard.org/courses/ap-english-literature-and-composition/exam.

The College Board. 2023. *AP English Literature and Composition Past Exam Questions*. New York: The College Board. https://apcentral.collegeboard.org/courses/ap-english-literature-and-composition/exam/past-exam-questions.

Common Core State Standards Initiative. 2010. *Appendix B: Text Exemplars and Sample Performance Tasks*. Washington, DC: National Governors Association Center for Best Practices and the Council of Chief State School Officers.

Crawford, Matthew B. 2009. *Shop Class as Soulcraft: An Inquiry into the Value of Work*. New York: Penguin Press.

Csikszentmihalyi, Mihaly. 1990. *Flow: The Psychology of Optimal Experience*. New York: Harper & Row.

Csikszentmihalyi, Mihaly. 1996. *Creativity: Flow and the Psychology of Discovery and Invention*. New York: HarperCollins.

Deakin, Roger. 2008. *Notes from Walnut Tree Farm*. London: Hamish Hamilton.

Diefenbach, Donald L. 2020. "The Impact of Television News on Mood and Mood Regulation." *Journal of Broadcasting & Electronic Media* 64, no. 3: 393–411.

Dillard, Annie. 1974. *Pilgrim at Tinker Creek*. New York: Harper's Magazine Press.

Dillard, Annie. 1989. *The Writing Life*. New York: Harper & Row.

Doctorow, Cory. 2017. *Walkaway*. New York: Tor Books.

Eisler, Benita. 1999. *Byron: Child of Passion, Fool of Fame*. New York: Alfred A. Knopf.

Eliot, George. 1871. *Middlemarch: A Study of Provincial Life*. Edinburgh: William Blackwood and Sons.

Eliot, T. S. 1922. *The Waste Land*. New York: Boni & Liveright.

English, James F. 2005. *The Economy of Prestige: Prizes, Awards, and the Circulation of Cultural Value*. Cambridge, MA: Harvard University Press.

Felski, Rita. 2015. *The Limits of Critique*. Chicago: University of Chicago Press.

Filgate, Michele, ed. 2019. *What My Mother and I Don't Talk About: Fifteen Writers Break the Silence*. New York: Simon & Schuster.

Flagg, Fannie. 1987. *Fried Green Tomatoes at the Whistle Stop Cafe*. New York: Random House.

Fredrickson, Barbara L. 2001. "The Role of Positive Emotions in Positive Psychology: The Broaden-and-Build Theory of Positive Emotions." *American Psychologist* 56, no. 3: 218–226.

Gallup. 2023. "Americans' Trust in Mass Media Remains Near Record Low." Gallup News, October 18, 2023. https://news.gallup.com/poll/512861/americans-trust-media-remains-near-record-low.aspx.

Gay, Ross. 2019. *The Book of Delights*. Chapel Hill, NC: Algonquin Books.

Gay, Ross. 2022. *Inciting Joy*. Chapel Hill, NC: Algonquin Books.

George, Nina. 2013. *The Little Paris Bookshop*. Translated by Simon Pare. New York: Crown, 2015.

Gerbner, George, Larry Gross, Michael Morgan, and Nancy Signorielli. 1980. "The 'Mainstreaming' of America: Violence Profile No. 11." *Journal of Communication* 30, no. 3 (September): 10–29.

Gibbons, Stella. 1932. *Cold Comfort Farm*. London: Longmans, Green.

Giono, Jean. 1953. *The Man Who Planted Trees*. Translated by Peter Doyle. Chelsea, VT: Chelsea Green Publishing, 1985.

Goldman, William. 1973. *The Princess Bride: S. Morgenstern's Classic Tale of True Love and High Adventure*. New York: Harcourt Brace Jovanovich.

Gottlieb, Lori. 2019. *Maybe You Should Talk to Someone: A Therapist, Her Therapist, and Our Lives Revealed*. Boston: Houghton Mifflin Harcourt.

Greer, Andrew Sean. 2017. *Less*. New York: Little, Brown and Company.

Grossman, Lev. 2023. *The Familiar*. New York: Astra House.

The Guardian. 2018–present. "The Upside: People and Innovations Trying to Find Answers to the World's Most Difficult Problems." Guardian News & Media. https://www.theguardian.com/world/series/the-upside.

Guillory, John. 1993. *Cultural Capital: The Problem of Literary Canon Formation*. Chicago: University of Chicago Press.

Hagelin, Sarah. 2022. *The New Female Antihero*. Chicago: University of Chicago Press.

Hanff, Helene. 1970. *84, Charing Cross Road*. New York: Grossman Publishers.

Harlen, Wynne, and Ruth Deakin Crick. 2003. "Testing and Motivation for Learning." *Assessment in Education: Principles, Policy & Practice* 10, no. 2: 169–207.

Hawkins, Anne Hunsaker. 1999. *Reconstructing Illness: Studies in Pathography*. 2nd ed. West Lafayette, IN: Purdue University Press.

Hemingway, Ernest. 1929. *A Farewell to Arms*. New York: Charles Scribner's Sons.

Herriot, James. 1972. *All Creatures Great and Small*. London: Michael Joseph.

Heschel, Abraham Joshua. 1951. *The Sabbath: Its Meaning for Modern Man*. New York: Farrar, Straus and Giroux.

Hickman, Caroline, Elizabeth Marks, Panu Pihkala, Susan Clayton, R. Eric Lewandowski, Elouise E. Mayall, Britt Wray, Catriona Mellor, and Lise van Susteren. 2021. "Climate Anxiety in Children and Young People and Their Beliefs About Government Responses: A Global Survey." *The Lancet Planetary Health* 5, no. 12: e863–e873.

Hogan, Patrick Colm. 2003. *The Mind and Its Stories: Narrative Universals and Human Emotion*. Cambridge: Cambridge University Press.

Hollander, Claire Needell. 2013. "Why Are We Teaching Sad Books to Teens?" *The New York Times*, July 6. https://www.nytimes.com/2013/07/07/opinion/sunday/why-are-we-teaching-sad-books-to-teens.html.

The Holy Bible, English Standard Version. 2001. Crossway Bibles.

Homer. 2017. *The Odyssey*. Translated by Emily Wilson. New York: W.W. Norton.

Hurston, Zora Neale. 1937. *Their Eyes Were Watching God*. Philadelphia: J.B. Lippincott.

Jackson, Virginia. 2005. *Dickinson's Misery: A Theory of Lyric Reading*. Princeton, NJ: Princeton University Press.

Jahren, Hope. 2016. *Lab Girl*. New York: Alfred A. Knopf.

Jamison, Leslie. 2014. *The Empathy Exams: Essays*. Minneapolis: Graywolf Press.

Jemisin, N. K. 2020. *The City We Became*. New York: Orbit Books.

Johnston, William M., and Graham C. L. Davey. 1997. "The Psychological Impact of Negative TV News Bulletins: The Catastrophizing of Personal Worries." *British Journal of Psychology* 88, no. 1 (February): 85–91.

Jones, Diana Wynne. 1986. *Howl's Moving Castle*. London: Greenwillow Books.

Kalanithi, Paul. 2016. *When Breath Becomes Air*. New York: Random House.

Karr, Mary. 2015. *The Art of Memoir*. New York: Harper.

Kaur, Rupi. 2017. *The Sun and Her Flowers*. New York: Andrews McMeel Publishing.

Keats, John. 1819. Letter to George and Georgiana Keats, April 21, 1819. In *The Letters of John Keats, 1814–1821*, edited by H. E. Rollins, vol. 2. Cambridge, MA: Harvard University Press, 1958.

Kimmerer, Robin Wall. 2013. *Braiding Sweetgrass: Indigenous Wisdom, Scientific Knowledge, and the Teachings of Plants*. Minneapolis: Milkweed Editions.

King, Stephen. 2000. *On Writing: A Memoir of the Craft*. New York: Scribner.

Klune, TJ. 2020. *The House in the Cerulean Sea*. New York: Tor Books.

Lamott, Anne. 1994. *Bird by Bird: Some Instructions on Writing and Life*. New York: Anchor Books.

Le Guin, Ursula K. 1968. *A Wizard of Earthsea*. Berkeley, CA: Parnassus Press.

Le Guin, Ursula K. 1969. *The Left Hand of Darkness*. New York: Ace Books.

Le Guin, Ursula K. 1974. *The Dispossessed: An Ambiguous Utopia*. New York: Harper & Row.

Le Guin, Ursula K. 1985. *Always Coming Home*. New York: Harper & Row.

Le Guin, Ursula K. 2000. *The Telling*. New York: Harcourt.

Leckie, Ann. 2013. *Ancillary Justice*. New York: Orbit Books.

Leopold, Aldo. 1949. *A Sand County Almanac: And Sketches Here and There*. New York: Oxford University Press.

Levitas, Ruth. 2013. *Utopia as Method: The Imaginary Reconstitution of Society*. London: Palgrave Macmillan.

Lichter, S. Robert, and Daniel R. Amundson. 1994. "A Day of TV Violence." *Media Monitor* 8, no. 2. Center for Media and Public Affairs.

Lindbergh, Anne Morrow. 1955. *Gift from the Sea*. New York: Pantheon Books.

Lodi-Ribeiro, Gerson, ed. 2018. *Solarpunk: Ecological and Fantastical Stories in a Sustainable World*. Nashville: World Weaver Press.

Markman, Keith D., Igor Gavanski, Steven J. Sherman, and Matthew N. McMullen. 1993. "The Mental Simulation of Better and Worse Possible Worlds." *Journal of Experimental Social Psychology* 29, no. 1: 87–109.

McAdams, Dan P. 1993. *The Stories We Live By: Personal Myths and the Making of the Self*. New York: Guilford Press.

McCall Smith, Alexander. 2000. *The No. 1 Ladies' Detective Agency*. Edinburgh: Polygon Books.

McGurl, Mark. 2009. *The Program Era: Postwar Fiction and the Rise of Creative Writing*. Cambridge, MA: Harvard University Press.

McIntyre, Karen E., and Cathrine Gyldensted. 2018. "Positive Psychology as a Theoretical Foundation for Constructive Journalism." *Journalism Practice* 12, no. 6: 662–678.

Mellor, Anne K. 1993. *Romanticism and Gender*. New York: Routledge.

Mindich, David T. Z. 2005. *Tuned Out: Why Americans Under 40 Don't Follow the News*. Oxford: Oxford University Press.

Mittell, Jason. 2015. *Complex TV: The Poetics of Contemporary Television Storytelling*. New York: New York University Press.

Montgomery, L. M. 1908. *Anne of Green Gables*. Boston: L.C. Page & Company.

Montgomery, L. M. 1926. *The Blue Castle*. Toronto: McClelland & Stewart.

Montgomery, Sy. 2015. *The Soul of an Octopus: A Surprising Exploration into the Wonder of Consciousness*. New York: Atria Books.

National Council of Teachers of English (NCTE). 1996. *Standards for the English Language Arts*. Urbana, IL: NCTE.

National Council of Teachers of English (NCTE). 2022. "Ponderings on Mental Health, Literature, and the Middle School Classroom." NCTE Blog, May 2022. https://ncte.org/blog/2022/05/mental-health-literature-middle-school/.

National Endowment for the Arts. 2004. *Reading at Risk: A Survey of Literary Reading in America*. Washington, DC: National Endowment for the Arts.

National Endowment for the Arts. 2007. *To Read or Not to Read: A Question of National Consequence*. Washington, DC: National Endowment for the Arts.

Newitz, Annalee. 2017. *Autonomous*. New York: Tor Books.

Nezhukumatathil, Aimee. 2020. *World of Wonders: In Praise of Fireflies, Whale Sharks, and Other Astonishments*. Minneapolis: Milkweed Editions.

Nolen-Hoeksema, Susan. 2000. "The Role of Rumination in Depressive Disorders and Mixed Anxiety/Depressive Symptoms." *Journal of Abnormal Psychology* 109, no. 3: 504–511.

Nolen-Hoeksema, Susan, Blair E. Wisco, and Sonja Lyubomirsky. 2008. "Rethinking Rumination." *Perspectives on Psychological Science* 3, no. 5: 400–424.

Nussbaum, Martha C. 1986. *The Fragility of Goodness: Luck and Ethics in Greek Tragedy and Philosophy*. Cambridge: Cambridge University Press.

Nussbaum, Martha C. 1990. *Love's Knowledge: Essays on Philosophy and Literature*. Oxford: Oxford University Press.

Nussbaum, Martha C. 1995. *Poetic Justice: The Literary Imagination and Public Life*. Boston: Beacon Press.

Nussbaum, Martha C. 2001. *The Fragility of Goodness: Luck and Ethics in Greek Tragedy and Philosophy*. Rev. ed. Cambridge: Cambridge University Press.

Nussbaum, Martha C. 2011. *Creating Capabilities: The Human Development Approach*. Cambridge, MA: Belknap Press of Harvard University Press.

Oatley, Keith. 2011. "Such Stuff as Dreams: The Psychology of Fiction." *Wiley Interdisciplinary Reviews: Cognitive Science* 2, no. 4: 425–430.

Ojala, Maria. 2012. "Hope and Climate Change: The Importance of Hope for Environmental Engagement Among Young People." *Environmental Education Research* 18, no. 5: 625–642.

Oliver, Mary. 2016. *Upstream: Selected Essays*. New York: Penguin Press.

Oliver, Mary. 2017. *Devotions: The Selected Poems of Mary Oliver*. New York: Penguin Press.

Owen, Wilfred. 1920. *Poems*. London: Chatto & Windus. (Original poem "Dulce et Decorum Est" written 1917.)

Palmer, Ada. 2016. *Too Like the Lightning*. New York: Tor Books.

Pennebaker, James W., and Janel D. Seagal. 1999. "Forming a Story: The Health Benefits of Narrative." *Journal of Clinical Psychology* 55, no. 10: 1243–1254.

Pew Research Center. 2021. "Who Doesn't Read Books in America?" Pew Research Center, September 21, 2021.

Pew Research Center. 2023. "Reading Habits in the Digital Age." Pew Research Center, January 2023.

Pooley, Clare. 2020. *The Authenticity Project*. New York: Pamela Dorman Books.

Potts, Richard, and Duane Sanchez. 1994. "Television Viewing and Depression: No News Is Good News." *Journal of Broadcasting & Electronic Media* 38, no. 1 (Winter): 79–90.

Powers, Richard. 2018. *The Overstory*. New York: W.W. Norton.

Rilke, Rainer Maria. 1929. *Letters to a Young Poet*. Translated by M.D. Herter Norton. New York: W.W. Norton, 1934.

Robertson, Christopher E., Stuart Soroka, and Tanya Collins. 2023. "Negativity Drives Online News Consumption."

Proceedings of the National Academy of Sciences 120, no. 15: e2217563120.

Robinson, Kim Stanley. 1990. *Pacific Edge*. New York: Tor Books.

Robinson, Kim Stanley. 1992–1996. *The Mars Trilogy*. 3 vols. New York: Bantam Spectra.

Robinson, Kim Stanley. 2020. *The Ministry for the Future*. New York: Orbit Books.

Robinson, Marilynne. 2004. *Gilead*. New York: Farrar, Straus and Giroux.

Ross-Bryant, Lynn. 2004. "Pilgrim at Tinker Creek and the Social Legacy of American Nature Writing." *Religion and American Culture* 14, no. 2: 175–204.

Rowland, Alexandra. 2019. "A Brief History of Hopepunk." Tor.com, December 2019. Accessed January 15, 2025. https://www.tor.com/2019/12/16/a-brief-history-of-hopepunk/.

Rumi, Jalaluddin. 1995. *The Essential Rumi*. Translated by Coleman Barks. San Francisco: HarperSanFrancisco.

Sartre, Jean-Paul. 1943. *Being and Nothingness*. Paris: Gallimard.

Sayers, Dorothy L. 1935. *Gaudy Night*. London: Victor Gollancz.

Scarry, Elaine. 1985. *The Body in Pain: The Making and Unmaking of the World*. Oxford: Oxford University Press.

Shaffer, Mary Ann, and Annie Barrows. 2008. *The Guernsey Literary and Potato Peel Pie Society*. New York: Dial Press.

Shakespeare, William. c. 1595. *A Midsummer Night's Dream*. In *The Norton Shakespeare*, edited by Stephen Greenblatt et al., 1055–1106. 3rd ed. New York: W.W. Norton, 2016.

Shakespeare, William. c. 1598. *Much Ado About Nothing*. In *The Norton Shakespeare*, edited by Stephen Greenblatt et al., 1485–1548. 3rd ed. New York: W.W. Norton, 2016.

Shakespeare, William. c. 1599. *As You Like It*. In *The Norton Shakespeare*, edited by Stephen Greenblatt et al., 1659–1724. 3rd ed. New York: W.W. Norton, 2016.

Shakespeare, William. 1611. *The Tempest*. In *The Norton Shakespeare*, edited by Stephen Greenblatt et al., 3115–3188. 3rd ed. New York: W.W. Norton, 2016.

Shepherd, Nan. 1977. *The Living Mountain*. Aberdeen: Aberdeen University Press.

Shields, Carol. 1993. *The Stone Diaries*. Toronto: Random House Canada.

Simard, Suzanne. 2021. *Finding the Mother Tree: Discovering the Wisdom of the Forest*. New York: Alfred A. Knopf.

Simmons, Andrew. 2016. "Literature's Emotional Lessons." *The Atlantic*, April 5, 2016. https://www.theatlantic.com/education/archive/2016/04/literatures-emotional-lessons/476772/.

Simonson, Helen. 2010. *Major Pettigrew's Last Stand*. New York: Random House.

Simsion, Graeme. 2013. *The Rosie Project*. Melbourne: Text Publishing.

Smith, Maggie. 2017. *Good Bones*. North Adams, MA: Tupelo Press.

Snyder, C. R. 2002. "Hope Theory: Rainbows in the Mind." *Psychological Inquiry* 13, no. 4: 249–275.

"Solarpunk: A Reference Guide." 2018. *The Solutions Journal* 9, no. 3.

Solutions Journalism Network. n.d. "What Is Solutions Journalism?" Accessed January 2025. https://www.solutionsjournalism.org/about/solutions-journalism.

Soroka, Stuart. 2012. "The Gatekeeping Function: Distributions of Information in Media and the Real World." *The Journal of Politics* 74, no. 2 (April): 514–528.

Soroka, Stuart, Patrick Fournier, and Lilach Nir. 2019. "Cross-National Evidence of a Negativity Bias in Psychophysiological Reactions to News." *Proceedings of the National Academy of Sciences* 116, no. 38 (September): 18888–18892.

Starhawk. 1993. *The Fifth Sacred Thing*. New York: Bantam Books.

Stegner, Wallace. 1987. *Crossing to Safety*. New York: Random House.

Strout, Elizabeth. 2008. *Olive Kitteridge*. New York: Random House.

Sword, Helen. 2012. *Stylish Academic Writing*. Cambridge, MA: Harvard University Press.

Tan, Amy. 1989. *The Joy Luck Club*. New York: G.P. Putnam's Sons.

Taylor, Brandon. 2021. "Brandon Taylor on the Pressure to Perform Trauma." Interview by Lauren Christensen. *The New York Times Book Review Podcast*, July 15, 2021. Audio, 12:45. https://www.nytimes.com/2021/07/15/books/brandon-taylor-the-new-york-times-book-review-podcast.html.

Tedeschi, Richard G., and Lawrence G. Calhoun. 2004. "Posttraumatic Growth: Conceptual Foundations and Empirical Evidence." *Psychological Inquiry* 15, no. 1: 1–18.

Tempest, Kae. 2020. *On Connection*. London: Faber and Faber.

Thich Nhat Hanh. 2017. *The Art of Living: Peace and Freedom in the Here and Now*. New York: HarperOne.

Thier, Karen, Kelsey Lough, and Alex Curry. 2022. "Does Solutions-Based Reporting Improve Optimism and Self-Efficacy? A Large-Scale Randomized Experiment of Audience Effects." *Journalism Practice*. Published online ahead of print. https://doi.org/10.1080/17512786.2022.2084728.

Tolkien, J. R. R. 1937. *The Hobbit, or There and Back Again*. London: George Allen & Unwin.

Tolkien, J. R. R. 1954–1955. *The Lord of the Rings*. 3 vols. London: George Allen & Unwin.

Towles, Amor. 2016. *A Gentleman in Moscow*. New York: Viking.

Trilling, Lionel. 1972. *Sincerity and Authenticity*. Cambridge, MA: Harvard University Press.

Trites, Roberta Seelinger. 2000. *Disturbing the Universe: Power and Repression in Adolescent Literature*. Iowa City: University of Iowa Press.

Twenge, Jean M. 2017. *iGen: Why Today's Super-Connected Kids Are Growing Up Less Rebellious, More Tolerant, Less Happy—and Completely Unprepared for Adulthood*. New York: Atria Books.

Valkenburg, Patti M., and Jessica Taylor Piotrowski. 2017. *Plugged In: How Media Attract and Affect Youth*. New Haven: Yale University Press.

Vuong, Ocean. 2019. *On Earth We're Briefly Gorgeous*. New York: Penguin Press.

Watson, Robert N. 1994. *The Rest Is Silence: Death as Annihilation in the English Renaissance*. Berkeley: University of California Press.

Watts, Erin. 2024. "Teaching Tragedies Following Personal Loss: Teachers' Emotions and the ELA Classroom." *English Education* 56, no. 3: 237–259.

Weir, Andy. 2011. *The Martian*. New York: Crown Publishers.

White, Michael, and David Epston. 1990. *Narrative Means to Therapeutic Ends*. New York: W.W. Norton.

Whitman, Walt. 1855. *Leaves of Grass*. Brooklyn, NY: Self-published.

Whittier College. 2013. "Shakespeare in Liberal Arts Education." Whittier College News, November 4, 2013.

https://www.whittier.edu/news/shakespeare-liberal-arts-education.

Wilder, Thornton. 1938. *Our Town: A Play in Three Acts*. New York: Coward McCann.

Williams, Florence. 2017. *The Nature Fix: Why Nature Makes Us Happier, Healthier, and More Creative*. New York: W.W. Norton.

Wohlleben, Peter. 2015. *The Hidden Life of Trees: What They Feel, How They Communicate—Discoveries from a Secret World*. Translated by Jane Billinghurst. Vancouver: Greystone Books.

Woolf, Virginia. 1927. *To the Lighthouse*. London: Hogarth Press.

Wulf, Andrea. 2015. *The Invention of Nature: Alexander von Humboldt's New World*. New York: Alfred A. Knopf.

Yanal, Robert J. 1999. *Paradoxes of Emotion and Fiction*. University Park: Penn State Press.

Zepeda, Cristina, et al. 2021. "Promoting Cognitive Flexibility through Cultural and Worldview Diversity." *Educational Psychologist* 56, no. 4: 283–299.

COMPLETE INDEX - THE SUFFERING CANON

A

Absence, narrative of, 39–40

Academy Awards. See Best Picture winners

Adolescent mental health, 16–17, 52–53, 89–96 CDC statistics, 18, 52, 89 Correlation with media consumption, 93–96 Persistent sadness rates, 89–90, 170

Alienation, institutionalization of, 83–85

Althusser, Louis, 62

Ambiguous/Integrated narratives (Category B), 31, 64, 200–204, 205–213

Anti-heroes, 34–35

AP English Literature exam, 49–50, 168–169 Free-response questions, 15, 49–50 Tragedy bias in, 49–51

Appendices, 189–242 Appendix H (Supplementary Tables), 243

Aristotle, 17–18, 67–68 Catharsis concept, 17–18, 67–68

Assessment, educational, 49–51, 168–169

Attention, cognitive, 131, 138, 144

Austen, Jane, 121, 126, 225, 227, 238

Authenticity, 78–80, 84, 156–157, 166 As suffering, 78–80, 84 In writing practice, 62–63, 156–157, 166

Autopsy vs. architecture, 143–144, 167

Awards culture, 30–37, 62–71, 155–164, 169–170

B

Balance, principle of, 166 In curriculum design, 142–143, 165–168 In news coverage, 132–133, 169 One-third principle, 142, 165

Beautiful death (Romantic ideal), 82–83

Beck, Aaron, 52, 91–92 Cognitive triad, 52, 92

Becker, George, 35

Best Picture winners, 31–35, 197–204 Analysis (1975–2024), 31–35, 197–204 Decade-by-decade patterns, 32–34, 199 Suffering-centered percentage (62%), 32, 197

Biographical focus on suffering, 35

Blueprints for better worlds, 122–123, 228–231

Bolton, Gillie, 158

Borderline cases (in coding), 119

Broaden-and-build theory, 133, 138, 144

Bruner, Jerome, 257

Byron, Lord, 78, 82–84 Byronic hero, 82–83 Gendered double standard, 84

C

Calhoun, Lawrence, 157

Camus, Albert, 83

Canon. See Flourishing Canon; High school literary canon; Suffering Canon

Carby, Hazel V., 254

Cathedral metaphor, 11–71, 106–107, 146, 168, 179–188 Dismantling of, 179–188 Foundation stones, 73–74 Windows in, 106–107, 146

Catharsis, 17–19, 67–69 Aristotelian concept, 17–18, 67–68 As defense, 17–19 Greek civic function, 67–68 Modern misreading, 17–19, 68–69

Category A (Explicit Suicide), 15, 189, 200

Category B (Deliberate Self-Destruction), 15, 189, 200

Category C (Thematic Self-Annihilation), 15, 189, 200

CDC (Centers for Disease Control), 18, 52, 89

Chambers, Becky, 122–125, 153, 158, 160, 164–165, 228–230, 239

Children's media, 38–45 Dead parent trope, 39–40 Developmental arc of despair, 41–42 Disney films, 39–40 Statistics on parental absence, 39–40

Christian tradition, 69–70, 73–74

Civic function, 67–68, 114–115, 131

Classroom cathedral, 46–61

Climate change narratives, 102–105 Climate anxiety, 103 Constructive hope in, 103–104

Coding methodology, 15–16, 31–32, 189–192, 195–196, 200–204

Cognitive development, 16–17, 41–42, 91–93

Cognitive schemas, 52, 91–93

Cognitive triad (Beck), 52, 92

Cohen's Kappa coefficient, 32, 197

College Board, 15, 49–50, 193

Combined prestige culture analysis, 66–71, 214–221 71% suffering-centered, 66–71, 112, 117, 145, 182, 214

Common Core State Standards, 15, 48, 168, 193

Community, narratives of, 121, 225–228

Competence, drama of, 120, 224–225

Composite characters, 14–15, 22–26, 38, 43, 47, 52, 100, 106–107, 110–111, 112–113, 115, 127, 131–132, 135, 142, 148, 151, 160, 163–164, 168, 170, 187

Conditioning, cultural, 7–10, 13–14, 30–31, 62

Connection, architecture of, 121, 225–228

Constructive hope, 103–104, 131

Consumptive aesthetic (Keats), 82–83

Costs of suffering canon, 88–117 Imagination drain, 100–107 Lost readers, 108–117 Mental health impact, 89–99

Counterfactual thinking, 141

Crawford, Matthew B., 120, 232, 241, 254

Creative nonfiction, 232–234

Creativity research, 138, 144

Critical thinking, equated with cynicism, 46, 51–53, 92

Critics and criticism, 34–35

Csikszentmihalyi, Mihaly, 138, 141

Curriculum design, 142–143, 165–168 Balance in, 142–143, 165–168 Mandated march through graveyard, 47–49 One-third principle, 142, 165 Reparative pairing, 126–127, 142–143

Cynicism, equated with intelligence, 46, 51–53, 92, 101–102

D

Daily Canon, 22–29, 131–143 As chronic stressor, 93–94 Rebalancing, 132–133 Three-part mass structure, 23–24

Data sources, 15, 193

Death Beautiful death (Keats), 82–83 In children's media, 38–45 In required reading, 13–21

Depression, 52, 85–86, 91–92 Cognitive schemas, 91–92 Depressive realism, 85–86 Rumination, 85–86, 91–92

Desensitization, 7–10

Developmental arc of despair, 41–42

Dillard, Annie, 125, 222, 234, 242

Disney animated films, 39–40

Doctorow, Cory, 229, 240

Drama (as genre), 234–235

Dystopian narratives, 102–105

E

Education, 46–61, 137–155, 165–169 As indoctrination, 46–61 Assessment, 49–51, 168–169 Classroom as imagination lab, 141–143 Curriculum design, 142–143, 165–168 One-third principle, 142, 165 Pedagogy of pathologizing, 51–53 Pedagogy of possibility, 137–155 Reparative pairing, 126–127, 142–143

Eisler, Benita, 82

Eliot, George, 36, 121, 225, 238

Eliot, T.S., 82–83

English, James F., 63, 169

Epston, David, 155

Essays (as genre), 232–234

Eucatastrophe (Tolkien's concept), 229

Everything Everywhere All at Once (film), 32, 63, 200, 219

Existentialism, 83

F

Fairness Doctrine (FCC), 24

Family practice, 162–163

Faulkner, William, 84

Felski, Rita, 254

Film Best Picture winners, 31–35, 197–204 Entertainment cathedral, 30–37 Prestige culture in, 30–37

Flagg, Fannie, 228, 238

Flow state, 138, 141

Flourishing Canon, 116–134, 222–242 Annotated list (100 works), 119–126, 222–242 Architecture of connection, 121, 225–228 Blueprints for better worlds, 122–123, 228–231 Criteria, 117 Drama of competence, 120, 224–225 Essays, memoir & creative nonfiction, 232–234 Foundations of wonder, 125, 222–224 Intelligence of repair, 119–120, 224 Poetry & drama, 234–235

Flourishing-centered narratives, 32, 64–65, 200–204 Definition, 200–201 In Best Picture winners (18%), 32, 197 In literary prizes (5%), 64, 205

Fredrickson, Barbara, 133, 138, 144

G

Gay, Ross, 153, 158, 160, 164–165, 232, 241

Gerbner, George, 26

Gibbons, Stella, 227, 238

Giono, Jean, 224, 237

Goldmere, Amara (composite character), 113, 115, 148

Goldman, William, 229, 239

Gottlieb, Lori, 234, 242

Greek tragedy, 17–19, 67–69 Catharsis, 17–18, 67 Civic function, 67–68 Modern misuse, 17–19, 68–69

Green Book (film), 33, 200, 219, 220

Greer, Andrew Sean, 64, 205

Grossman, Lev, 64, 205, 211

Guillory, John, 254

Guilty pleasure hierarchy, 112–113, 155–156

H

Hanff, Helene, 227, 239

Hemingway, Ernest, 83–84 Stoic nihilism, 83–84

Herriot, James, 120, 126–127, 224, 237

Heschel, Abraham Joshua, 233, 241

High school literary canon, 13–22, 46–61, 189–192 68% suffering-centered, 15, 16, 65, 189 17 out of 25 texts (suicide/self-annihilation), 13, 15, 170, 189 25 most-taught texts, 189–192 Coding categories, 15, 189–192

Historical foundations, 67–87

Hogan, Patrick Colm, 254

Hollander, Claire Needell, 18

Hope Constructive hope, 103–104, 131 Hope theory (Snyder), 131

Hurston, Zora Neale, 119–120, 127, 225, 238

I

Imagination As cognitive infrastructure, 138–139 Imagination drain, 100–107 Rebuilding, 137–155

Indoctrination, educational, 46–61

Information streams, 132–133, 161

Institutional levers, 155–164, 169–177

Intelligence, equated with cynicism, 46, 51–53, 92

Intelligence of repair (genre), 119–120, 224

Inter-rater reliability, 32, 197

Ironwood, Mike (composite character), 22–26, 28–29, 131, 135, 142, 160

J

Jackson, Virginia, 85

Jahren, Hope, 120, 223, 237

Jamison, Leslie, 62, 233, 241

Jemisin, N.K., 230, 239

Jones, Diana Wynne, 224, 237

Journalism, 22–29, 131–143, 169 Negativity bias in news, 23, 93, 131, 161 Solutions Journalism, 27, 131–143, 169 Three-part mass of catastrophe, 23–24

K

Karr, Mary, 234, 242

Kaur, Rupi, 235, 242

Keats, John, 82–83 Beautiful death, 82–83 Consumptive aesthetic, 82–83

Kimmerer, Robin Wall, 125, 223, 236

King, Stephen, 156, 159

King's Speech, The (film), 201, 218

Klune, TJ, 227, 239

L

Lab Girl (Jahren), 120, 223

Lamott, Anne, 156, 158–159, 234, 242

Le Guin, Ursula K., 122–123, 158, 228–230, 239

Learned helplessness, 102, 133

Leckie, Ann, 230, 240

Leopold, Aldo, 224, 237

Less (Greer), 64, 205, 208, 219

Levitas, Ruth, 101

Lichter, S. Robert, 23

Lindbergh, Anne Morrow, 233, 241

Literary prizes, 62–71, 205–213 78% suffering-centered, 63, 72, 151, 205 Period analysis, 64–65, 205, 209–210 Pulitzer Prize for Fiction, 63–70, 205–213 National Book Award for Fiction, 63–70, 205–213

Lodi-Ribeiro, Gerson, 256

Lord of the Rings, The (Tolkien), 122, 127, 217, 229, 235, 240

Lost readers, 108–117 Democracy problem, 114–115 Silenced stories, 113–114 Voluntary exiles, 110–111

M

Marginalized writers, 62–63, 113–114

Martyrdom, 69–70, 73

Master of Fine Arts (MFA) programs, 62–71, 150–164 As seminary, 62–71 Flourishing Draft workshop, 151 Wound mandate, 62–63, 150

McAdams, Dan P., 256

McGurl, Mark, 153

Mean world syndrome, 26

Meaning-making, 157–158

Mellor, Anne K., 84

Memoir (as genre), 232–234

Mental health crisis (adolescent), 89–106 44% persistent sadness, 89, 93, 170 CDC statistics, 18, 89 Correlation with curriculum, 93–96

Methodology, 15, 195–196, 200–204

MFA programs. See Master of Fine Arts programs

Middlemarch (Eliot), 36, 121, 166, 225

Million Dollar Baby (film), 202, 217

Mindich, David T. Z., 24

Ministry for the Future, The (Robinson), 122, 230

Mittell, Jason, 34

Modernism, 81–87 Alienation institutionalized, 83–85 Despair mandate, 81–87 World War I impact, 81–82

Montgomery, L.M., 226, 238

Montgomery, Sy, 125, 223, 237

Moonlight (film), 201, 218

Moorley, Siobhan (composite character), 112–113, 115

Most-taught texts. See High school literary canon

N

Narrative therapy, 155

National Book Award, 63–70, 205–213

NCTE (National Council of Teachers of English), 48, 168

Negative schemas, 52, 91–92

Negativity bias, 131, 138, 161 In news, 23, 93, 131, 161

Nezhukumatathil, Aimee, 125, 223, 237

News media, 22–29, 131–143 As Daily Canon, 22–29, 131–143 Balanced information, 132–133 Mean world syndrome, 26 Negativity bias, 23, 93, 131, 161 Rewiring, 131–143 Solutions journalism, 27, 131–143 Three-part mass structure, 23–24

Newitz, Annalee, 231, 240

Nolen-Hoeksema, Susan, 85–86, 91 Rumination research, 85–86, 91

Nomadland (film), 200, 219

Nussbaum, Martha, 18, 36, 67, 233, 241, 254

O

Oatley, Keith, 43

Odyssey, The (Homer), 127, 235, 242

Ojala, Maria, 256

Oliver, Mary, 233–234, 241–242

One-third principle, 142, 165

Oppenheimer (film), 33, 63, 65, 200, 219, 221

Ordinary People (film), 204

Overstory, The (Powers), 119, 125, 208, 218

Owen, Wilfred, 82

P

Palmer, Ada, 231, 240

Parasite (film), 200, 218

Parents, absence in children's media, 39–40

Pathography, 35

Pedagogy Of pathologizing, 51–53 Of possibility, 137–155 Reparative pairing, 126–127, 142–143

Pennebaker, James, 158

Pew Research Center, 111

Play and flow, 141–142

Poetry (as genre), 234–235

Policy implications, 101–102

Pooley, Clare, 228, 239

Post-traumatic growth, 157–158

Powers, Richard, 119, 125, 208, 210

Prestige culture, 30–37, 62–71, 150–164 71% suffering-centered (combined), 66–71, 112, 117, 145, 182, 214 Awards, 30–37, 150–164 Catechism of, 34–35 In film, 30–37 In literature, 62–71 Television, 34–35

Profundity, redefinition of, 117, 166–167

A Psalm for the Wild-Built (Chambers), 122–125, 228 Deep dive, 123–125

Publishing industry, 155–164, 169, 171–172

Pulitzer Prize for Fiction, 63–70, 205–213 80% suffering-centered, 69, 209

R

Reading lists, 47–49, 142, 165 Mandated march, 47–49 Rebalancing, 165–168

Readers, lost. See Lost readers

Realistic, conflated with pessimistic, 101, 166, 176

Redemptive suffering, 69–70

References, Consolidated, 244–260

Religious foundations, 69–74 Christian tradition, 69–70, 73–74 Greek tragedy, 67–69

Reparative pairing (pedagogy), 126–127, 142–143

Reparative reading, 155, 162

Representation, principle of, 167

Resilience, 16, 42–43 Post-traumatic growth, 157–158

Rigor, principle of, 166–167

Rilke, Rainer Maria, 234, 241

Robinson, Kim Stanley, 122, 229–230, 240

Robinson, Marilynne, 119, 120, 210, 222, 236

Rocky (film), 204

Romanticism, 78–87 Byronic hero, 82–83 Cult of sensibility, 79–80 Gendered double standard, 84–85 The Romantic virus, 78–87

Romeo and Juliet (Shakespeare), 13, 73, 93, 189 As secular martyrdom, 73

Ross-Bryant, Lynn, 256

Rowland, Alexandra, 256

Rumination, 85–86, 91–92, 93

Rumi, Jalaluddin, 235, 242

S

Sand County Almanac, A (Leopold), 224

Sartre, Jean-Paul, 83

Sayers, Dorothy L., 229, 239

Scarry, Elaine, 70

Schemas, cognitive, 52, 91–93

Science fiction, 102–105, 122–123, 228–231

Self-annihilation In curriculum, 13–22, 189–192 Thematic, 15, 189, 200

Seminary of suffering (MFA), 62–71

Sensibility, cult of, 79–80

Sentimental, as critique, 63, 166

Seventeen texts (suicide/self-annihilation), 13, 15, 170, 189

Shaffer, Mary Ann, 120, 226, 238

Shakespeare, William, 48, 73, 189, 235, 242–243 In curriculum, 48 Romeo and Juliet, 73

Shape of Water, The (film), 33, 200, 219, 220

Shepherd, Nan, 224, 237

Shields, Carol, 120, 224, 238

Silverdale, Keiko (composite character), 151, 168

Simard, Suzanne, 224, 237

Simmons, Andrew, 51

Simonson, Helen, 227, 239

Simsion, Graeme, 227, 239

Slumdog Millionaire (film), 65, 201, 217

Smith, Maggie, 235, 242

Snyder, C.R. (hope theory), 131

Social media, 90, 94

Solutions Journalism, 27, 131–143, 169 Definition, 131 Research on effects, 131

Solutions Journalism Network, 131, 133, 169

Soroka, Stuart, 23

Spotlight (film), 201, 218

Starhawk, 229, 239

Statistical overview, 243 See also Appendix H

Statistics, key 17 out of 25 texts, 13, 15, 170, 189 44% adolescent sadness, 89, 93, 170 62% Best Picture (suffering), 32, 65, 197 68% high school canon, 15, 16, 65, 189 71% combined prestige, 66–71, 112, 117, 145, 182, 214 76% literary prizes, 63, 72, 151, 205 80% Pulitzer-specific, 69, 209 Synthesized overview, 243

Stegner, Wallace, 121, 225, 238

Stonefield, Miguel (composite character), 110–111, 115, 127, 148

Strengths-first critique, 155–156

Strout, Elizabeth, 119, 121, 208, 226, 238

Suffering Canon Combined statistics (71%), 66–71, 112, 117, 145, 182, 214 Costs of, 88–117 Definition, 200 Historical foundations, 67–87 In children's media, 38–45 In education, 13–22, 46–61 In film, 30–37 In literature, 62–71 In MFA programs, 62–71 In news media, 22–29

Suffering-centered narratives Definition, 200 Prevalence, 13–14, 15, 32, 63, 197, 205

Suicide In curriculum, 13–22, 189–192 Explicit (Category A), 15, 189, 200 17 out of 25 texts, 13, 15, 170, 189

Supplementary Tables (Appendix H), 243 High school canon breakdown, 243 Key statistics across analyses, 243 Period analysis of prestige winners, 243

Sustainability, principle of, 167–168

Sword, Helen, 34

T

Tan, Amy, 121, 225, 238

Taylor, Brandon, 63

Teachers, 46–47, 51, 143, 165 As imagination stewards, 143 Not responsible for system, 47

Tedeschi, Richard (post-traumatic growth), 157

Television, prestige, 34–35

Tempest, Kae, 233, 241

Testing. See Assessment, educational; AP English Literature exam

Thematic self-annihilation (Category C), 15, 189, 200

Their Eyes Were Watching God (Hurston), 119–120, 127, 225

Thich Nhat Hanh, 233, 241

Three-part mass of catastrophe (news structure), 23–24

Titanic (film), 202

Tolkien, J.R.R., 122, 127, 229–231, 235, 240 Eucatastrophe, 229

Tortured artist myth, 35, 78–87, 167

Towles, Amor, 120, 226, 238

Tragedy Greek tragedy, 17–19, 67–69 In curriculum, 13–22, 46–61 Tragic canon. See Suffering Canon

Trauma As credential, 35, 62–63, 113–114 In children's media, 38–45 In MFA programs, 62–63, 150 Post-traumatic growth, 157–158 Working with, 157–158

Trilling, Lionel, 85, 84

Trites, Roberta Seelinger, 41

Twenge, Jean, 90

Twelve Years a Slave (film), 201, 218

Twenty-five most-taught texts, 189–192

U

Utopian thinking, 101–102

V

Vuong, Ocean, 153, 158, 164–165

W

Waste Land, The (Eliot), 82–83

Watership Down (Adams), 223

Weir, Andy, 120, 234, 242

Westbridge, Jennifer (composite character), 14, 19, 46–47

"What if better?" thinking, 141

White, Michael, 155

Whitman, Walt, 235, 242

Wilder, Thornton, 235, 243

Williams, Florence, 234, 242

Wintermere, Noah (composite character), 38, 43, 47, 52, 100, 106–107, 115, 127, 142, 170

Wohlleben, Peter, 223, 237

Wonder, foundations of, 125, 222–224

Woolf, Virginia, 84

Workshop culture (MFA), 62–71, 151–159 Flourishing Draft, 151 New workshop logics, 154–156 Reparative reading, 155 Strengths-first critique, 155–156 Wound mandate, 62–63, 150

World War I, 81–82 As cultural breaking point, 81–82

Wound mandate, 62–63, 150, 156–159

Writers Liberated practice, 158–159 Marginalized, 62–63, 113–114 Refusing wound mandate, 156–159 Working with wounds, 157–158

Writing practice. See Master of Fine Arts programs; Workshop culture

Wulf, Andrea, 223, 237

Y

Yanal, Robert J., 256

Youth mental health, 18, 89–90

Z

Zepeda, Cristina, 256

www.ingramcontent.com/pod-product-compliance
Lightning Source LLC
Chambersburg PA
CBHW070637160426
43194CB00009B/1486